Second E[dition]

GCSE
HUMANITIES FOR AQA

WITHDRAWN

Mick Gleave Philip Ashton Jonathan Plows Graham Read Edward W[

HODDER
EDUCATION
AN HACHETTE UK COMPANY

The Publishers would like to thank the following for permission to reproduce copyright material:

Photo credits 3 *l* Ilpo Musto/Rex Features, *cl* Les Wilson/Rex Features, *c* The Travel Library/Rex Features, *cr* Photodisc/Getty Images, *r* Educationphotos.co.uk/ Walmsley; **5** Sipa Press/Rex Features; **8** *t* Michael St. Maur/Corbis, *c* Terrance Klassen/Alamy, *b* The Art Archive/Museo Prenistino Palestrina/Dagli Orti; **13** *l* Tiziana and Gianni Baldizzone/Corbis, *r* ABACA/Press Association Images; **15** Mary Evans; **16** Photodisc/Getty Images; **22** *tl* The Image Works/Topfoto, *tr* Joe Macdonald/Corbis, *cl* Clay Perry/Corbis, *cr* Topham Photri, *bl* Peter Frischmuth/Still Pictures, *br* David Turnley/Corbis; **25** Kevin Fleming/Corbis; **33** Peter Cavanagh/Alamy; **34** Murad Sezer/AP/Press Association Images; **37** Crispin Hughes/Photofusion; **43** The Art Archive/Musée des Beaux Arts Valenciennes/Gianni Dagli Orti; **44** Ken Straiton/Corbis; **46** Sipa Press/Rex Features; **47** *t* Yann Arthus-Bertrand/Corbis, *bl* Worldwide Picture Library/Alamy, *br* Gustavo Gilbert/Corbis SABA; **48** Collart Herve/Corbis Sygma; **50** David Turnley/Corbis; **53** *l* Kenra Luck/San Francisco Chronicle/ Corbis, *r* Chris Lobina/Alamy; **65** *t* Andy Hibbert/Ecoscene/Corbis, *ct* Photodisk/Getty Images, *c* Nailah Feanny/Corbis SABA, *cb* Anthony Cooper/ Ecoscence/Corbis, *b* Steve Lindridge/Eye Ubiquitous/Corbis; **67** Photodisk/Getty Images; **69** *l* Owen Humphreys/PA Wire/Press Association images, *r* Janine Wiedel Photolibrary/Alamy; **70** David Hoffman Photo Library/Alamy; **72** Natalie Fobes/Corbis; **73** Greenpeace/Greig; **77** *t* K.M. Westermann/ Corbis, *b* Carl & Ann Purcell/Corbis; **78** *l* & *r* Mick Gleave (author); **82** Jeff Moore/Press Association Images; **83** Greenpeace/AFP/Getty Images; **84** John Birdsall/Press Association Images; **85** David Zimmerman/Corbis; **86** Greenpeace-Steve Morgan; **87** Alik Keplicz/AP Photo/Press Association; **89** Sipa Press/Rex Features; **95** *t* KPA/Zuma/Rex Features, *b* KPA/Zuma/Rex Features; **97** Photofusion Picture Library/Alamy; **99** *l* Marc Serota/Reuters/Corbis, *r* Sam Morgan Moore/Rex Features; **100** Barry Batchelor/PA Archive/Press Association Images; **107** *t* J. Redden/UNHCR via Getty Images, *b* INTERFOTO/Alamy; **108** Gerald Scarfe, www.geraldscarfe.com; **110** Rex Features; **115** Spencer Platt/Getty Images; **116** Fraidoon Pooyaa/AP/Press Association Images; **122** *t* Mary Evans, *b* Bettman/Corbis; **123** The Granger Collection, NYC/TopFoto; **124, 125, 126** & **127** Bettman/Corbis; **132** Poster © ADAGP, Paris and DACS, London 2009/ Photo ©National Museum in Poznań; **133** Bettman/Corbis; **135** Tim Page/Corbis; **136** Bettman/Corbis; **137** Eddie Adams/AP/Empics; **139** Bettman/Corbis; **143** Educationphotos.co.uk/Walmsley; **144** Fiona Hanson/PA Archive/Press Association Images; **152** Imagestate Media; **155** Hulton-Deutsch Collection/Corbis; **156** & **157** Akg-images; **160** Commission for Racial Equality; **161** Sayyid Azim/AP Photo/Press Association; **163** Adam Davy/Press Association; **165** *A* Ingram Publishing Limited, *B* Peter Turnley/Corbis, *C* Royalty-free/Corbis, *D* McPHOTO/Still Pictures, *E* Kevin Fleming/Corbis, *F* Mark Peterson/Corbis, *G* Owaki-Kulla/Corbis, *H* Liba Taylor/Corbis; **166** Jonathan Hordle/Rex Features; **171** Joel Robine/AFP/Getty Images; **172** Lucianne Pashley/age footstock/Photolibrary.com; **174** *l* Issouf Sanogo/AFP/Getty Images, *r* http://www.flickr.com/photos/didbygraham/517825526 /Released under Creative Commons Attribution 2.0 Generic (on 10 June 2009); **178** Elizabeth Dalziel/AP Photo/Press Association Images; **179** *b* North Wind Picture Archives/Alamy, *t* & **180** Olivier Asselin/AP Photo/Press Association; **181** Johnson Space Center/NASA; **183** Eduardo Martino/Panos Pictures; **187** *t* Alexander Joe/AFP/Getty Images, *b* Olivier Laban-Mattei/AFP/Getty Images; **188** Cameron Spencer/Getty Images; **190** imagebroker/Alamy; **199** Bob Krist/Corbis; **200** Picture Partners/Alamy; **205** *t* Blend Images/Alamy, *b* Jupiterimages/Pixland/Alamy; **211** Blend Images/Alamy; **214** Mick Gleave (author); **216** The U.S. National Archives, http://www.flickr.com/photos/ usnationalarchives/, CC BY 2.0; **219** *l* Peter Muhly/AFP/Getty Images, *r* Ingram Publishing Limited; **223** epf model/Alamy; **224** MGM/RGA; **225** Adarchives.

Acknowledgements Jared Diamond: Map of the world showing spread of humans (adapted) from *Guns, Germs and Steel* (Vintage, 1998); Population Reference Division: 'World Population Prospects'; and estimates (United Nations, 1998 Revision); Deborah Zabarenko: Extract from 'Global warming may cause world crop decline' from *Reuters* (12 September 2007); R. Cooke: Figure: Soil pollution from farms (University of Reading, 2000); Greenpeace: Website information from www.greenpeace.org/international/campaigns (2009); World Resources Institute: Chart: Greenhouse gas emissions from www.infoimagination.org/politics/images/kyoto.gif (2000); UNICEF: 'Child Rights and Child Poverty in Developing Countries' from *Summary Report to UNICEF* (Centre for International Poverty Report, University of Bristol); BBC News, In voices: Ada Hussain (adapted); Debt trap (adapted) from www.MakePovertyHistory.org (2009).

Every effort has been made to trace all copyright holders, but if any have been inadvertently overlooked the Publishers will be pleased to make the necessary arrangements at the first opportunity.

Although every effort has been made to ensure that website addresses are correct at time of going to press, Hodder Education cannot be held responsible for the content of any website mentioned in this book. It is sometimes possible to find a relocated web page by typing in the address of the home page for a website in the URL window of your browser.

Hachette Livre UK's policy is to use papers that are natural, renewable and recyclable products and made from wood grown in sustainable forests. The logging and manufacturing processes are expected to conform to the environmental regulations of the country of origin.

Orders: please contact Bookpoint Ltd, 130 Milton Park, Abingdon, Oxon OX14 4SB. Telephone: (44) 01235 827720. Fax: (44) 01235 400454. Lines are open 9.00 – 5.00, Monday to Saturday, with a 24-hour message answering service. Visit our website at www.hoddereducation.co.uk

Cover image by David Angel at DebutArt
Illustrations by Oxford Designers and Illustrators
Typeset in 12pt Adobe Garamond by DC Graphic Design Limited, Swanley, Kent.
Printed in Italy

A catalogue record for this title is available from the British Library

ISBN: 9780340986790

Contents

INTRODUCTION

About the book

This book is for students studying AQA GCSE Humanities. It covers the content of the specification as well as providing support for the examination.

The book contains six main chapters. The first two chapters cover the content for Unit 1: Humanities Core in the specification. In this unit you must study both parts of the core:

• Core 1: Culture and beliefs
• Core 2: Environmental issues

The next four chapters cover the content for Unit 2: Humanities Options in the specification. In this unit you must study any two of the following options (although in this book People and work is not covered):

• Option 1: Conflict and co-operation
• Option 2: Prejudice and persecution
• Option 3: Global inequality
• Option 4: Family and socialisation
• Option 5: People and work

In the specification the description of what each topic in the Core and Option Units should cover is divided into three categories: concepts, focus, and content.

Concepts

Each unit has four concepts. These are broad statements which guide you through the main issues explored in the topic.

For example, Concept 1 in Culture and beliefs states that: 'There are common and contrasting aspects of culture.' The concept outlines one theme of the topic, which can be approached using materials chosen by the teachers to illustrate the point and be interesting and relevant to the students' own experiences.

This book interprets the concepts and shows different ways that they can be explored, using current issues and drawing from different perspectives such as History, Geography, Citizenship, Religious Studies, Sociology and other subjects in the curriculum. The book makes links between concepts and these are important if the topic is to be fully understood. For example, in the Conflict and co-operation chapter, causes and effects of conflicts are intertwined: effects can become causes of other conflicts. Similarly, in Family and socialisation, the changes that have taken place in the family (Concept 4), are intimately bound up with different external influences on the family (Concept 3).

Focus

The focus section in the specification gives more details and guidance on what specific aspects of the concept have to be explored, and the nature of the case studies which must be taught and which will be assessed in the examination. Each topic requires you to explore three case studies covering different issues.

For example, the focus section for Culture and beliefs for Concept 1 says that students must be familiar with:

• *'Culture in the UK today. The similarities and differences from at least one other European country.'*
• *'A case study of culture in two contrasting societies: the UK today and one other (a primitive/less developed/historical example).'*

The points in the focus sections are explored in depth in this book, through explanations, illustrations and relevant detailed case studies. You are expected to use knowledge and information from case studies in answers to examination questions. Some of the case studies in the book are relevant to more than one concept, and you should be aware of this when these case studies are used. The case studies in the book are intended as guides and examples rather than specific case studies which must be learned.

Content

The content section in the specification is basically a list of terms, phrases and names which you are expected to understand. They give you a clear picture of what you need to know. The terms will be used in examination questions, and you should use them appropriately in your answers where they are relevant to the question.

For example, the content section for Culture and beliefs for Concept 1 is:

'Customs, traditions, norms, attitudes, values, religious beliefs and practices, rites of passage, identity, gender roles, communication, technology, social organisation.'

The words and ideas in the focus and content sections are used, explained, and illustrated in the relevant chapters of this book. At the beginning of each section there is a list of each of these terms to help you check that you know and understand them. They also appear in the glossary with short definitions.

Concepts are outlined and explained at the beginning of each chapter and the content of each chapter is then broken down into sections covering the four concepts in the specification.

Key terms, phrases and names from the content section of the specification, and a few additional terms that are useful for understanding this chapter, are outlined at the beginning of each concept section in the chapter.

Case studies, examples and sources support the focus sections of the specification and illustrate the key concepts.

Key words and concepts are highlighted in small capitals the first time they appear in a chapter and are defined in the glossary.

Activities check your basic understanding of the key concepts and give you practice in applying these to analyse, interpret or evaluate a case study, source or example.

Investigations give you ideas for extension and research work.

About the written examination

The Core and Optional Units are assessed through a written examination. There are two papers – one for the Core Unit and one for the Optional Unit. Each paper accounts for 37.5 per cent of the total marks. For each of the written papers you will be given a source booklet in February of the year of the examination. There will be questions on the sources in the examination as well as other questions to test your knowledge and understanding of the subject content. There is more information and advice about the examination questions on pages 227–229 of this book.

About controlled assessment

Controlled assessment is worth 25 per cent of the total marks. It is an investigation task set by the examination board linked to one of the topics you are studying. There is more information and advice about controlled assessment on pages 229–231 of this book.

CULTURE AND BELIEFS

INTRODUCTION

> This chapter will explain what culture is and why it is important. The culture and beliefs chapter is based on four concepts:
>
> 1. There are common and contrasting aspects of culture.
> 2. There is a wide variety of factors that influence an individual's culture and identity.
> 3. Interaction between cultures can bring benefits and can cause conflict and change.
> 4. Individuals and groups have different beliefs, attitudes and values.

In this chapter, you will explore the ways in which CULTURE influences the behaviour, attitudes and beliefs of groups and individuals. You also need to understand culture and how it affects our lives to understand the other parts of your Humanities course.

People live in groups. Groups live in many different ways. The word 'culture' sums up how a group of people lives. First there are the BELIEFS, ATTITUDES, VALUES and language that those in a group share. These decide how its members behave.

BEHAVIOUR covers all the practices that characterise a group. These include their CUSTOMS and TRADITIONS, art, literature, the things they make (AESTHETICS), and the roles they play. So culture is the pattern of learned and shared behaviour among the members of a group.

The word 'culture' is useful and powerful because it helps us explain the different ways people behave. This ability to explain different types of behaviour can lead to better relations between people of different cultures. Let us look at an example.

In Britain and most European countries it is the custom to greet someone with a firm handshake while looking each other in the eye. This is based on the belief that these actions show that you are friendly and not a threat to them. In Japan, the normal greeting is a graceful bow, while avoiding eye contact, indicating non-aggression. In Japan, it is believed that a firm handshake is aggressive, as is making eye contact. An understanding of each other's culture would clearly help avoid misunderstanding and provide the opportunity to learn new things from a different culture.

> *Cultural ignorance can be expensive*
> Pepsi Cola lost its dominant market share to Coca-Cola in South East Asia when Pepsi changed the colour of its vending machines and coolers from deep 'regal' blue to light 'ice' blue. Many people were put off buying a drink from these machines because light blue is associated with death and mourning in these cultures.
>
> *Cultural ignorance can be offensive*
> Mombasa is a Kenyan city on the beautiful East African coast. A large number of its inhabitants are Muslim. Many European holidaymakers walk around the city in swimming trunks and bikinis. This offends the religious beliefs of many Muslims.

'English culture'

One way of building up an understanding of the word culture is to look at how people in other countries see us in England. Study the pictures A–E opposite.

These photographs are based on what a cross-section of visitors to England said they thought was 'typically English'.

We can see that they give clues to the culture that has evolved in England. The pictures reveal our past and how it has shaped present culture. They suggest what is believed, valued, celebrated and more.

Now, we would probably agree that these images of English culture do not tell the whole story. We might want to add things. Below is a diagram setting out the key aspects of any culture.

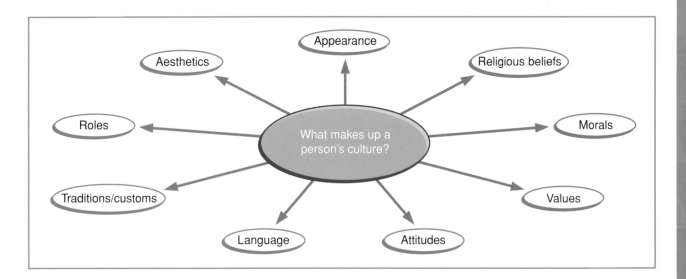

ACTIVITIES

Complete Activities 1–3 to help you become confident of the meaning of the word 'culture'.

1 a) Match the following terms to the photos A–E. Each phrase sums up an aspect of culture in England. You may need to discuss these.
   i) Custom; **ii)** RELIGION; **iii)** ROLES;
   iv) Aesthetics (art, architecture, literature, dance, design, etc.); **v)** Values.

   b) Create a table like the one below to record your decisions.

Photo	Aspect of culture	Explanation	How typical is it?
a) Tea and cake	Custom	A traditional English drink and snack in the afternoon	Mainly older people

2 Discuss the following views in a small group and decide which you agree with most. You may not agree with any of them and decide to come up with your own statements.

   • 'The photos give a complete guide to English culture.'
   • 'The photos give a reliable guide to English culture.'
   • 'The photos give a false guide to English culture.'

3 Create a collage of aspects of English culture. Plan it first. It may help to work in pairs. You could use the diagram above, magazines, newspapers, or the internet to help. Your challenge is to make a more accurate display of English culture than photos A–E.

CONCEPT 1

There are common and contrasting aspects of culture

In this concept section, you will learn about:

- How living in groups builds up cultures.
- Social organisation and common roles in cultures.
- Why there are different cultures.
- The factors that influence common and contrasting aspects of culture.

The following are ideas and terms that you will need to know from this concept section:

customs • traditions • norms • attitudes • values • religious beliefs • religious practices • rites of passage • identity • gender roles • communication • technology • social organisation

On the previous two pages, we explained that the word 'culture' could be used to describe a group of people who have certain beliefs and behaviours in common. But why do people live in groups anyway?

The explanation lies in the nature of human beings.

On our own, we are weak. If we look at the evidence of Early Man (over 1–2 million years ago) we can see that human beings alone were no match for the animals they hunted, such as sabre-toothed tigers, cave lions and woolly mammoths. So they got together in groups to improve their chances of survival. They also found they could search for fruits and berries more efficiently in small groups than on their own. Once they learned to act together, they could not only survive, but also begin to thrive.

The strength of human beings comes from our ability to work together in groups. When we are alone, we sense our weakness. We become afraid and want to feel we belong.

Co-operation and its consequences

Living in groups, or tribes, however, meant that Early Man had to co-operate. This meant in turn that other aspects of culture became important.

- To co-operate, you need to have an agreed way of doing things. These are known as NORMS. For example, in many early cultures, it was the norm to share out all food fairly within the group. Norms would guide the individuals in the group so they knew what to do as a team. They would be passed on from one generation to the next. When this happens, the norms would become traditions, which the members of the culture would follow for many generations. Some norms would become a formal set of rules, which would then be enforced through SANCTIONS (rewards or punishments).
- People would learn their roles within the tribe or group. For example, some would become specialist hunters or shelter builders, others care for children or make weapons. This would build up trust within the group and give each individual a sense of belonging. The tribes that co-operated best became the most successful.
- The drive to co-operate better led to improved ways of communicating. This is why language developed. The bigger a group becomes, the more important it is that everyone knows what needs to be done, and who is responsible for it.

Finding food

One example of communication was the way people within a tribe would share their knowledge about the animals and plants around them. In this way, they could improve their knowledge of the animals' feeding habits, making it easier to hunt them. They would also learn more quickly which plants were poisonous and which were good to eat.

Fire

Another example of communication is how groups of humans shared the knowledge of how to make fire. Fire gave groups:

- protection from predators, as most animals were afraid of fire. This gave groups more choice about where they camped.
- confidence to MIGRATE into colder regions.
- the ability to cook food. Cooked food is safer to eat.

This meant the youngest and oldest members of the group had more chance of survival.

1 How important was co-operation for the survival of Early Man? Give your reasons.
2 Study the cave painting and caption below. How would co-operation within a group have allowed art to develop?

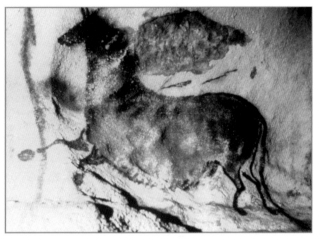

Modern humans, known as Homo sapiens, have only been around for the past 120,000 years. By 40,000 years ago, they had learned how to make tools out of bone, antler, ivory, stone and wood. By 17,000 years ago, they were producing fine artwork like this cave painting found in Lascaux, in South West France.

Living in groups today

Nowadays we can't imagine how to survive without co-operation. We are members of several groups at the same time: our FAMILY, school, workplace, PEER GROUP, sports team, and our local, national and international COMMUNITY. We belong to each group because they still help to satisfy our needs and desires better than if we tried to live independently. You only have to study where your food, clothes and other possessions come from to realise we have become a world community where we depend on each other.

Learning how to co-operate

We are not born knowing how to co-operate, however. We learn to do so as we grow up. First, our parents teach us through smiles, frowns and other sanctions what is and is not 'acceptable'. They show us how to play and share. We learn that we have to give to the group in order to receive from the group.

In each group we have a set of rules or norms. We have a role to play so that the group achieves its purpose. People depend on us and we depend on them. It makes us feel secure to belong to a group. We fear being on the outside, alone. By learning to co-operate we develop the ability to work together and so play our part in the group. This gives us our identity.

A person's identity is made up of all the groups they belong to, their beliefs and attitudes, and the things they do in groups and in society. Identity helps people to feel accepted by society.

Sadly this feeling of security is not everyone's experience, however, as the story below shows.

Hayley's story

Hayley was neglected as a baby. If she cried, she would be shouted at, even smacked. As a child, her parents did not play with her, take her for walks or read to her. She was shouted at if she got into trouble. Her parents took little interest in what she did at school. She began to get into trouble at school for disrupting lessons. She began shouting at her teachers. She started truanting. When she was 15, Hayley left home and moved into a flat with some 20-year-olds who regularly took drugs. She had a baby. If the baby cried, she shouted at him.

3 Suggest reasons why Hayley was disruptive at school. Use the following words to help:

   Love; Co-operation; Norms; Sanctions; Learn

4 What help should be given to Hayley and her baby? Why? Who should give it?

5 a) Why does co-operation require trust?
   b) How difficult would it be to live totally independently today?
   c) What are the disadvantages of living in groups?
   d) How important is it for a group to have sanctions for people who break the norms?
   e) How might a culture be affected if the experiences described in Hayley's story become widespread?

CULTURE AND BELIEFS

Why are there different cultures?

Having studied why people live in groups on pages 4–5, we will now look at why these groups have developed different cultures around the world. By learning why there are different cultures, you can begin to understand some reasons why people have different values and attitudes about the way we should live.

A) All children have the right to an education.

B) The voting age should come down to 16.

C) The tradition of ARRANGED MARRIAGES should be stopped.

D) Families should be responsible for looking after their elderly relations.

E) There should be CAPITAL PUNISHMENT for 'terrorists'.

F) People should do more to reduce GLOBAL WARMING.

G) People in the West should do more to help reduce hunger.

H) All countries should accept ASYLUM SEEKERS.

I) More should be done to reduce under-age drinking of alcohol.

ACTIVITIES

1 On your own:
   a) Organise the beliefs above (A–I) into those you agree with and those you disagree with.
   b) Put them into a rank order, starting with the issues you consider most important. Give reasons for your order.
   c) Now, in small groups, discuss and complete the following tasks:

   • As a group, come to a decision on which beliefs your group agrees with and which it opposes.
   • Now compare your rank orders of importance.
   • Reach a group decision on rank order.

   Appoint/elect someone to keep a record of the discussion and decisions and to report back at the whole-class discussion.

2 As a group or class, discuss the following questions about Activity 6c):
   a) What difficulties were there in completing Activity 6c)?
   b) What aspects of culture can help explain your differences of opinion? (Beliefs, values, traditions?)
   c) What part did co-operation and COMPROMISE play in your discussions?
   d) On which issue(s) was it easiest to put up with opposing views? Why?

It is likely that there was some disagreement in your group in Activity 1 on page 6. Around the world there are differences both between and within cultures on these and other beliefs. Having done this activity should help you understand this quotation:

'We are moving into an age when different CIVILISATIONS will have to learn to live side by side in peace, learning from each other, studying each other's history, art and culture to enrich each other's lives. The alternative in this overcrowded little world is misunderstanding, tension, clash and catastrophe.'

Lester Pearson, former Prime Minister of Canada and NOBEL PEACE PRIZE winner, 1957

Emergence of different cultures

Human beings have basic physical needs that must be satisfied if they are to survive: food, water, shelter. We also have emotional needs such as love, security and identity. Living in groups makes it easier to provide for these needs. Different groups have found very different ways of achieving these goals. This has led to the emergence of many different cultures with different beliefs and values.

How has this come about? To answer this we need to look at the map below and learn a little history.

ACTIVITIES

1 What would be your three main pieces of advice to help 'different civilisations learn to live side by side'?
2 'We are all IMMIGRANTS.' How true is this statement? Use the map to support your answer.

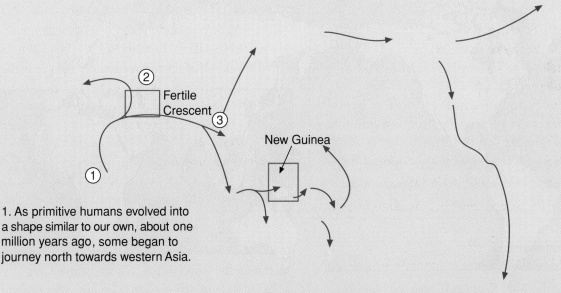

3. Others crossed Asia to the east. From there they migrated southeast to Australia or northeast, across the Bering Straits to America. They could do this either by walking over a land bridge of ice 1,610 km (1,000 miles) wide, during the last Ice Age, which ended about 10,000 years ago, or by boat across the sea, which was only 80 km (50 miles) wide. They then travelled on down the west of North and South America. Here the earliest remains are only about 12,000 years old.

2. In western Asia they divided, some turning northwest towards Europe (earliest remains 500,000 years old).

Fertile Crescent

New Guinea

1. As primitive humans evolved into a shape similar to our own, about one million years ago, some began to journey north towards western Asia.

From about seven million years ago, there have been various types of human being evolving and spreading around the world. Evidence in the form of human fossils and bones and crude tools have helped us piece together the map shown above. This traces the MIGRATION of human beings from their origins in eastern Africa.

A map of the world showing how human beings have spread across the continents from Africa, based on skeleton remains. (Adapted from: *Guns, Germs and Steel* by Jared Diamond)

Natural environment

Groups adapted to survive. They were beginning to develop their own distinct culture. Local materials would be used for clothing and shelter; animals and plants would be hunted or gathered. The beliefs and languages that developed would reflect their particular natural ENVIRONMENT. The power of the environment to influence culture can be seen in New Guinea today.

Case study: Cultural groups in New Guinea

New Guinea is a large island near the equator north of Australia (see map on page 7). There are 6,000 languages spoken in the world and 1,000 of them (one sixth) are to be found on this island. How can this be explained?

The island is very rugged and very mountainous. There are swamps at sea level and dense rainforest covers most of the island. There are glaciers capping the highest mountains. It has one of the heaviest rainfalls in the world, so there are many very fast flowing rivers. These have divided the slopes into deep gorges and valleys. It is usual for a three mile journey to take all day.

Since travel is so difficult, the people living in one valley rarely contact those living in the next valley. So over time the population has divided into thousands of separate cultural groups. Each has adapted to living in different natural environments: by the sea, in the deep tropical valleys and high in the mountains, developing its own language, traditions, norms and values.

The variations in culture around the world are just a larger version of the variations that have occurred on this one island.

ACTIVITIES

1 Using the New Guinea Case Study as an example, explain why are there so many different languages around the world.
2 How do you think the different 'house' designs shown in the pictures on this page were influenced by differences in the natural environment?

'House' design

Natural environment influenced the shelters people developed, some examples of which are shown in the photos below.

Beehive hut in West Ireland – made from local stone and built layer by layer.

Tipi in North America – made from the tanned hides of bison or elk. They were made to be moved because the Native Americans lived off these animals and had to follow the herds as they migrated in search of grazing grounds as the seasons changed.

Mud from the banks of the Nile was shaped into bricks, dried out and used to build homes in Ancient Egypt. This needed a dry climate.

1 Research building designs and materials in different cultures today and make a presentation of your findings. How big are the differences you found? How far do they reflect differences in environment and climate?

Wealth and technology

Some natural environments turned out to be more helpful to humans than others. This is a major cause of differences between cultures. While some human groups struggled to survive in harsh environments, others thrived in 'kinder' environments.

Case study: The Fertile Crescent

One 'kinder' environment is an area stretching from the Eastern Mediterranean to the Persian Gulf, known as the Fertile Crescent (see map, page 7). Here, vegetation grows very easily in the warm, wet winters and hot, dry summers. Large areas of land are relatively flat. This is the region where human beings first learned how to farm successfully. For example, the first farmers grew wheat and rye 13,000 years ago in Syria.

When a culture turned to farming for its food instead of hunter-gathering, some very important changes in their way of life took place.

- Instead of wandering around hunting wild animals, they could now settle in one place.
- This made it worthwhile to design permanent buildings.
- Storing food surpluses became possible. This allowed some people to be released from farming and to develop other skills.

People from this region invented writing and made huge progress in maths and building design. They created the first cities, CIVILISATIONS and EMPIRES in the world.

Evidence suggests that the earliest writing developed in three fertile areas – Egypt, Mesopotamia (Iraq, Syria, Iran) and Harappa (Pakistan) between 3500BCE and 3100BCE.

Other environments

As groups migrated to other parts of the world, such as to Australia, they became very cut off from the peoples in Europe and Asia.

They would not have heard about any of the important developments, so they could not share what had been learned. Also the environments they learned to survive in were very different. They found fewer plants for food and far fewer animals that could be domesticated (for example, no sheep, horses or donkeys).

In some areas wildlife and game were plentiful, so there was no need to look for alternative sources of food or to develop farming. In other areas the environment was too harsh for farming to work. In such areas, people remained hunter-gatherers.

Back in Africa, where Homo sapiens had originated, the Sahara Desert and the equatorial rainforests proved to be huge barriers to communication and trade. The widely different natural environments provided few animals to domesticate. There were not many crops to farm. So, in Africa too, many cultures remained hunter-gatherers.

Peoples in Arctic regions, Africa, Australia and America developed their own distinct cultures due to their isolation. They did not develop powerful civilisations like the ones that grew up in Asia and Europe.

Even the great empires of the Incas and Aztecs in South and Central America were eventually held back by their lack of crops and farm animals. This limited the development of technology and communications and contributed to their defeat by the Europeans in the sixteenth century.

Spread of ideas

Cultures living in 'kinder' natural environments used horses to help them travel between settlements. New ideas spread across Asia and Europe; trade increased. Places on the same latitude would benefit most from learning about improved farming methods because they had similar climates.

Progress

These cultures grew wealthier. They could use this WEALTH to develop their art and TECHNOLOGY. This in turn led to progress in architecture, sciences and government.

Although cultures traded with each other, they also competed with each other for power. This encouraged the development of more things to trade and more powerful weapons of war.

Farming could support a denser population than hunting and gathering. The cultures that adopted the best farming methods became the most populated. This enabled them to have the biggest armies.

ACTIVITIES

1 There are three main reasons why different cultures have emerged. These are:

- different environments
- differences in wealth
- different technology.

These reasons are all linked. Draw a diagram with notes to explain the links between the reasons and why they caused different cultures to emerge. You can use the words listed below to help you:

Crops for farming; Horses/cattle; Settlements; Surplus; Wild animals for hunting; Latitude; Trade; Technology; Size of population; Isolation

2 'The reason that some cultures are more wealthy and powerful today than others is mainly down to luck.' How far does the evidence on pages 6–9 support this opinion? Discuss this in groups, then write up the discussion.

3 Why did the cultures that developed farming methods gain an advantage over those that remained mainly hunter-gatherers?

This competition for power strengthened the mistrust and fear between the different cultures, such as the rivalries between the Phoenicians, Greeks and Romans to control the lands around the Mediterranean 2,000–3,000 years ago.

As a result, men and women in different cultured groups have developed different roles, norms, beliefs, languages, and traditions.

Conclusion

So, even though human beings had learned that living in groups and co-operating was the best way to survive, they learned to do this in different ways. Some were more successful than others. At the same time they learned to be cautious, even hostile, towards 'outsider' groups.

As a result, men and women in different cultural groups have developed different roles, norms, beliefs, languages and traditions.

Investigation

2 Research one or more of the following peoples. They each have, or had, their own distinct culture.
   a) Yanomami of South America
   b) Bushmen of the Kalahari
   c) Inuit of North America
   d) Native Americans of the Plains

For each culture:

- identify and describe the people's natural environments
- explain how well the culture has adapted to its environment
- explain what you consider to be the strengths and weaknesses of the way the people adapted
- identify what problems the people face today.

This Case Study looks at the similarities and differences between the cultures of Spain and the UK.

Similarities

The cultures of most European countries are similar in many ways. The people have similar lifestyles. They live in wealthy, industrialised economies, where most people live in cities and towns. Most people have a job, a comfortable home and enough food. They use advanced technology such as computers, mobile phones, high speed trains and modern cars in their daily life. Most people are healthy and can expect to live into their seventies or eighties, and the state provides free education and basic healthcare.

The POLITICS of European countries are similar too. They are democracies, which means that the population vote in an election for political parties, and the winner of the election runs the country until the next election.

The cultures of most European countries have been influenced by immigration and invasions by other groups. The impact of other cultures on the UK is described in detail in the section on English culture (pages 26–30) and in the chart on page 31.

Spanish culture has also been deeply influenced by the impact of other cultures, especially by Islamic culture.

History and culture

As they did in the UK, the Romans invaded Spain. They arrived in 218 BCE, stayed there for about 700 years and brought their language and building skills to the country.

However, the major influence on Spanish culture was the arrival of the Arabs in the eighth century, who brought Islamic culture to Spain. These invaders were called the Moors in Spain. For another 700 years, despite constant battles with Christians who were trying to drive them out of Spain, the Moors introduced mathematics, geography and astronomy, and also high skills in architecture and building to Spanish culture. The Moorish influence is seen in Spanish food and architecture, and in lifestyles and culture.

The Moors finally left Spain 500 years ago, but, since then, influences from North Africa and other

European cultures have ensured that Spain has experienced a mix of powerful outside influences for far longer than the UK. This explains why the culture of Spain is far more diverse than that of most European societies.

Climate and culture

The biggest difference between the UK's and Spain's culture is the influence of climate and the environment. The weather makes Spanish everyday life and work very different from life in Britain. For most of the year, much more of life takes place in the open air. People meet and eat in squares or parks, or in pavement restaurants.

The summer heat in central and southern Spain means that most activities take place in the coolest parts of the day. Most shops close and work stops in the afternoon, and most of the population disappear from the streets from one until four in the afternoon.

The evening is the busiest time of day in Spanish life, and this has changed eating habits in most Spanish cities. Work and social activities start again in the early evening: shops open, people meet for a drink, then often go home until late evening, when they go out to dinner or to socialise, and stay out until after midnight. This lifestyle is becoming more common among young people in the UK, but it is still the case that most of the adult UK population go to bed when the Spaniards are going out.

Becoming part of the EU has changed this pattern a little, as businesses follow the European timetable, but the traditional Spanish day remains. This lifestyle encourages much wider social interactions in the community, especially in the areas that are not tourist centres.

Regional cultures

The UK is made up of four separate countries. Scotland has a separate government and the Scots see themselves as having a different culture from the English. Wales and Northern Ireland also have their own cultural identity and separate political assemblies that promote slightly different cultures. They have different languages, and different accents, and are proud of their separate cultures.

However, the Spanish culture is much more divided by regions and the people's identity is much more based on their home region, rather than being Spanish. From the map on page 12, you can see that the country is divided into different climates and regions. People from different regions speak different languages, eat different food, follow different occupations, and have very different lifestyles to each other. Their weather and their history have created different cultures.

Examples of regional cultures

1 Galicia and Asturias

This is the wettest part of Spain, particularly in autumn and winter. In Galicia, summers are cooler and wetter than the rest of the country. It is a rural area that relies on fishing and farming more than on industry. It is not as popular with tourists as the southern coastal areas and the language is Gallego.

In Asturias the people were never taken over by the Moors and are more closely linked to the Celts – they play bagpipes and drink cider. There is a tradition of challenging the Spanish government.

2 Castilla and Madrid

This area has a continental climate: there are heavy snowfalls in winter and temperatures regularly fall to minus 20ºC. Summer is very hot. As the Castillians say, 'nueve meses de invierno y tres meses de infierno' ('nine months of winter and three months of hell'). Madrid is the centre of government and the people who live there are often seen as the traditional Spanish leaders. The language is Castillian.

3 Basque Provinces: Navarra, Catalonia and Aragon

This area has a Mediterranean climate: the eastern and southern coasts have mild winters and cooler, more comfortable summers.

The people from the Navarra and Catalan regions are called Basques. They speak a language called Euskada and see themselves as a separate culture. Many of them want an independent state. This has led to some violence by some nationalist groups.

The main city in this area is Barcelona, which the locals say is the main city in Spain, much more attractive and important than Madrid. The city and region is also seen by the locals as the centre of Spanish culture, especially the art and architecture.

4 Valencia, Murcia and Andalucia

This area has a semi-arid climate: very hot and dry. Average winter temperatures are above 14ºC and average summer temperatures are high. Rainfall is very low. This is the area of Spain that holidaymakers flock to for reliably sunny days.

The area was the centre of Moorish culture but the cultures of the three territories are very different.

Murcia is virtually a desert, and provides very little work for local people. By contrast, Valencia is very fertile, and is a major agricultural area, still using many of the Moorish farming techniques, which are best for dry areas.

The local food is influenced by Moorish tastes. Sweet dishes are much the same as those found in Arab countries, using lots of honey and nuts.

Different territories

Regions in Spain.

ACTIVITY

1 Explain how the Spanish cultures described above are different from your own culture.

1 CULTURE AND BELIEFS

CONCEPT 2

There is a wide variety of factors that influence an individual's culture and identity

How are people shaped by the cultures they are born into? In this concept section you will learn about:

- Nature and nurture, and the contrasting evidence in the nature versus nurture debate.
- The influence of primary and secondary agents of SOCIALISATION.
- The importance of beliefs to a culture.

The following are ideas and terms that you will need to know from this concept section:

education • family • peer group • mass media • religion • ethnicity • work • role models • genetic and environmental influence • socialisation • nature and nurture debate

ACTIVITY

1 In Source A, the man of the Wodaabe and the western European model both use make-up. Which is regarded as normal and which is regarded as abnormal behaviour in England? Give reasons for your answer.

How is culture acquired?

The questions dealt with in this topic are: 'How do we actually "get" our culture? Are we born with it or do we learn it as we grow up?' This is part of what is known as the 'nature v nurture' debate.

Nature and nurture

Which has the more powerful influence on us as a person: our GENES or the people around us? Simply put, the two sides of the debate are as follows:

- nature – supporters of this side argue that genes are the major influence on our INTELLIGENCE and behaviour.
- nurture – supporters argue that our intelligence, behaviour and culture are learned through a complex process known as socialisation. On page 5 we saw that socialisation means learning how to behave in society.

It is difficult to set up experiments in a laboratory to find answers that help us decide which side of the debate to support. However, look at the following evidence (Sources A–I, pages 13–16), collected over the last 100 years or so.

Source A

Wodaabe man of Niger (western Africa) preparing for a party.

A western European model.

Think about it

If nurture (socialisation) is more influential than nature (genes), then our parents have a big role to play in influencing us. Should parents be held more responsible for their children?

If intelligence, criminal and addictive behaviour are due to our genes, then what should happen to those people with 'bad genes'?

Other reasons why this is an important debate will come out as you research the arguments in this section.

Source B

As a result of evolving separately, the tribes in New Guinea developed more than language differences (see Case Study on page 8). For example, GENDER ROLES are different.

In her famous research, the ANTHROPOLOGIST Margaret Mead described three tribes. These are some of her findings.

- The Arapesh expected both men and women to be gentle and play an equal part in bringing up their children.

- The Mundugumor, however, were the opposite. Both men and women were forceful and women detested having and looking after children.

- The Tchambuli were different again. The women were self-assertive, practical and ran the HOUSEHOLD. They shaved their heads and did not wear any necklaces, rings or bracelets. The men wore lovely ornaments, did the shopping, gossiped and loved dancing.

ACTIVITIES

1 Look up the following terms in the glossary and learn their meanings:

Genes; Socialisation; MALE; FEMALE; MASCULINE; FEMININE; Gender roles; Intelligence

2 a) Create a table like the one below. Put the terms you looked up in Activity 1 into the columns you think are correct. In the fourth column, add the reasons for your choice.

Nature	Nurture	Both	Reasons

b) Decide whether Source A (page 13) supports the nature or nurture argument, or both, and add to the table. Then select an appropriate statement from the list below to write into the 'Reasons' column.

- 'Masculine behaviour is different in different cultures.'
- 'It is not natural for men to wear make-up.'
- 'Gender roles are learned through socialisation.'
- 'Gender roles are determined by our genes.'
- 'The way each person's brain works is determined by our genes.'

c) Now do the same with Source B.

d) Study the following sources C–I (pages 15–16) and add each source to your table with reasons for your decisions, just as you did for Sources A and B, creating your own sentences for the 'Reasons' column.

e) When you have completed d) think about the nature v nuture debate. Write down your own opinion about which has the most powerful influence on us as a person (you may well be undecided). What are the most important pieces of evidence on both sides?

Source C

The 'Jim Twins'

Studies of twins who have been brought up apart could help resolve the debate. If twins have identical behaviour, even though they have been socialised differently, then this would suggest that nature is more powerful than nurture in determining our behaviour and culture. Thomas Bouchard, a psychologist at the University of Minnesota in the USA, conducted the most famous of these studies. One of the cases he researched was that of the 'Jim Twins'.

Born in 1940, Jim Springer and Jim Lewis were adopted by different families four weeks after birth. In 1979, they were reunited for the study at the age of 39. The Jim twins caused a public stir, as they shared remarkably similar lives. Similarities were striking and included the following:

- did well in maths at school and had problems with spelling
- the same hobbies: mechanical drawing and carpentry
- similar habits: chewing their fingernails, chain smoking Salem cigarettes
- headaches at the same time every day
- the same colour and model Chevy car
- first wives named Linda and second wives named Betty.

Other similarities included naming their dogs Toy, their sons James Allan and taking holidays in the same place each year. Their IQ scores were as close as one person would get doing the test twice.

Source D

Eyesight

A recent study of British twins has revealed that the need to wear glasses is largely genetic. Only 15 per cent of short-sightedness is caused by environmental influences such as using computers or reading a lot of small print.

Source E

There have been a number of reports of feral children – children who have grown up without human parenting. Here is one of the more famous cases. More can be researched on the internet.

Kamala and Amala, the 'Wolf Girls'

In 1920, in India, two young girls were discovered under the care of a she-wolf. The girls were taken to an orphanage. Kamala, aged eight and Amala, aged 18 months, behaved exactly like small wild animals.

- They slept during the day and woke by night. They slept curled up together in a tight ball. They growled and twitched in their sleep.
- They remained on all fours, enjoyed raw meat, and would bite and attack other children if provoked. They had spent so long on all fours that their tendons and joints had shortened. It was impossible for them to straighten their legs and even attempt to walk upright.
- They could smell raw meat from a distance.
- They had an acute sense of sight and hearing.
- Amala died one year later, but Kamala lived for nine years in the orphanage. She died of illness at the age of 17.
- Kamala found it very difficult to learn to speak. She only learned a few words.

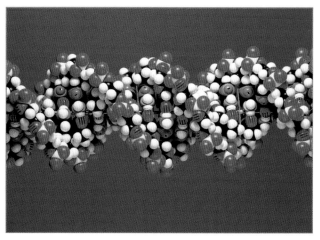

A DNA double helix, which contains our genetic instructions. How important are our genes in making us who we are?

Source F

Intelligence: a summary of views

- Some scientists believe you can measure intelligence just as you can measure eyesight. In the early part of the last century they put forward the idea that you can control the human race by selective breeding (eugenics). If intelligence is controlled by our genes, for example, what is the point of education for those with a low intelligence? Why not breed them out?

- In 1994, Hernstein and Murray's book, *The Bell Curve*, argued that differences in intelligence test scores between racial groups reflect BIOLOGICAL differences. Belief in the Bell Curve and in the genetic, rather than social, basis for intelligence has encouraged many racist ideas.

- Other scientists say that genes work by interacting with the environment. Social factors will also influence intelligence.

- Intelligence tests may be more of a test of social factors, such as your education. For example, the US military tested recruits and found that black applicants scored lower than whites. However, an analysis of the recruits found this was because of educational differences. Black recruits scored very low until the 1950s, when their scores increased as a result of better education for black children.

- Many researchers believe there are many ways of measuring intelligence.

- It is impossible to set questions that don't have some sort of bias towards a particular cultural background or are easier for men than for women or the other way round. For example, boys tend to do better in working with shapes and patterns whereas girls score higher on language skills.

- Diet is also an important factor. Good diet helps people to function well physically and mentally.

Source G

Aggressive genes?

For 26 years, researchers followed what happened to 1,037 children born in 1972 in Dunedin, New Zealand. They found that children were much more likely to grow up to be aggressive if they had inherited a particular version of a gene called 'MAOA', which affects how the brain works.

But people with MAOA only went off the rails if they had had an abusive upbringing. Carriers with good parenting were usually completely normal.

Source H

Smoking

Smoking during pregnancy causes the baby to weigh less – a clear example of the effects of nurture. However, recent research shows that this effect is mostly confined to women who have particular types of two genes, CYP1A1 and GSTT1.

Source I

A gene's influence

Recent research in Italy shows that families in which the women are very fertile also contain a high frequency of homosexual men. It is suggested that the link is a gene responsible for both.

How does socialisation work?

As our ability to understand and identify genes grows, there is growing evidence that genes play a part in many aspects of human behaviour and development. However, some of the evidence in the sources you have studied shows that socialisation plays at least some part in making us the person we are. Exactly what the balance is, however, between nature and nurture is still open to debate. Human beings do not have the whole answer to this and more research is needed. Whatever the outcome of this debate, there is no doubt that much of our culture is learned. So, now let us look at how it is learned.

Primary socialisation

Evidence shows that those who look after us in our first months and years, play a central part in moulding us (see page 5). It is from our immediate family that we learn to talk, walk and use various objects. They are also the ones who first teach us what is right and wrong behaviour and how to relate in a 'proper' way to different people such as grandparents, friends, strangers and so on.

So already we are learning norms, MORALS, values, language through our family. The family is the primary agent of socialisation. Methods of learning include:

- *imitation*, copying Mummy when washing
- *identification*, baby follows older brother around
- *role learning*, for example, helping to clear up after a meal
- *conditioning*, rewards to encourage certain behaviours and sanctions to discourage others.

A child is learning the basics of co-operation, and how to behave. These blueprints are the ones most firmly imprinted in the brain. Once these blueprints have been set up, research shows that they are often there for life.

This is one of the key reasons why it has proved so hard to re-socialise feral children when they are found. They have already been socialised, but not in a human way.

ACTIVITIES

1 List the four methods by which a child learns through primary socialisation and give one more example for each.

2 'Give me a child until she/he is five and I will give you the woman/man.' Explain this statement using your understanding of primary socialisation. Refer to Source E, page 15, about feral children. Does this source support it? Give your reasons.

Other agents of socialisation are shown in the diagram below.

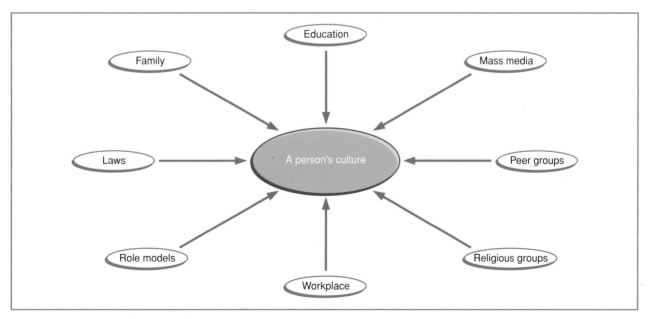

How do we acquire our culture?

These are the other agents of socialisation identified in the diagram on page 17 and explained in the diagram below. These are called secondary agents of socialisation.

- **Education:** Schools teach about a culture's values, traditions, attitudes and language.

- **The mass media:** Advertising can have a huge influence on our values, attitudes and behaviour. The headlines, articles and pictures on the TV, internet and in newspapers and magazines are likely to be part of our socialisation too.

- **Laws:** These are formal norms with sanctions. Laws set out clear-cut rules about what is acceptable behaviour in society. If someone breaks a law, there are consequences if they are found out. This individual will be punished either by removal from society (prison), fines (material cost) or rejection by the rest of society. This has a powerful influence on most people's behaviour. Other laws, for example, laws against DISCRIMINATION (see page 146) at work have helped improve the treatment of women, homosexuals and ethnic minorities.

- **Peer groups:** This is particularly powerful during teenage years. The desire to belong to a group is strong.

- **Religious groups:** In some cultures, these affect almost everyone (see page 21).

- **The workplace:** The way we are organised at work and our relationships within it contribute to our socialisation. The hours we work and the type of work we do are also important influences.

- **Role models:** Senior or famous members of a culture play a key part in maintaining or adapting it. They may reinforce or challenge behaviour, values and traditions that others want to copy.

These influences are not all of equal importance for all cultures. For example, the mass media is clearly more powerful in a culture where everyone can read and each household has access to a TV and radio. Religious organisations have real influence on culture in some parts of the world. Examples include South America (Catholic Christian), the Middle East (Islam) and parts of the US (evangelical Christian).

The different agents of socialisation can also CONFLICT with each other. For example, in England, a young person may learn to conform to one set of norms with their family concerning such values as swearing and sexual relationships, but experience another set of norms with their peers or on the TV. As we mature we usually learn to manage these conflicting pressures. In such a SOCIETY, individuals have to work out their own beliefs and values. As you will see on pages 21–25 there are some cultures that go out of their way to keep the mass media away from the socialisation process.

Case Study
Gender and sex – what's the difference?

In order to show how socialisation works, we shall consider the way we learn our gender roles. There is often much confusion between the nouns *gender* and SEX. The word 'gender' means the way we are expected to think and behave by our culture according to whether we are male or female. In other words, it is to do with our ideas of masculine and feminine. 'Sex', on the other hand, covers our biological and INNATE CHARACTERISTICS. It is simply whether we are male or female.

We are born into a culture that already has a set of beliefs and values. All the people who are involved in the raising of a child will have ideas about how children should behave. As soon as we are born, we are sent signals as to what is expected of us. As we go through life, gender role norms are usually then reinforced by secondary socialisation.

The table below shows some familiar examples of the ways gender roles can follow traditional patterns of choices for jobs and education.

LANGUAGE	IMAGES	ROLES
'Go and help Mummy/Daddy'	Blue theme in bedroom and for clothes for a boy; pink themes for a girl	Boy helps Dad wash the car Girl helps Mum cook
GIRLS: 'Isn't she sweet!' 'Girls should not be rowdy' 'She is so kind' 'Doesn't she look pretty!'	TOYS FOR GIRLS: Pram/doll Role-play set: nurse, hairdresser Make-up kit	OCCUPATIONS, 2006: Health and social work: 79 per cent female Childcare workers: 98 per cent female Construction: 90 per cent male Manufacturing: 75 per cent male High court judges: 94 per cent male Surgeons: 90 per cent male 70 per cent of women are in the worst paid jobs
BOYS: 'He's a real lad' 'He's so forceful' 'Isn't he big and strong!'	TOYS FOR BOYS: Action man figures Model cars Skateboard/football kit/bike/violent video games *James Bond* film poster	FURTHER EDUCATION CHOICES, 2006: Hairdressing and beauty: 93 per cent female Engineering and technology: 87 per cent male Computer science: 81 per cent male

ACTIVITIES

1 Divide into small groups and consider the following statements:

- All boys are interested in is sport.
- Girls should wait for boys to invite them out.
- Boys show off more than girls.
- Girls are better at modern languages than boys.
- Girls are more concerned about their appearance than boys.
- Boys should pay for girls when they take them out.
- Girls are less confident than boys.
- Boys are better at maths.
- Girls are more caring than boys.
- Groups of boys are more rowdy than groups of girls.

a) For each statement, take it in turns to say whether you agree or disagree.

b) Record the group's views, including whether you all agreed or not.

c) Reflect: are you guilty of stereotyping each other? In other words, do your answers suggest that you have 'hidden' expectations based on your assumptions about how males and females should behave? Where have these assumptions come from?

2 Study the table above and use examples to show how primary socialisation can affect our career choices.

Different gender roles

The norms in England for gender, however, are not the same for every cultural group. The fact that gender roles can vary from culture to culture suggests that gender is learned rather than inherited.

Source B shows how some of the agents of primary and secondary socialisation give us our culture. The research opportunities suggested in 'Investigations' (right) will help you extend your understanding of these influences.

Investigations

1 Get a shopping catalogue and analyse the adverts for children's toys.
   a) Are these adverts a form of primary or secondary socialisation? Give your reasons.
   b) How does the catalogue use colour to suggest which pages are for boys' toys and which are for girls'?
   c) Why are there children shown playing with many of the toys?
   d) What later roles are the toys preparing children for? Explain.

2 Look up the films on TV for the next week. Identify those that promote 'masculine' and 'feminine' roles. How do these films affect our socialisation?

3 a) Collect information about numbers of students at a coeducational school taking options. Identify those options where there seems to be a male/female bias.
   b) Design a questionnaire to find out the main influences on the students' choices.

How important are beliefs to a culture?

You can use the case study of the Amish to understand what you have learned about the theory of culture (what it is and how you acquire it).

You can also use it as a model for a future study of another culture.

Case Study
The Amish culture

Introducing the Amish

Imagine what it would be like if you had never watched TV or if you had never heard music on an MP3 player. What would your life be like if you did not have a mobile phone, or a fridge, or a washing machine in your home, or have the use of a car?

This is how the Amish live. They refuse to have or use any of these items in their lives.

Why?
It is not because they are poor. It is because they believe it is wrong to have them.

Why?
Read on.

Today, most Amish live in Pennsylvania, Ohio and Indiana in the USA. They choose to live separately from other US citizens and have a distinct culture.

The information on pages 22–25 gives you some clues about the Amish. You can research their culture further either on the internet, where there is a range of useful sites, or through your library. You may design your own research or use the activities below. The film *Witness* paints a vivid picture of Amish life. The documentary *The Devil's Playground* shows how the Amish try to give their children a free choice of what lifestyle to follow.

ACTIVITIES

1 Start by studying the six photos A–F and their captions on page 22.

On your own or with a partner, write down any questions about the Amish culture these pictures suggest to you. You can then plan how to research answers to them.

2 Having studied the information on pages 22–25 about the Amish, sort the following sentence starters and enders:

a) The Amish do not wear buttons because	i) they believe it will cause their communities to drift apart and pursue material wealth.
b) The Amish will not join the US army because	ii) it is a sign they are married.
c) The Amish do not educate their children beyond 14 years of age because	iii) they believe it will cause conflict and make it more difficult for them to concentrate on following Jesus' teachings.
d) The Amish do not live with people from other cultures because	iv) it is a way of enforcing their norms.
e) The Amish do not have modern technology because	v) they believe that they, the people, are the Church.
f) The Amish use shunning as a sanction because	vi) they believe these are a sign of pride and they want to be humble.
g) Some Amish men grow beards because	vii) they are pacifists. They believe this is what God and Jesus want us to be.
h) The Amish do not have church buildings because	viii) they believe they will get distracted by worldly ambition and 'the ways of the English', and not stay close to God's way.

A

Amish men are wearing traditional black suits and hats. Women are also in traditional black, with aprons and bonnets.

B

The Amish follow a life based around farming, using horses and simple farm machinery.

C

This woman is making quilts. You can also see her bonnet and traditional clothes.

D

The Amish have a very clear DIVISION OF LABOUR. The men do the barn raising while the women prepare and serve the food.

E

Amish women making pretzels. Can you see any electrical items?

F

Children are taught from a very young age to help out on the farms and around the home. They stop going to school at the age of 14.

Background to the Amish

In Switzerland, in the early sixteenth century, a group of Christians was led by Jacob Amman. They wanted to practise Christianity differently to the way the Pope and the kings and queens of Europe at that time thought was right. They wanted to:

• simplify prayer and church service
• wait until children grew up before baptising them.

Because of this, other Christians persecuted them. For example, many were put in sacks and thrown into rivers.

So they gave up trying to live in Europe. In the seventeenth century they settled in Pennsylvania, USA. Here they could rebuild their way of life based on farming and their Christian beliefs. The way they live has scarcely changed since those days.

Today, they live away from other cultures in small, tight-knit communities. Among themselves, they speak a form of German. Most Amish have very little to do with anyone outside of the Amish faith. Those who are not Amish are still referred to as the 'English'. Eighty per cent of the Amish live in Pennsylvania, Ohio and Indiana.

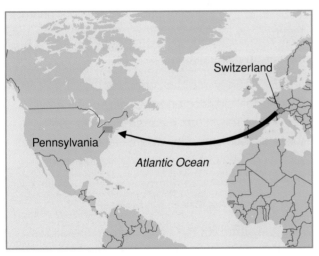

Map showing migration of Amish from Europe to Pennsylvania, USA, in the seventeenth and eighteenth centuries, where many settled.

What are Amish principles?

The Amish believe that living how God wants them to is essential. They believe God wants them to submit to his guidance and serve others – giving up any selfish thoughts. This way of life is called *Gelassenheit* and is summed up in Source A below. The Amish believe that modern technology such as electricity, television, cars and the telephone all undermine these principles. This is because they are means of bringing the outside world into the community. If they used modern technology, they believe their communities would be pulled into the modern world and their beliefs would be watered down or lost.

ACTIVITY

1 What reasons can you give for the Amish being afraid that modern technology such as electricity, television, cars and the telephone will break up their communities?

Source A

The basic beliefs of the Amish
The Amish say:

• the Bible is God's word.

• God loved the world so much that he gave his only son, Jesus, to die on the cross for us. We must be humble at all times and try to live as Jesus said we should.

• we believe in peace at all times, the use of violence is never right.

• faith calls for a lifestyle of learning, good work, serving others and holy living.

• the Church is separate from the state. The Church is the people, not a building.

Rules

Amish communities live by a set of rules. These rules are guidelines for living. They cover all aspects of clothing, leisure activities, work, worship and giving birth. Every rule has a reason that links back to their beliefs. See Source B below for some Amish rules.

Source B

Some Amish rules

Beards

A man does not shave his beard after he becomes married. Moustaches, however, are associated with the military and therefore are forbidden as they symbolise violence and pride. Amish men should be humble.

Clothes

Women and girls wear dresses made from one solid colour. They always wear long sleeves. Their skirts must be longer than halfway between their knees and the floor. They cannot cut their hair. It is always worn in a bun on the back of their heads. If they are married, they wear a black bonnet on their heads. If they are single, they wear a white one.

Buttons are not allowed because the Amish believe they are a sign of pride.

Men must wear a solid coloured shirt, dark trousers, braces and a straw or broad-rimmed hat. The Amish feel that these clothes make them separate from the outside world.

ACTIVITY

1 How do Amish beliefs in Source A (page 23) explain their rules for beards and clothes (Source B)?

Shunning

The Amish will never use violence. They use shunning to enforce their beliefs and rules. If someone is shunned, no one buys from, sells to, or even eats at the same table as the shunned person. All members that leave the Amish Church are shunned, as are those who marry outside the Amish faith. This idea also comes from the Bible:

'But now I am writing to you that you must not associate with anyone who calls himself a brother but is sexually immoral or greedy, an idolater or a slanderer, a drunkard or a swindler. With such a man do not even eat.'

1 Corinthians 5:11

Tourism

The second largest Amish community is in Lancaster, Pennsylvania. It has become the centre of 'Amish tourism'. It is near many cities – close enough for people to take day trips there.

On the one hand, tourism is resented because:

- it means the community becomes crowded. Their farm and schoolwork is disrupted
- tourists take photos of the Amish – which they do not like as it is a sign of pride to have your photo taken.

However, tourism also has benefits:

- It brings money into the community.
- It increases 'outsider' understanding of the Amish way of life. This in turn means the government tolerates them and does not interfere. For example, Amish children can legally stop going to school at 14.

Teenagers

When they turn 16, the Amish community allows teenagers the freedom to explore the customs of the outside world – including alcohol, drugs and sex – before deciding whether to join the Amish Church for life and be baptised, or leave the community altogether.

Source C

The Devil's Playground

The Devil's Playground is a documentary by filmmaker Lucy Walker. It tells of hundreds of Amish teenagers from ten different states who congregate in 'barn hops' and 'hoedowns'. Large fields are filled with cars and horses and buggies. Many get drunk.

One of the teenagers in *The Devil's Playground* is 16-year-old Gerald of Indiana. He moves out of his parents' house to live in a trailer. In the film he says: 'I didn't tell my parents for like a month. If I was living at home, I couldn't have 200 channels of DirecTV, a stereo and Nintendo, and a fridge full of beer.'

Faron is an 18 year old with an increasingly serious drug problem. His music idol is the late rapper Tupac Shakur. Yet Faron says he hopes to follow his father into the Amish ministry.

Despite the freedom to experiment, or maybe because of it, 85–90 per cent of the teenagers actually decide to return to the Amish ways and join the Church by getting baptised. You can read more on the internet and view video clips by putting *The Devil's Playground* into a search engine.

Amish teenagers.

ACTIVITIES

1 According to Source C, what does *The Devil's Playground* tell us about the influence of the following agents of socialisation on Amish youth? Give your reasons.

The mass media; Peer groups; Religion; The family

2 Study all the information and sources about the Amish on pages 21–25. Use the spider diagram of what culture is on page 3 as a model to create your own concept map of the Amish culture. An example of how you might start this is given below:

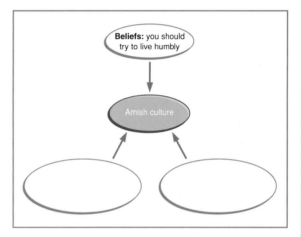

3 What are the main religious beliefs of the Amish? How do they influence other aspects of their culture? Refer to examples in the information and sources on pages 21–25 to support your answer.

4 Why is interaction with the 'outside' culture such a problem for the Amish?

5 Does this study of the Amish support or challenge the argument that nurture is more important than nature in making us who we are?

6 What do you consider are the strengths and weaknesses of the Amish culture? Give your reasons.

CONCEPT 3

Interaction between cultures can bring benefits and can cause conflict and change

What happens to different cultures when they interact with each other? In this concept section you will learn about:

- The causes and effects of immigration into the UK.
- How the UK became a multi-cultural society.
- Whether there is a single culture in this country – a British cultural identity.

The following are ideas and terms that you will need to know from this concept section:

push and pull factors • immigration • emigration • multi-culturalism • nationality • human rights • freedoms • refugees • cost/benefits • rights and responsibilities • ethnic minority groups • citizenship • shared values • democratic society

Migration into the UK

Over the past 2,000 years, many different ETHNIC GROUPS have lived in 'the British Isles'.

Migration

Migration means moving from one country (or region) to another. When someone leaves a country/region it is called EMIGRATION; when someone moves to a country/region it is called IMMIGRATION.

Push and pull factors

When people decide to migrate they usually have powerful reasons. It is not an easy decision to leave relatives, friends and your home.

People are *pushed* out of their homeland and *pulled* towards a new home. The chart below shows the push and pull factors that have influenced people's decisions to migrate over the years.

History of migration into the UK

People have been living in the islands that make up the UK for at least ten thousand years. Early migrants were usually people travelling to find a safe and fertile place to live. The first two push and pull factors in the chart below were the usual causes of early migration.

Later changes in population were the result of powerful empires seizing territory for power and wealth.

The culture in the UK now is the result of the merging of the many tribes and invaders who have lived on the British Isles for thousands of years.

PUSH FACTORS: WHY PEOPLE WANT TO EMIGRATE	PULL FACTORS: WHY PEOPLE CHOOSE TO MOVE TO ANOTHER COUNTRY
Poverty in their homeland.	To escape poverty.
Shortage of food and/or housing.	Better living conditions.
Limited opportunities to get work or make a living wage.	More jobs, better wages, better opportunities in careers.
Poor education, with no chance to improve knowledge.	More opportunities to learn and develop knowledge and abilities.
Unhealthy environment, poor healthcare.	Healthier environment and better medical facilities.
Intolerance of their culture and/or religious beliefs.	A safer life, with less threat of persecution, more freedom to choose lifestyle.
Political disagreements and threats to their safety.	Prefer the political and legal system, feel more secure. Less corruption.
Bad weather.	Good weather.

The Celtic tribes

Celtic tribes spread from central Europe from 500BCE onwards. They settled in areas now known as France, Belgium, Britain, Ireland and Spain.

- Daily life – the Celts lived in large family groups. They made clothes from wool woven into tartan patterns. They also became outstanding metalworkers by learning from tribes living in western Asia. They used these skills to make beautiful images of sacred birds and animals in bronze and gold.
- Religion – the Celts believed in many gods and goddesses. They worshipped in temples. Druid priests (Ancient Celtic priests) taught about the importance of life after death.
- Food – the Celts were good hunters. They also knew how to grow crops. They invented a harvesting machine. The Romans thought this was such a good idea that they copied and developed it further.

> If we are to end the fighting and remain in control, we must encourage the Celts to become more like us. We must offer their leaders gifts like mirrors, furniture and new cooking tools. We must make sure they see how much better we live. When they see our superior buildings, stone streets, public baths, large town villas with under-floor heating, our painted and plaster-covered walls, they'll realise that it is worth accepting our laws and other customs. They'll accept the need to speak our language. Most will then want to stop fighting us and join us instead.

ACTIVITIES

1 Give two examples of Celtic beliefs and two examples of other aspects of Celtic culture.

2 Describe and explain two ways cultures benefited from interacting with each other.

The Roman invasions

The Romans invaded Britain in the first century BCE and again in the first century CE. The Romans saw Britain as a useful source of metals (especially tin), corn, meat, skins and wool.

The Celts fought hard to stop the Romans taking over their lands. There were uprisings and rebellions. The Romans wanted to bring this to an end and to start trading with the Celts. The quote in the speech bubble above from a Roman General to his advisers sums this up.

This plan eventually worked. The Celtic islanders actually became Romans, both culturally and legally. Roman CITIZENSHIP gave the Celts political status. By 300 CE, almost everyone in 'Britannia' was Roman, even though they were descended from Celts and still mostly speaking 'Celtic' dialects. Roman rule brought cultural change.

The Romans did not conquer the Celts in Scotland, Ireland, Wales and Cornwall. In these areas, the Celts remained independent, keeping their own language and culture for many centuries to come.

ACTIVITIES

3 Get into pairs. Imagine you are Celts. You have heard a report of what the Roman General said (above). Prepare a speech either for or against co-operating with the Romans. Use arguments based on the information in the speech above and your knowledge of the Celts.

4 What was likely to happen to the Celtic culture if they did/did not co-operate with the Romans?

Angles, Saxons and Jutes

After the Romans finally left in the fifth century CE, tribes from northern Europe began invading Britain.

The Angles, Saxons and Jutes landed and settled in the eastern and southern parts of Britain. These tribes came from areas in what is now mainly Germany. They mixed with each other over the years, leading to a common Anglo-Saxon culture. Their language became known as 'Angle-ish' or English. Their land in the south and east became known as 'Angle-land' – England.

Vikings

Meanwhile, the Vikings from Norway, Sweden and Denmark (also known as the Norsemen – the men from the north) began arriving in the eighth century CE. They invaded large parts of northern Britain where their language and culture became the main influence. For over 200 years on and off there were battles between Viking descendants and their Anglo-Saxon rivals for control of the island.

Normans

In 1066, the Norman invasion led to the defeat of both the Saxons and the Vikings. The Normans took strict control of the defeated people. Norman language (French) and culture now became dominant over most of Britain. One example of this can be seen in the way words for our food change from farm to table (from peasant worker to nobleman). 'Pig', 'cow' and 'sheep' are Anglo-Saxon words. These are the words used on the farm. When the meat arrives at the table, they become 'pork', 'beef' and 'mutton'. These are French-based words (*porc*, *boeuf* and *mouton*).

The English language we speak today has grown from the mixing of languages spoken by all these invaders.

ACTIVITIES

1 What is the origin of the word 'English'?

2 How true is it to say that English is a pure language? Explain your answer.

3 How important is a common language in developing a common culture?

Source A

LATIN (ROMAN) VERBS	FRENCH	MEANING	ENGLISH WORDS
duco, duxi, ductus	duc	to lead	conduct, induction, duke
mitto, misi, missus	mettre, mis	to send	mission, message, emit
scribo, scripsi, scriptum	écrire	to write	inscribe, scripture, script

Source B

Some regional dialects in spoken English

Na then, me China Plate, would ya loike ter Scapa Fla daahhhn ter the bloomin' Noah's Ark for a ball of chalk wif me? (Cockney: London)

Noo then, me skip, ood yoo loike ter goo dowl ter the park for a walk with me? (Birmingham)

'Na' then, mi bonnie lad, ood thee li' ta nip on darn ta t' park for eur walk wi' mee? (Yorkshire)

Neeo then, wor bairn, wud yee leek tuh gan doon tuh the wreck fo' a wark wi' wor? (Newcastle)

ACTIVITIES

4 Look at Source A. Can you think of five more French words that are linked to English words?

5 With a partner, try speaking aloud the phrases in Source B in the different dialects. Now try translating the phrase. Which did you find easier to translate – why?

Other settlers

Later settlers in Britain often migrated because of some of the other push and pull factors listed in the chart on page 26.

Huguenots

During the sixteenth and seventeenth centuries, over 60,000 Protestant (Huguenot) refugees from Belgium, Holland and France fled to Britain to escape religious PERSECUTION.

They settled in London and in towns like Norwich and Canterbury. Most finally settled in London. Some were expert in making clocks and scientific instruments. Others were goldsmiths, silversmiths, merchants and artists.

Their skills at weaving silk and velvet helped expand the silk weaving industry in Spitalfields. During the eighteenth century, wealthy Huguenots gave a lot of money to support the army.

Germans

Between 1850 and 1914, the number of Germans who chose to live in Britain rose from 4,000 to 40,000. They brought with them new ideas in banking and other industries. Companies that are world famous today, like ICI (chemicals) and Siemens (computers and electronics) were started by Germans settling in Britain during this time.

Russian and Polish Jews

Between 1870 and 1914, about 120,000 Russian and Polish Jews fled to Britain to escape racist and religious persecution. Many settled in London, Manchester and Leeds where they were free to practise their religions. Some set up their own textile businesses, providing good clothing. Many went to work in factories, sometimes playing a leading role in trade union struggles.

Irish

Irish labourers worked on the building of new roads, canals and railways during the Industrial Revolution in the eighteenth and nineteenth centuries.

Sailors

As the British Empire developed so did trade, bringing new peoples to Britain. Lascars (sailors from South East Asia and India) came along with seamen from countries like China, West Africa, and those known today as Somalia and the Yemen.

Textile workers

During the twentieth century, immigrants from Cyprus, Pakistan and Bangladesh have come to work in textiles.

Italians

In the first half of the twentieth century, many Italians came to Britain. The Clerkenwell district of London became known as 'Little Italy'. Italians introduced street vending of ice cream and worked in the catering trade as waiters, chefs, bakers, confectioners and café owners. Later on, in the 1940s and 1950s, men and women from the south of Italy were recruited to work in factories in Luton and Bedford. Some went on to open Italian restaurants and pizzerias.

Other imported delicacies including curry and chow mein, smoked salmon and fried fish have all been introduced by people from overseas and are now part of everyone's diet.

After the Second World War

After the Second World War, there was a labour shortage. People forced from their homes in Poland, Italy, Ukraine and Germany filled their jobs. Later, the National Health Service (NHS) and organisations like London Transport recruited men and women from the Caribbean to work for them.

Immigrants have brought new musical sounds like bhangra and dub. Some have become sporting heroes and founders of many well-known businesses. Today, health and transport services continue to be supported by nurses, doctors and managers from overseas. In towns and cities, there are not only churches but also synagogues, mosques, gurdwaras, Hindu and Buddhist temples.

ACTIVITY

1   Using the information on pages 26–29 – and any other you have researched – create a presentation that highlights the ways England has benefited from the immigration of people from other cultures over the past 500 years.

The main phases in the growth of the population of Britain.

Time period (approx.)	Population (millions)	Ethnic groups involved	Emigration (E) or Immigration (I)	Comments on population and reasons
500BCE–43CE	1	Celtic tribes	I	Celtic tribes from North Europe settled in England, Scotland and Wales. Searching for good land.
43–410CE	1.5	Romans	I	There is still much evidence of the Roman occupation. There were over 125,000 Roman soldiers and their families living here. Tin and farming.
450–865	1.5	Anglo-Saxons	I	Came from northern Europe. Gradually took control of the whole of England.
865–1000	1.5	Vikings	I	From Scandinavia. Took control of most of Scotland, Wales and Northern Ireland.
1066–1348	3.5	Normans	I	From North France. Took over all England and Wales.
1350–1642	6	English, Belgian, Dutch, French	Some E and I. Migration from towns began. Some emigration to the USA. Some immigrated from Europe to the UK.	Many fled to avoid religious persecution.
1700–1850	21	English, Scottish, Irish	Mainly I. Migration from countryside to towns. Immigration from Ireland.	Massive growth of cities due to Industrial and Agricultural revolutions. Religious persecution.
1850–1910	37	English, Scottish, Welsh, Irish Lithuanian, Polish, Russian	E and I. Emigration to mainly USA, Canada. Some immigration from Europe.	Mainly to USA. Highland clearance, Irish potato famine.
1914–45	49	English, Scottish, Welsh, Irish, European	E and I. Migration within UK. Three million emigrated before the Second World War. Immigration of refugees.	Continuing Industrial Revolution. New start in colonies and USA. Religious persecution in Europe.
1945–99	58.6	English, Scottish, Welsh, Irish, European, Caribbean, African, S. E. Asia	E and I. Migration within UK. Immigration from colonies. Emigration to Canada, USA, Australia and South Africa.	Sharp fall in UK city populations 1950–80. Active recruiting in colonies due to labour shortages in UK. UK citizens leave to start new life. More emigrate than immigrate during this period.

Investigation

Study the table above. It has been completed using data collected from the social history page of the BBC website. Research whether there is an English culture. Consider:

- The role of the Celts/Romans/Normans/ other ethnic groups in influencing culture in the UK.
- Further examples of Latin, Greek and French influences on English language.

- The experiences and contributions of immigrants to England since the first century CE. See Channel 4 (Originations) and the museum-based website called 'movinghere' for an excellent start to this research.
- What the statistics in the table show. Overall, have more people migrated from or to Britain over the last 200 years?

Beliefs – the basis of culture?

Cultures are held together by shared beliefs. For example, the Amish culture is based on their version of Christianity. Cultures in many countries are based on religious beliefs and the norms and values which come from those beliefs.

Most Western cultures are based on Christian values taken from the Bible, but over the years these values have become part of the legal systems of the culture. Ideas about peace and human rights have their roots in religious teachings (for example, the Bible tells us to 'love thy neighbour' and that 'Thou shalt not kill').

However, in the UK today, people follow many different religions – the UK is a multi-faith society. Also, generally speaking, religion itself is not such an important part of many people's daily lives.

1 **a)** The Amish's behaviour is based on their Christian beliefs. Which, if any, of the following words and phrases help to describe the beliefs underlying culture in England? Are there others you would use?

Non-violent; Calm/relaxed; Liberal; Multi-cultural; Caring; Tolerant; Traditional; Modern; Christian; Atheist; Family-based; Respectful; Freedom of choice; Success is measured by wealth; Competitive; Fashion-driven

b) With a partner, make a list of what you think are the top five of these words and phrases. Then have a class discussion to decide the top three.

2 Here is a poem written by Daniel Defoe in 1701 (he is probably most famous for his novel *Robinson Crusoe*). Take the last two lines as the title and discuss whether they are true *or* write an up-to-date version of his poem, including more modern references.

The True Born Englishman
In eager rapes, and furious lust begot,
Between a painted Briton and a Scot:
Whose gen'ring offspring quickly learnt to bow.
And yoke their heifers to the Roman plough:
From whence a mongrel half-bred race there came,
With neither name nor nation, speech or fame:
In whose hot veins now mixtures quickly ran,
Infus'd betwixt a Saxon and a Dane.
While their rank daughters, to their parents just,
Receiv'd all nations with promiscuous lust.
This nauseous brood directly did contain,
The well-extracted blood of Englishmen …
… A True Born Englishman's a contradiction!
In speech, an irony! In fact, a fiction!

What religions are there in the UK in the twenty-first century?

The UK is a multi-faith society. Everyone has the right to religious freedom. This is now part of the European human rights law.

Although religious faith in the UK is mainly Christian, most of the world's religions are practised. Due to immigration in the last century there are important Hindu, Jewish, Muslim and Sikh communities. There are also smaller communities of Bahá'í, Buddhists, Jains, and Zoroastrians, as well as followers of new religious movements.

There are beliefs underlying all our actions. They do not have to be religious. For example, a feature of culture in England is the payment of taxes to support the armed forces. This is done because the government believes it is right to do so. The majority of people accept it.

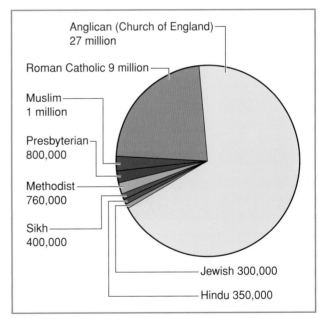

- Anglican (Church of England) 27 million
- Roman Catholic 9 million
- Muslim 1 million
- Presbyterian 800,000
- Methodist 760,000
- Sikh 400,000
- Jewish 300,000
- Hindu 350,000

Approximate numbers of religious followers in the UK out of a total population of 60 million (2005).

Source C

CAMPAIGN TO GET BRITAIN OUT OF EUROPE

NOW

The 'Get Britain out of Europe' campaign is a pressure group determined to change government policy on Europe. Throughout the history of this proud NATION, we have been independent. We have never had anything to do with Europe in the past and we do not intend to start now! What has Europe ever done for us? Nothing! In fact, we have often found ourselves fighting them. We, the British, have always led the world in technology and business.

We say it is time to stop the slide into Europe. We have a distinct British culture and we want to keep it that way.

Keep Britain out of Europe!

ACTIVITY

1 **a)** What facts has Source C got wrong?
   b) Now write a letter to the campaign organisers to explain to them in what ways they are wrong.

Case Study
What is a multi-cultural society?
The UK today

A multi-cultural society is one where there are many different cultures. In the UK, the term multi-cultural also refers to other cultural diversity such as religious beliefs, attitudes to gender and sexuality, or lifestyles.

To most people, a 'multi-cultural society' doesn't simply mean that there are people from other ethnic groups living here, but that their cultures and ways of life are accepted as part of that society. The idea that all cultures should be accepted and given the freedom to follow their traditions is called multi-culturalism.

Democracy

To live in a society that works well, the people have roles and responsibilities which they must fulfil. The UK, like other countries in the EU, is a democratic society, where the citizens have the right to elect their government, and they also have human rights, as citizens, to social support and fair treatment. Some examples of these rights are the right to education and health care for everyone, the right to protection from violence and crime, and the right to be helped if they live in poverty.

In exchange for these rights, citizens have responsibilities, such as having to obey laws, contributing to society through work, and treating others with respect and honesty.

The cost to the government of providing civil and social rights comes from taxes paid by the citizens.

You can see from this brief description of democracy that members of a society need to share attitudes, expectations and values if this equation of rights and responsibilities is going to balance. When immigrants from different cultures join a multi-cultural society, the government has to try to make sure that the society still has a shared culture, or it may start to disintegrate.

The challenges of multi-culturalism

• **The number of immigrants** from other cultures who have come to live in the UK in recent years have worried some of the UK population. What they fear is that different cultures are becoming separate groups in the UK, living together in their own communities and becoming isolated from the rest of society. As a result, they are integrated in their own ethnic or religious group, but feel little attachment or involvement with UK culture. The government has attempted to change this by introducing Citizenship classes into all schools, and has tried to provide all adult immigrants with English language classes to help them integrate into work and the wider community.

• **Fears for jobs:** In recent years there has been a feeling that immigrants who were prepared to work for low wages were taking all the jobs. In 2006, there was much media coverage on the influx of Polish and other East European workers who were taking jobs in the building industry. The *Daily Mail* reported that:

More than 600,000 immigrants, half of them from Poland, have arrived in the UK since the former Soviet bloc nations joined the European Union in 2004 – more than 25 times the number originally predicted by the Government.

A similar number are expected to come to Britain from Romania and Bulgaria, which are joining the EU in January.

Tim Shipman, Daily Mail Online, 6 October 2006.

Such stories led to calls to reduce immigration, to protect UK jobs. The government's other official sources said that the immigrant workers had boosted the economy by paying taxes and by spending their money in the UK.

- **Feelings of injustice and resentment:** The numbers of immigrants and refugees and asylum seekers who entered the country in the period from 2003–08 led some people in poor areas to express feelings of unfairness that newcomers were given housing and financial help, when people who had lived and worked in the UK all their lives were still waiting for housing and receiving less financial help. The government said that it would continue to help refugees for humanitarian reasons and as part of EU and UN agreements, and that voluntary immigrants received little financial help and no housing priority.

They stated that the majority of immigrants were in work and contributing to the economy.

- **Political and religious conflict:** The UK's involvement in the war in Iraq in 2003 has led to conflict between Britain and some Muslims, who believe the war was an attack on all Islamic nations and the religion itself. Terrorist attacks by Islamic fundamentalist groups in America, Europe, Asia, Glasgow and London have resulted in widespread distrust of Muslims in the UK. The fact that a terrorist attack in London was carried out by British Muslims, and that some Muslim fundamentalists in the UK have openly said that they believe it is their duty to kill all opponents of Islam, has led to prejudice against Muslims in the UK.

Over recent years there has been a strong rise in numbers of British Asian youths showing support for the Taliban and other extremist Islamic groups. In the face of such prejudice from many British people, it is not too surprising that some Muslims feel their identity and loyalty is with their faith rather than with the UK.

The effect of this tension has been an increasing separation of Muslim communities and the rest of the UK. Many Muslims feel they are stereotyped as terrorists by some people, and the vast majority of Muslims who are not in sympathy with terrorism are made to feel like unwanted outsiders.

These women are wearing the niqab.

Alevis are followers of a faith rooted in the beliefs of Shia Islam, but many of their religious practices are very different from those of other Shia Muslims. Here, they perform semah dance, which is a ritual dance characterised by turning and swirling.

Recently, wanting to assert their identity, many Muslims have adopted the traditional clothes that show Islamic faith. This has intensified the separation of cultures, and this has influenced many people to challenge the idea that multi-culturalism can exist in a united society.

Multi-culturalism: Can it work?

The basic belief in multi-culturalism is that all cultures should be given respect and acceptance in a society. This idea is based on the principles of human rights, and stands against prejudice, racism and PERSECUTION. It is a moral decision that it is better to be friendly, generous and tolerant, than to be aggressive, selfish, and bigoted.

It is also based on self-interest, because the evidence is that co-operation is less painful, less expensive, and more likely to lead to lasting peace than conflict and aggression.

The tension between Islamic and Western values is likely to diminish when the political and military conflicts in the Middle East are resolved, which will take some time, and will depend on co-operation and compromise.

If multi-culturalism results in a divided society where different cultures live separate and isolated lives, living in segregated areas, and remaining ignorant of each other's values, beliefs and skills, it will be a major loss for all cultures. If those cultures live under separate different laws, there will be no possibility of a united society, and probably conflict between the groups.

The historical evidence is that, over time, different cultures are influenced by other cultures and find a way of integrating their ways of living, agreeing on basic values and developing and using each other's skills and knowledge. When this happens, the evidence from history is that, by accepting new cultures, societies develop and grow strong with the knowledge and wisdom gained from the new cultures.

Will the UK continue to be a multi-cultural society?

This is a question no one can answer with complete certainty, but there is a strong probability that it will for the following reasons:

- The UK has been a multi-cultural society for thousands of years (see pages 26–34).
- The populations of the world are likely to continue to migrate. The movement of people between countries has increased since travel across the world has become easier and cheaper. Some will leave the UK and some will come to settle.
- The sharing of cultural ideas has brought benefits, as the examples of the contribution of immigrants to Britain have demonstrated.
- The world is now a global community. No country can progress and develop without contact and trading with other cultures. This will lead to all cultures spreading across the world to teach, learn and to trade.
- The effect of climate change will increase the migration of people around the world as they look for environments that can support them. If the UK is a hospitable environment, people will come.
- The hostility to newcomers in the UK is generally much less intense in the twenty-first century than it was in the twentieth century as people have grown accustomed to widespread migration. The racism directed at Afro-Caribbean immigrants in the 1950s, and Ugandan Asian immigrants in the 1960s has ceased to be such a problem.

CONCEPT 4

Individuals and groups have different beliefs, attitudes and values

People have different beliefs on how to live. This includes beliefs about what is morally the 'right' and 'wrong' way to behave. This concept section will help you to think about your own and others' morals, values, attitudes and beliefs. You will learn about:

- What moral issues are and why they are important to all cultures.
- The different ways of making moral decisions.
- How to go about researching a moral issue.

> The following are ideas and terms that you will need to know from this concept section:
>
> issues: cultural, moral, political, religious, social • perspectives

What is a moral issue?

A moral issue concerns beliefs about whether an action is right or wrong in the sense of it being good or bad. We can use 'wrong' to mean immoral and 'right' to mean moral. The words 'right' and 'wrong', however, can be used in different contexts. Consider the following choices:

1 Which pair of shoes *should* I buy?
2 What answer *should* I give to this maths problem?
3 *Should* I take the £10 note that is sticking out of someone's pocket, or warn them they are about to lose it?

Each of these decisions is right or wrong in a different sense:

1 Which shoes represents the best value? Which looks the best?
2 Which answer can be proved?
3 Which action is the most honest?

Only the third is a moral decision. We *all* make moral decisions, even if we do not think about it.

ACTIVITY

1 The school receptionist is collecting money as students arrive for a 'no uniform day' for charity. A 15-year-old student sees some of this money lying in a container unattended. They pocket it while the secretary is distracted by an emergency phone call.

   a) Which of the following statements do you agree with most?

   - The student is stealing. I believe stealing is wrong because you have no right to take something that does not belong to you.

   - The student is not exactly stealing. The money is not being taken from someone so there is no victim.

   b) Attempt to explain the beliefs you hold that influence your decision. Give your reasons for rejecting the argument you do not agree with. Consider:

   - your beliefs about fairness, justice, rights
   - your beliefs about survival, looking out for yourself.

The moral issue in the activity is to do with stealing and whether we consider stealing 'wrong' or immoral. We are usually socialised to believe that stealing is immoral. This is, in turn, based on other beliefs. There is no *proof* that stealing is immoral, as there is in, say, maths, that $2 + 2 = 4$, or in history, that Henry VIII had six wives. Instead, we have to look for the most persuasive line of reasoning.

In a moral issue, this line of reasoning may be about fairness, justice and the purpose of life. It may be about obeying a code of behaviour as set out in any religion.

Moral issues, then, are any issues requiring a decision based on beliefs about what is 'good' or 'bad' behaviour.

Norms of behaviour

As human beings live in groups, norms of behaviour are set up. Every culture has a set of norms that guides behaviour. Many of these norms are based on the beliefs of that culture.

For example, the Amish refuse to use violence in any situation (see pages 21–25). This is a norm of their culture. It is based on the belief that using violence is always wrong. This comes from their acceptance of what Jesus taught: that God wants us to love each other:

'Love thy neighbour'
'Blessed are the peacemakers'.

These are sayings of Jesus that the Amish interpret in their everyday lives. This says that violence is always wrong. To apply this belief, they refuse to join in the US armed forces. They forbid the use of any weapon in their communities. They will never hit another person. If someone breaks this norm they will shun them to show their disapproval.

Decision making

Moral	A moral decision is about basic human values (for example, fairness, individual freedoms, respect for others). For instance, you may decide that giving money to help disaster victims is a moral act.
Immoral	An immoral decision is the exact opposite of a moral decision. For example, you might think that shoplifting is immoral.
Amoral	An amoral decision or action is taken when you have *no* moral beliefs. For example, a child hits his brother in the eye and hurts him simply because he wants to see what will happen. He did not have any understanding of right and wrong.
Non-moral	A non-moral decision does not concern the 'big questions'. A non-moral decision is more to do with practical, day-to-day decisions. For example, deciding what to wear in the morning is a non-moral decision.

Adapted from the BBC Education website at
www.bbc.co.uk/education

ACTIVITIES

1 Draw a diagram to show the links between the Amish's Christian beliefs and their attitude towards capital punishment.

2 a) 'It is always wrong to carry a weapon.' Write down in bullet points your thoughts on this view. State whether you agree or disagree, with reasons. How do your beliefs about violence affect your answer?

  b) Interview another student to compare notes. Share your ideas in a class debate.

3 Do you believe it is better to be aware of your own morals? Explain, using the decision making table below.

4 In order to survive, cultures have to establish norms on a range of moral issues such as the taking of life, sexual relationships, use of violence and rights concerning private property. In small groups, discuss your beliefs about some of these issues. Link your attitude to the moral issue and the belief on which your attitude is based.

What are the different ways of making a moral decision?

There are two ways of arriving at moral decisions.

1 By using your beliefs as *rules* for living, which may never be broken. These are principles. For those of us who have religious beliefs, we have to obey the teachings of that religion. These lay down rules for right and wrong behaviour. Christians and Muslims believe that Jesus and Muhammad both taught that life is sacred, that only God can create life and only God has the right to take it.

The technical term for this approach: deontological

Therefore followers may argue that capital punishment, abortion and euthanasia are all, always, immoral.

2 By looking at the *outcome* of a decision. For example, lying may be justified if it protects someone against an INJUSTICE. Humanists believe that human beings should be in control of their lives. They believe that all actions should have loving, caring outcomes. Therefore, they would argue, abortion can be justified if the pregnant

The technical term for this approach: consequentialist

woman feels it would bring her peace of mind in a situation where she is distraught at being pregnant following a rape, for example.

There are difficulties with both approaches.

- In the first approach, does anyone have the right to decide that their rules or beliefs are more important than anyone else's?
- In the second approach, who decides which outcome is the most desirable? What is the timescale for deciding the 'final' outcome?

Very often, moral decisions involve choosing between options that are both undesirable. For example, if you are very poor and your child is hungry, you can face a choice between stealing some food, which you believe to be wrong, and letting your child suffer, which is also wrong.

ACTIVITY

1 Which approach to reaching a moral decision – deontological or consequentialist – would an atheist be more likely to adopt? Explain your reasoning.

How do we learn right from wrong (our moral code)?

We learn what is right and wrong through the various agents of socialisation.

1 Initially, a child will learn from its parents and immediate family. This may be through the methods shown in the diagram below.

2 As we grow up, we come across other agents of socialisation such as school, the mass media and peer groups. Often what is morally acceptable in that culture will be very clear, but there can be some strong disagreements.

3 In multi-cultural societies people can be exposed to conflicting messages. Cultural groups do not always have the same impact.

4 PEER PRESSURE is a powerful force in all cultures. It is very strong for teenagers. However, the morality of an action is never decided by how many people approve of it.

Even if we are members of an organised religion, we still have to make moral decisions. This is particularly so in cases where only morally wrong alternatives seem available.

For example, you believe it is always wrong to tell lies and you also believe racism is wrong. What would you say to a violent racist who threatened you and asked you where a particular asylum seeker was hiding, if you knew where they were?

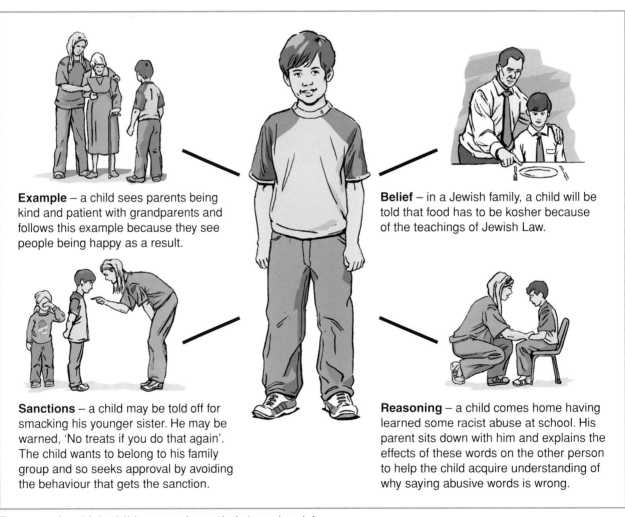

Example – a child sees parents being kind and patient with grandparents and follows this example because they see people being happy as a result.

Sanctions – a child may be told off for smacking his younger sister. He may be warned, 'No treats if you do that again'. The child wants to belong to his family group and so seeks approval by avoiding the behaviour that gets the sanction.

Belief – in a Jewish family, a child will be told that food has to be kosher because of the teachings of Jewish Law.

Reasoning – a child comes home having learned some racist abuse at school. His parent sits down with him and explains the effects of these words on the other person to help the child acquire understanding of why saying abusive words is wrong.

Four ways in which children may learn their 'moral code'.

How important is a shared moral code?

Our beliefs decide our morals and our morals decide our behaviour. If people in a culture have widely different ETHICS, or moral codes, then even though they may share the same language and eat similar food, there will be little shared behaviour. So, a shared moral code is central to the survival of any culture. The moral code guides people's behaviour. If behaviour is not shared then the people will not feel a common identity. The culture will break up and people will form into new groups that do share a moral code.

Why do we need to discuss moral issues?

We are living through a period of great change, both nationally and globally. This means we have to constantly think about ethics in new situations.

History teaches us what happens to cultures that fail to adapt: they die out. This means there is a need for discussion of different views. Many cultures have become democracies to allow these discussions to take place.

So cultures have to allow for different views and try to keep their traditions. This creates tensions within cultures around the world.

Until recently, there was little interaction between people of different cultures. Armies were led by the rulers of one culture against another culture to sort out which culture controlled what. There was little contact apart from that. This allowed people to believe their ways were the only right ways. This is known as ETHNOCENTRISM.

Cultures were based on clear religious traditions. Moral codes based on them were enforced ruthlessly by those who held power.

Cultural changes

Things have changed in recent times. These changes are caused by:

- The increasing influence of the mass media. This means there are more people and organisations influencing us.
- We are more aware of different, often conflicting, values in our own and others' cultures.
- In many societies, organised religion has little influence over the majority of the people. This is true in the UK and many other countries.

Technological and scientific changes

Humans have developed the technology of the mass media. We have also extended the scale on which we EXPLOIT NATURAL RESOURCES. We are now influencing the climate and ECOSYSTEMS of this planet.

Other scientific advances mean we can now genetically modify crops, animals and humans. We can extend life in ways that could not even be imagined 200 years ago.

These changes challenge us in two ways.

1 They place before us new moral questions. For example, should research into the cloning of human embryos be allowed?

2 They increasingly require internationally agreed decisions. A country can ban abortion but it cannot prevent someone travelling to another country where abortion is legal.

Can we rise to these challenges?

ACTIVITIES

1 Study page 38.
   a) Draw a diagram to show the main ways you 'learned' your moral code.
   b) Were there any 'conflicting messages' about right and wrong in your childhood?
   c) How did this affect you?

2 Why does a culture need a shared set of morals?

3 How has moral decision making changed over the last 200 years?

As part of the culture and beliefs module, you will explore an issue where there is no agreement about the right way to behave. The disagreement is because the people involved have different beliefs about what is right or wrong.

These differences could be based on religious, political, cultural or scientific beliefs. Explain:

- What the issue is.
- What are the different values, attitudes and beliefs about the issue.
- Which groups hold these values, attitudes and beliefs, and why they hold their views.
- What you think is the right response, after you have examined the different views.

Case Study
Euthanasia

Here is some guidance on researching the moral issue of euthanasia. The aim of the research is to:

- find out what arguments or reasoning are used
- see how opponents of that view deal with each argument.

This is followed by a list of other moral issues that can be researched and debated in a similar way.

Possible research title

Why do people hold different views on whether euthanasia should be legalised?

Research this question and prepare to debate it formally according to your teacher's instructions.

> Your research should:
> - define key terms (for example, 'euthanasia', 'moral')
> - explain what moral issue is raised by euthanasia. Examples of moral issues here are: sanctity of life, right to control own life
> - identify groups supporting different views
> - explain why the groups hold their views and say what is the source of their beliefs
> - state and explain your conclusion.

Definitions

There are two groups with different views on euthanasia. The first is the Pro-Life Alliance, which is against euthanasia. The second is the Voluntary Euthanasia Society, which is in favour of euthanasia. Those who argue in favour of the right to euthanasia have a different definition from those who argue against. Euthanasia has many definitions.

The Pro-Life Alliance defines it as:

'Any action or omission intended to end the life of a patient on the grounds that his or her life is not worth living.'

The Voluntary Euthanasia Society looks to the word's Greek origins – '*eu*' and '*thanatos*', which together mean 'a good death' – and says a modern definition is:

'A good death brought about by a doctor providing drugs or an injection to bring a peaceful end to the dying process.'

Different viewpoints

Some arguments used when discussing whether euthanasia is immoral include the following:

a) Patients can recover after being 'written off' by doctors.

b) It can quickly and humanely end a patient's suffering.

c) Life is a gift from God. It is sacrosanct. Only God can take life away.

d) Old people might feel they are a nuisance to others ('in the way'). They may choose this course of action without really wanting to.

e) It can help reduce the grief and suffering of the patient's loved ones.

f) Everyone should have the right to decide when and how they should die.

g) It would change the role of a doctor.

h) A patient may not be able to make a rational decision, or might change their mind and not be able to communicate this.

i) It would help everybody if a decision could be made before the patient entered the very last stage of suffering.

j) It would help others to face death if they realised they could die with dignity.

k) If it became legal it could be used too widely, or abused.

l) There are now many painkilling drugs that can relieve suffering.

m) If the law were changed, doctors could legally act on a patient's desire to die without further suffering.

Investigation

a) Sort the arguments given on page 40 into those supporting euthanasia and those against.

(When sorting out the arguments, be aware that it is possible to argue that a person has the right to make a certain decision but not support the decision he/she actually makes.)

b) Now carry out further research to find out more about these arguments and others for and against euthanasia.

Alongside each argument, note any key terms you find as a result of your research such as:
- sanctity of life
- human rights
- doctors' Hippocratic Oath
- palliative care
- suffering
- right to dignity
- humanist.

There are some very good books and websites to support this research. These are difficult terms, so ask your teacher if you need help with any of them. Keep an exact record of all the sources you have used: website addresses, authors, book titles.

c) Develop your research by identifying conflicting beliefs and attitudes. Find quotations from books, or speeches the various groups for and against use to back up their views. Websites for various religious groups can also be a useful source. Draw a flow diagram that links attitudes towards euthanasia to the underlying beliefs. Use the evidence/quotes to back this up.

d) Reflect on your research and consider possible conclusions. Make sure your conclusion follows on logically from your evidence and analysis.

Examples of other moral issues for research and debate

- **Abortion**: should women have the right to terminate a pregnancy?
- **Animal rights**: can experimenting on animals be justified?
- **Arranged marriage**: should parents have the right to arrange a marriage for their children?
- **Asylum seekers**: is it immoral to turn away an asylum seeker?
- **Boxing**: can the fight industry be justified?
- **Bullfighting**: is killing bulls for entertainment morally acceptable?
- **Capital punishment**: is the taking of someone's life as a punishment morally justifiable?
- **Censorship**: should there be controls on what information people have access to?
- **Divorce**: should married couples have the right to separate?
- **Euthanasia**: should a person who is terminally ill have the right to help in ending their life?
- **Genetic engineering**: is it wrong?
- **Global warming**: is it immoral to waste the world's resources?
- **Human cloning**: should research into the cloning of human embryos be allowed?
- **Is there a God?**: what makes some people believe in God and why do others disagree?
- **The law**: is breaking the law always wrong?
- **Life after death**: what do different groups of people believe happens when you die?
- **Lying**: is lying always wrong?
- **Monarchy**: should we all be proud of our royal family, or should we leave the past behind?
- **Plastic surgery**: can plastic surgery on the NHS be morally justified?
- **Poverty**: is it immoral to allow millions to starve when there is more than enough food in the world to feed everyone?
- **Recreational drugs**: is the use of recreational drugs wrong?
- **School uniform**: is the requirement to wear school uniform a moral issue?
- **War**: can war be morally justified?

ENVIRONMENTAL ISSUES

INTRODUCTION

This chapter will help you understand the relationship between people and the natural environment. The environmental issues chapter is based on four concepts:

1. Individuals and groups use the environment in different ways.
2. Our use of the environment has negative consequences.
3. Individuals and groups have different attitudes and values and make different responses to environmental issues.
4. Environmental problems can be solved in different ways.

There will be a section on each concept, but some case studies will cover several concepts.

Concerns, problems and worries about the natural environment are called environmental issues. The natural ENVIRONMENT is the part of the planet that is already there (such as land, sea, rivers, atmosphere, vegetation), not made by people.

ACTIVITY

1 **a** Make a list of *six* environmental issues (problems) you have heard about.
  b Put your six issues in *rank order*, showing which you think are the greatest threats to human life. (Make your most serious issue number 1, all the way through to your least serious at number 6.)
  c Explain why you picked the most serious (1) and least serious (6).

No one wants to destroy or damage their environment. The environment is where we live,

our homeland. It is where we find the things we need to survive, like food, materials for shelter, tools to make things, fuel for heat and light and power. It is where we take our rest and leisure and enjoy our lives. You would think that no sensible person would deliberately destroy their environment.

People have always used the NATURAL RESOURCES of the planet. Over the years, as the human population has grown, and as demand for food and material goods has expanded, we have taken more and more resources from the natural environment.

Now, at the beginning of the twenty-first century, there are many people who believe that the natural environment cannot regenerate or recover as it used to do. Some people fear that we have taken so many resources and are doing so much damage to the natural environment that it will become increasingly difficult for humans to survive on the planet.

The first question we should ask is: why are these environmental problems happening now? There are three main reasons:

• Population growth.
• Developments in science and technology.
• Growing world demand for food and material goods.

Reason 1: Population growth

There has been a massive increase in the world population over the last 200 years.

• In 1800 the world population was about 800 million.
• Two hundred years later the world population was six *billion*, nearly eight times larger.
• At the moment, over 75 million more people are added to the world population each year.
• By 2050 the world population is expected to be nine billion.

World population growth, 1750–2050

Population (in billions)

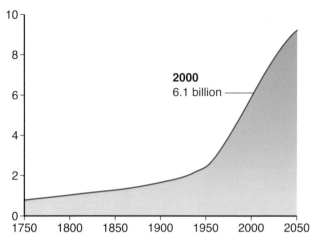

2000
6.1 billion

United Nations, 'World Population Prospects', the 1998 Revision; and estimates by the Population Reference Bureau.

ACTIVITY

1 Describe three ways in which the natural environment will have been changed by this increase in population.

Reason 2: Developments in science and technology

Our scientific understanding and advanced technical skills have resulted in most of the world using a lot more TECHNOLOGY in their daily lives.

This has meant that we use more and more natural resources on a daily basis. Natural resources are the raw materials (such as coal, oil and wood) we take from the environment and use to make things or use to make ENERGY (like electricity). When these resources are used, they change the environment and create by-products such as carbon dioxide and toxic chemicals.

ACTIVITY

2 Using the two photos on pages 43 and 44 to help you:
  a Draw and label five examples of technology that we did not have 200 years ago.
  b Take three of your examples and explain how these make use of natural resources.

This is a painting from 1837. What technology is being used by the farmers?

Reason 3: Growing world demand for food and material goods

Many people's desires and expectations for their lives have changed. Put simply, people want more material things. This is because the MORE ECONOMICALLY DEVELOPED COUNTRIES (MEDCs), such as the UK, Japan, North America, Germany, have become much richer. Most people in these places have enough food and good housing, and have come to expect a comfortable lifestyle with lots of luxuries. Other people who live in LESS ECONOMICALLY DEVELOPED COUNTRIES (LEDCs), for example, in Zaire or Indonesia, want the same lifestyle as people in MEDCs.

This is a scene of modern city life from Tokyo, Japan. Japan is a more economically developed country – an MEDC.

ACTIVITY

1 a Make a list of the things you would like to have when you set up home on your own.

b Get together in groups and make a combined list of ten things that everybody wants.

c Copy the table below and add the items in your list. Alongside each item, write what raw materials will be needed to make them and what natural resources will be used.

Thing we want	Materials needed	Resources used
Car	Steel, rubber, plastic, glass, leather, petrol	Iron ore, oil, sand, animal skin, chemicals
Plasma screen TV	Glass, plastic, metals, rubber, copper, electricity supply	Sand, oil, metal ores, silicone, copper, electricity from a coal, oil or nuclear power station

CONCEPT 1

Individuals and groups use the environment in different ways

In this concept section you will learn about:

- ECOSYSTEMS and the rainforest ecosystem.
- Exploitation of natural resources.
- RENEWABLE and NON-RENEWABLE RESOURCES.
- Energy generation in the UK today, and in the future.

In your work on culture and beliefs (pages 6–12) you have learned that CULTURES across the world are different. They have different goals, beliefs, technology, and lifestyles. As a result, groups from different cultures use the environment in different ways.

Even within the same culture, individuals and groups might want to use the same environment for different purposes; an area of land might be used for growing food, mining minerals, building houses, or kept as a attractive landscape to be enjoyed by people for its beauty. Decisions have to be made, but these decisions affect the natural environment on a much wider scale than you might think.

> The following are ideas and terms that you will need to know from this concept section:
>
> ecosystem • natural resources • energy generation • renewable and non-renewable resources • alternative energy: solar, wind, tidal, thermal, nuclear • biofuels • fossil fuels • hydroelectric power

What is an ecosystem?

All parts of the natural environment are part of a larger scale ecosystem. An ecosystem is a system consisting of many organisms (plants, animals, insects, etc.) that depend on each other to exist in a particular environment. The environment itself provides the conditions (climate, supply of water and minerals) needed for the organisms to live and stay healthy.

If an ecosystem is disturbed, for example, by plants or animals being removed or damaged, there will be knock-on effects on all other parts of the ecosystem. So, if a certain type of plant disappears from an area, all the living organisms that relied on that plant to survive will die out, or move from the area. This will have further knock-on effects on other living organisms.

Rainforests

Tropical rainforests are a very important ecosystem for the planet. A third of the world's trees grow there. Half of the world's species of plants and animals exist there and many of them can be found nowhere else. They contain a largely unexplored BIO-DIVERSITY that could provide the world with new medicines and foods, and knowledge that could benefit all the world's population.

They have a huge influence over the world's climate and in controlling the atmosphere that we breathe. Trees absorb carbon dioxide and produce oxygen. This process cleans and purifies the atmosphere. Rainforests also absorb solar radiation. If there are no trees, more radiation bounces back into the atmosphere and raises the temperature of the atmosphere. This could alter the patterns of air circulation, which change rainfall and influence weather across the world. For example, recent hurricanes in the Gulf of Mexico, droughts in Ethiopia, Kenya and Somaliland, flooding in the UK, and bushfires in Australia are partly the result of changing air currents and cloud movement.

Rainforests also play a role in recycling the earth's water as moisture is absorbed by the trees and evaporated into the atmosphere to return as rainfall in other parts of the world. Without the forests' ability to store water, streams can disappear during the dry season and the land will become dry and infertile.

What has happened to the rainforests?

In 1950, about 15 per cent of the Earth's land surface was covered by rainforests. Today, more than half of the world's tropical rainforests have been cut down or burned, and the rate of destruction is still accelerating. This is called DEFORESTATION.

There are no accurate figures for the loss of trees, and estimates vary, but 20,000 square miles of rainforest lost per year is a figure that is accepted by many experts. This amounts to two football pitches disappearing each second, an area larger than New York City each day, and an area larger than Poland each year.

In some places the tropical rainforest has almost completely disappeared: Nigeria and the Ivory Coast are two such areas. In many places forests are down to 20 per cent of the size they were in 1960: for example, in Thailand, the Philippines, Mexico, Vietnam.

Why did this happen?

In the last 40 years the value of the rainforest trees and the land they cover has been recognised and exploited by many different people and groups. The following case study examines different uses for the rainforest.

Case study
The Brazilian rainforest

This case study will look at why the world's largest rainforest, the Brazilian (Amazonian) rainforest, is being cut down. This is not a unique problem – trees in other rainforests around the world are being cut down for the same reasons. These reasons are shown in the photos on pages 46–48.

Logging: Deforestation in the Amazon Basin rainforest – trees are being converted into timber to sell abroad, especially hardwoods (mahogany, sapele, ebony), which are in demand in MEDCs. The big trees are transported and sold, but smaller trees and plants are ripped up and left to die.

ACTIVITY

1 Use the photographs on pages 46–48 to answer these questions:
   a) What advantages does the exploitation of the rainforest bring to different groups?

   b) What problems has this exploitation brought to the survival of the rainforest and the health of the planet?

Extraction of minerals: Minerals are extracted from the land beneath the trees (these might include iron ore, diamonds, precious metals – this photo is of a gold mine near Pocone in Brazil). This involves clearing many trees so that companies can mine or quarry and build transport systems. This creates wealth, and environmental destruction.

Small-scale farming: The clearance of the rainforest has provided plots of land for the rapidly growing population who need food and jobs. For many local people, farming land cleared from the rainforest has changed their lives for the better. This photo shows a typical settlement with turtle-breeding pens at the waterside.

Cattle ranching: The first stage is clearing the land by burning (as in photo). Then grass grows over the burnt land, but often only lasts a year or two before the land is worn out and the cattle have to be moved to another area where the forest has been cleared.

Major engineering projects: These include dams for hydroelectric power, building roads, building settlements for farmers, loggers, miners and others living in the forest. These projects bring great advantages to local people, opening up territory for farming, or bringing electricity to the area, but at the same time, they destroy the rainforest. This photo shows the Samuel Dam on the Jamari river in Brazil. 654 km² (253 square miles) of forest were drowned when the lake formed, but the dam provides electricity for Porto Velho, which has a population of over 650,000.

Most of the uses for the rainforest described and shown in the photos above and on pages 46 and 47 are connected with ECONOMIC DEVELOPMENT of the countries involved.

How do these activities affect the rainforest ecosystem?

- The removal of the trees destroys plants, including rare or unknown species, wiping some out altogether.
- This in turn will affect other species that relied on them to survive.
- Once the trees are uprooted, the soil will be washed away by rain storms. Before deforestation, the leaves and roots protected the ground.
- Rainforest soil is only a thin layer and contains few nutrients, so it will not last long without fertiliser.
- Without trees holding water, the area will dry out.
- The trees will no longer absorb carbon dioxide or release oxygen, and dead trees will produce more CO_2 and methane. This will have a major effect on the quality of the planet's atmosphere, and release greenhouse gases.

Once the ecosystem is disturbed, these changes will have an impact on the whole planet.

Exploitation of other natural resources

As well as timber and minerals, individuals and groups use many other natural resources from the environment.

What do we mean by 'the exploitation of natural resources'?

The word 'exploit' means to make use of something for the benefit of individuals or groups. The word can also mean 'use to make a profit'. Exploiting resources is not in itself bad. All living things survive by making use of the environment to provide what they need, for example, food and materials for shelter.

Timber, metal ores and minerals from the land are not the only resources that we exploit. We also exploit:

- Fresh water.
- The sea and sea life.
- FOSSIL FUELS such as coal, oil and natural gas.
- Gases in the atmosphere.
- Animal and plant life.

ACTIVITY

1 Draw a table like the one below and fill it in
   to show how humans exploit natural
   resources.

Natural resource	How is it exploited?
Fossil fuels	Burned to provide heat and light, used as fuel for vehicles
Land	Grow crops, dispose of waste
Water	
Sea and sea life	
Animals and plants	

As the population grows, we use more and more of
these resources. For example, water is essential for
human life. Although a person can survive without
food for several weeks, without water most people
will die within days. Apart from that, water is
essential for crops and animals. But, in addition,
we need water for cleaning, many manufacturing
processes, and as an essential ingredient in many
products.

In some parts of the world there is still plenty of
water, but in others the shortage of water has made
living nearly impossible.

The next case study on the Aral Sea shows how
exploiting another ecosystem will have far-reaching
effects. It shows that, unless the environment and
the resources it contains are understood fully,
attempts to change it may have unexpected
consequences.

Case Study
The Aral Sea

The Aral Sea was once the fourth biggest inland sea
in the world. Fishing and a busy shipping trade
provided a healthy livelihood for several hundred
thousand people. The Aral Sea surface was
66,100 km² (25,520 square miles). The salt content
was one per cent.

Then, in the 1960s, the flow of water into the sea
began to drop alarmingly. The Soviet government
had set up a major irrigation scheme in order to
grow huge amounts of rice and cotton in the area to
help the Russian economy. This scheme involved
diverting water from the rivers that flowed into the

Aral Sea to areas where the rice and cotton were
planted. This irrigation scheme sucked out more
than 90 per cent of the natural flow of water into the
sea. As a result, 27,000 km² (10,425 square miles)
of former sea became a dried-out desert.

About 60 per cent of water volume was lost. The
sea level fell 14 metres. The water became twice as
salty. Every year, about 200,000 tonnes of salt and
sand are being carried away by wind.

Map of the Aral Sea.

The effects on the Aral Sea area

Climate
Because of the draining of the sea, important
climatic changes have taken place. The water of the
sea used to moderate the temperature. It made
winters warmer and summers cooler. Now winters
are colder and summers hotter. Rainfall has declined
because there is less water to evaporate and the
area is much drier. The area is always dusty because
the wind has increased.

Desertification
The salt in the air damages the farming area,
destroying pastures and creating a shortage of food
for domestic animals. Deserted and sandy areas are
extended by the dust being carried further by the
wind. As the DESERTIFICATION increases, there is more
toxic dust in the air from the wind blowing over the
exposed seabed.

Work

The cotton and rice industries are failing. The fishing industry has collapsed. The harbours are now miles from the sea, and fish could not survive in the over-salted polluted water. Other businesses such as boat-building and papermaking have closed down completely, or work half days only.

All these issues are destroying the traditional social life of the region. Many people are unemployed, there is widespread poverty, and many of the old workforce are having to leave the area.

Water supply

The water the people need to drink, wash, and use for SANITATION is in very short supply. The water that is available is polluted.

Human health

The drying up of the sea, the reduction in the quality and quantity of water, and the salty and dust-laden air, has had a damaging effect on the health of the people, and the animal and plant life as well. Diseases like anaemia, cancer, tuberculosis, and allergies are common problems.

A fishing boat which is now stranded 11 km (7 miles) from the nearest seawater. The man on the boat is its former captain.

The Soviet government had not worked out in advance what might happen to the local ECOLOGY. The impact of the irrigation system on the local communities was never considered. Poor planning and management left the local people in desperate conditions.

ACTIVITIES

1 Draw a diagram to show what happened to the Aral Sea.
2 Explain why groups had different attitudes to the way the water was used.
3 What were the effects on the people in the area?

The production of energy

This section focuses on the production of energy and the need to provide increasing amounts of energy as the world population grows and societies become more INDUSTRIALISED.

We will look at:

- Different sources of energy, both non-renewable and renewable.
- The problems associated with these sources of energy.
- How SUSTAINABLE DEVELOPMENT could be achieved in the future.

What are non-renewable resources?

Non-renewable natural resources are simply described by saying that, once we have used up this type of resource, there will be no more created. The best known examples of these are fossil fuels: coal, oil and natural gas. For most of our history, since the Industrial Revolution, our energy needs have been mainly supplied by non-renewable fossil fuels.

Nuclear power is strictly speaking a non-renewable energy source as it uses uranium, which could run out. However, this is unlikely to happen for a very long time. Therefore, this is treated as an alternative to fossil fuels and is included in the section on renewable energy sources.

Non-renewable sources of energy were responsible for the great advances in industry, transport and domestic living that have taken place over the last 200 years. Over the last 100 years, the use of these non-renewable resources has increased seventeen-fold. MEDCs use them most. The USA uses six times as much as the average used by other countries, though developing countries such as China and India will soon make as great an impact on remaining resources.

Fossil fuels are still relatively cheap to use (though prices can rise steeply), flexible, and are reasonably efficient in producing the power needed to keep industry and transport growing. But there are problems.

Fossil fuels are running out

Each year we use a huge amount of fossil fuels that took about a million years to be made. There is still about 200 years' supply of coal, but oil and gas are close to being used up. Estimates vary, but most say 60–70 years before we run out. This figure does not take into account increases in demand for oil or gas.

Fossil fuels cause pollution

Widely used fuels such as coal and oil/petroleum contain carbon, hydrogen, sulphur and nitrogen, which form carbon dioxide, sulphur oxides and nitrogen oxides when burned. These gases cause climate change (see pages 60–63). They also produce ACID RAIN.

Petrol and diesel fuels produce many chemical by-products, which create PHOTOCHEMICAL SMOG. In big cities this smog is a major health risk to people in the area. Natural gas is cleaner, but produces much carbon dioxide.

Fossil fuels still provide almost 80 per cent of the word's total energy needs and more than six billion tonnes of carbon emissions are produced annually from burning these fuels.

The future for fossil fuels

Although the problems of low reserves and POLLUTION make fossil fuels a poor choice for the future, these fuels have two very big advantages as power sources today:

1 Despite recent rises in cost, fossil fuels are still cheaper than other methods of generating energy.

2 Most of our technology in industry, transport and in producing electricity, is based on these fuels, and our investment in this technology is massive. To scrap power stations and our methods of transport (which include ships and aircraft as well as road vehicles) would cost an almost unthinkable amount of money.

The answer that most environmental researchers and many governments have agreed is that we need to develop different energy sources to add to, and eventually replace, fossil fuels. These sources should minimise pollution and use energy efficiently. This means we need renewable energy sources.

What are renewable energy sources?

They are sources of energy that occur naturally and are always available. They do not run out with use.

So the question is: if fossil fuels pollute the world and are running out, and renewable energy is so much cleaner and will not run out, why do we not use renewable sources for all our power needs?

All of the renewable energy sources described here are being used today across the world. But all of them create difficulties that need to be resolved before they can be used to replace fossil fuels. Pages 51–57 list the major sources of energy we can tap into and some of the problems associated with them.

1 Power from rivers

HYDROELECTRIC POWER makes use of the movement of fresh water in rivers, using the flow of water to generate electricity by passing the water through a turbine. The diagram on page 52 shows how a hydropower plant works.

Hydropower does not cause much pollution and water is a renewable resource, but there are some problems in using it:

- The cost of building dams is enormous. It takes years before the cost of a dam is covered by the cheap electricity produced. However, dams can produce a lot of electricity.
- They can only be built in a limited number of places.
- To build them, a great deal of land has to be flooded, farms and towns disappear, and many people have to be displaced. One very big dam built in China recently, the Three Gorges Dam, meant 1.2 million people were forced to move home when the area behind the dam was flooded.

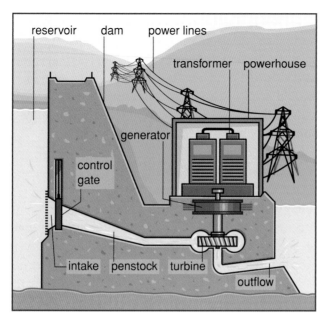

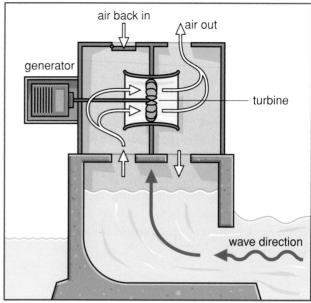

How hydropower works.

How wave power works.

- The local ecosystem is damaged (both plants and animals) and the environmental impact is widespread. Think of the fish that cannot get to breeding grounds or that get killed by turbine blades.
- Water in huge reservoirs is lost through evaporation, especially in hot countries.

2 Power from the sea

- Tidal power uses the tidal movement of the sea in a similar way to hydropower: water flows in and out of a basin moving a wheel or turbine.
- Wave power uses the movement of waves to produce energy by converting this movement into electricity.

In theory, the vast energy of the sea should be a major source of power, but attempts to use tides and waves to drive turbines have not always produced very good results. It is expensive to build anything in the sea, and the problem of linking turbines with rising and sinking levels of water or the movement of waves has not been effectively solved except at enormous expense.

Where it has been tried, there was large-scale disruption to the ocean ecosystem and relatively little energy was produced. However, both tidal power and wave power generators have been built, and more are planned. New technology, and greater understanding of how to build wave powered generators means that they will eventually be effective suppliers of electricity, but the cost of building them will always be high.

3 Power from the sun

SOLAR ENERGY makes use of the heat and light of the sun. Photovoltaic cells (solar panels) can convert light to electricity. They can be placed on buildings, or large numbers can be set up in sunny areas. The sunlight strikes a solar panel and is converted into electricity. Other simpler solar systems run water between panes of glass, which provide hot water for a building.

Unlike hydropower and wind power, solar energy is not used to provide much power. In theory, the sun could provide us with thousands of times our energy needs, but it is difficult to capture this resource to produce energy on a large scale.

Solar cells have many advantages – the fuel is free, they cost virtually nothing to maintain, they create no pollution – but they are expensive to make, and they are not very efficient in converting sunlight to energy (about 15 per cent efficient).

- Some houses in sunny areas can produce enough power to heat water and provide lighting, but large-scale solar power is very expensive to produce.

The size of this installation in the Mojave Desert gives some idea of how much space and expensive technology is needed to produce a useable quantity of power for industry. This plant produces enough energy to power over 50,000 homes.

- Although they can operate in a climate such as Britain's, at the moment photovoltaic cells can only work on a small scale and are very expensive to produce. However, in Denmark, buildings that use special designs to collect solar energy and retain heat have been made to be self-sufficient and show that, even in the north, solar power has a chance of working.

4 Power from the wind

Wind energy makes use of wind to power electrical generators. These act like windmills. The wind turns large vanes that provide power for a turbine, which produces electricity.

Wind farms have a dramatic effect on the countryside. Some people think they are very ugly, but others think they add interest to a landscape.

The use of wind power is growing. It does not cause pollution through waste or gas emissions; it does not need fuel or cooling liquids.

It is the British government's favoured alternative to fossil fuel power generation. The government have decided that off-shore wind farms are the best idea, because they have almost constant wind, and people object to them less. A massive wind farm called the London Array will be built in the outer Thames estuary, 12 miles off the

Wind farms sited at sea are becoming a popular option as they can rely on almost constant winds, and they are more acceptable to nature conservationists.

Kent and Essex coasts, and when finished will have 271 turbines across a 90 square mile site. The first phase, consisting of 175 turbines, could be completed by 2012.

However, there are practical problems:

- Wind turbines are expensive to build.
- Many wind turbines are needed to produce a fair amount of electricity, which take up a lot of space.
- They are noisy, especially in a high wind.
- The wind does not blow all the time, so there will not be a consistent supply of electricity. Wind generation of electricity has to be backed up by other methods of producing electricity.
- There are other objections to wind farms as the newspaper headlines below show.

TURBINE BLADES RESPONSIBLE FOR DEATH OF RED KITE

Low-frequency noise causes migraines and insomnia

PROPERTY PRICES SLUMP AS WIND FARM BUILT

BLIGHT ON OUR LANDSCAPE – THE RESIDENTS FIGHT BACK

However, in 2009, the Royal Society for the Protection of Birds (RSPB) has withdrawn its objections to wind turbines. There is a growing popular demand to ignore objections to the siting of these wind farms on the basis that they are more important to the survival of the planet than the concerns of local residents about house prices and the way they look.

5 Power from plants

Biofuels are an energy resource derived from biological materials, most often plants. These create less pollution than conventional fuels and are a renewable resource. The energy produced by biological materials is called 'bio-energy'. These biological materials are called 'bio-mass'.

Bio-energy can be used to provide heat, make fuels and generate electricity. Wood, which people have used to cook and keep warm for thousands of years, continues to be the largest bio-mass resource. There are many other types of bio-mass we can use to produce energy. These bio-mass resources are mostly plants that can be used to make vegetable oil (such as palm oil, rapeseed oil), but we can also use waste from agricultural and forest industries, landfill gas, aquatic plants as well as that produced by cities and factories.

Today, bio-energy provides about three to four per cent of energy used in the USA and 12 per cent across the world. We are learning how to produce materials and chemicals from bio-mass, which could replace petrol or diesel oil. In fact, everything we get from fossil fuels could be made from bio-mass.

However, there are problems:
- An enormous amount of land is needed to grow crops for biofuels. The world also needs to grow food, and the increasing population has already put a strain on food supplies. As a result, food is getting more expensive. In the future, there will be greater shortages and bigger problems. Grow crops for food or grow crops for energy?
- The planting, harvesting, producing and transporting of these crops produces air pollution and adds to global warming. The burning of vegetable oil releases CO_2 and other greenhouse gases into the atmosphere.

Scientists have produced damning evidence to suggest that biofuels could be one of the biggest environmental con-tricks because they actually make global warming worse by adding to the man-made emissions of carbon dioxide that they are supposed to curb.

Independent, *8 February 2008.*

6 Power from below the Earth's surface

The centre of the Earth is molten rock at around 6,000 degrees Celsius. Even a few kilometres down, the temperature can be over 250 degrees Celsius.

In volcanic areas, molten rock can be very close to the surface. This can heat underground water, and sometimes we can use that heat to power electrical generators, or even provide central heating for houses. This is called GEOTHERMAL POWER.

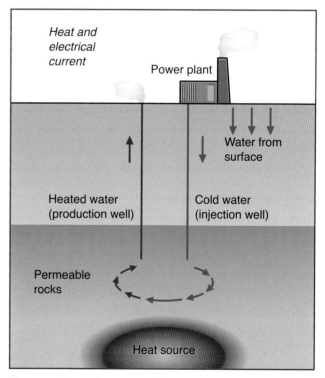

How geothermal power works.

The diagram above shows the basic principles. Cold water is pumped underground to a point where geothermal power heats it up, then the hot water is pumped back up to the surface where it is used to drive turbines, or sometimes it is simply piped to radiators in houses.

Obviously this method of producing power is only easily available in places where volcanic, hot areas are near to the Earth's surface. Examples of where it is used are New Zealand, Iceland, Japan, the Philippines and the USA. Geothermal power only provides about one per cent of power across the globe – but Iceland, for example, gets almost all its power from this source.

Advantages
- Geothermal energy does not produce pollution or contribute to the greenhouse effect.
- The power stations do not take up much room, so there is not much impact on the environment.
- Once a geothermal power station is built, the energy is almost free.
- It may need a little energy to run a pump, but this can be taken from the energy generated.

Disadvantages
- The main problem is that there are few places where conditions are right to build a geothermal power station. Hot rocks of a suitable type are needed, at a depth where they can be drilled down to.
- A geothermal power station can be difficult to design and build, so they are costly.
- Delivering hot water to where it's needed will involve pipelines, often for many kilometres.
- Geothermal sites are not predictable as volcanic areas are unstable. This adds to difficulties in construction and the power can consequently be unreliable.

ACTIVITIES

1 Using the information on pages 51–55, explain the advantages and disadvantages of these sources of energy:
   - Hydroelectric power
   - Tidal and wave power
   - Wind power
   - Solar power
   - Biofuels
   - Geothermal power
   - Nuclear power
2 As a group, discuss which of these renewable sources of power could be used in the UK to replace fossil fuels.

- Hazardous gases and minerals may be produced, and are difficult to dispose of safely.

7 Nuclear power

Nuclear power stations use a non-renewable resource – uranium. This could run out eventually but experts are not too worried because more is being discovered, and nuclear reactors are being made more efficient as technology progresses. In 2008, nuclear power provided 26 per cent of the UK's power needs.

Advantages
- Nuclear power stations do not produce as much air pollution like fossil fuels. It is nearly 'clean power'.
- A shortfall in power that a country needs to keep going is called the 'energy gap'. Building more nuclear power stations is the most efficient and quickest method of filling the energy gap left when we stop using fossil fuels.
- Once the power station is built, the power is reliable and cheaper than power produced using fossil fuels.

Disadvantages
- Nuclear power stations are extremely expensive to build, and they are very expensive to maintain and keep running safely.
- They also only last about 30 years before they have to be closed down and dismantled.
- The nuclear waste produced is very hard to dispose of safely. The Irish Sea is polluted by waste from Sellafield nuclear power station. There are no methods of storing nuclear waste that are completely safe.
- An accident, like the reactor fire at Chernobyl in 1986, can make the land 50 miles around the power centre uninhabitable for a hundred years or more.
- Even a smaller accident, such as a leak of radioactive coolant water, can be lethal to humans and animals.
- There is always a security risk that radioactive materials could be stolen and used to make nuclear weapons.

Energy generation in the UK today, and in the future

How should the UK generate energy in the future? The chart below shows how we do it now.

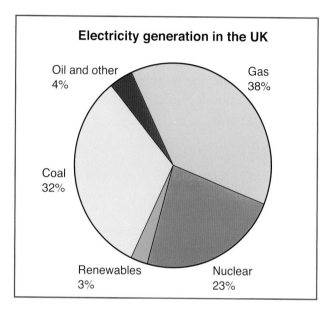

Electricity generation in the UK

Oil and other 4%
Gas 38%
Coal 32%
Renewables 3%
Nuclear 23%

You can see from the above chart that we depend on fossil fuels – non-renewable sources of energy – to generate most of our electricity.

Without electricity we could not live or work as we do now, and the economy would grind to a halt. But depending on fossil fuels raises problems:

- The world is going to run out of oil and natural gas fairly soon. Before these run out they will become more expensive as countries use more.
- If we want to prevent further global warming, we have to cut down our carbon emissions, which means we must phase out fossil fuels.
- There is more coal, but burning coal causes more air pollution than the other fossil fuels.
- Nuclear power stations are getting old, so new ones will have to be built to replace them.
- The UK does not want to depend on importing electricity or sources of energy generation.

With these problems facing us, the government has decided we must make more use of renewable sources of energy to generate electricity.

- This means we have to turn to wind, solar, or water power from rivers, tides, or waves (the UK has little geothermal power available).
- Bio-energy is a possibility, but this will still produce greenhouse gases and will mean using land for biofuel crops rather than for growing food.

UK energy: Wind power?

Wind power is the government's preferred method, because it is clean, and because once wind farms are set up they will be cheap to run. The government has set a target of using wind turbines to produce one-third of all UK electricity by 2020: this will be 35 gigawatts of electricity. (The gigawatt is the equivalent of 1,000 megawatts, or one thousand million watts. One gigawatt of electricity would meet the energy needs of over 600,000 UK households, around one per cent of the UK's energy needs.)

To do this the industry will have to build 15,000 turbines on land and at sea. It will be difficult to do, and it will be very expensive. Some people say this can't be done in the timescale.

On land

Huge numbers of wind farms and pylons will lead to massive protests about beautiful landscapes being ruined, and delays in getting planning permission may go on for years. Even once agreed, they are likely to take years to build.

At sea

One plan is to build giant wind farms 10 to 20 miles off-shore. Some are already planned, for example, in the Bristol Channel, and off coasts in Wales and Yorkshire. These will be so costly to build that big companies like Shell have already pulled out because of the cost and technical difficulties. Securing wind turbines with 110-metre-long blades to the seabed is going to be a major engineering problem.

UK energy: Solar energy?

Solar energy can add to our supply of electricity, but it relies on regular sunshine – this means our weather isn't reliable enough for the UK to depend on it. There will have to be some form of back-up for cloudy days. At the moment, solar panels that are large enough to produce electricity to power a factory or a few hundred houses are very expensive to make, but, as technology improves, this may not be true for long.

UK energy: Power from the rivers and sea?

Energy from tides, waves, or rivers is possible. Like wind turbines, these generators can be difficult and expensive to build.

However, new designs are being developed. At the moment, these are small scale and still experimental, but they have had promising results.

One issue still to be resolved is that they can cause environmental problems by disrupting the ocean's ecosystem and causing coastal erosion. This solution could cause a new set of environmental problems.

UK energy: Nuclear power?

One final possibility is to use nuclear power to generate electricity. It's clean because it doesn't produce much CO_2 or other forms of air pollution. It's possible to build new nuclear power stations to replace the old ones quicker than we can build wind farms to produce the same amount of electricity. It's expensive, but cheaper than using fossil fuels. We currently produce 26 per cent of our electricity this way, so we already understand how to use it.

However, many people are very nervous about the risks of radiation leaks, terrorist threats, and the problem of disposing of nuclear waste. Nonetheless, experts and supporters say that nuclear power stations are much safer than they used to be, that security can be made as strong as it is for nuclear weapons, and that this method is the most efficient for replacing fossil fuels.

How should the UK generate electricity in the future?

You can see there are no easy answers. But if we want to go on making electricity, and reduce pollution and carbon emissions, we have to make hard decisions.

What we and the government have to weigh up is:

- Can we save energy and reduce our need for electricity?
- Can people be persuaded to accept the impact of wind turbines, solar power cells, and wave generators on the environment?
- Can the technology be developed to make these methods efficient enough to replace non-renewable sources?
- Can nuclear power stations be made safe enough to reduce people's fears?
- Can we afford to spend the huge amount of money that is needed to phase out fossil fuels and convert to renewable energy sources in the near future?
- Can we properly assess how these new technologies will affect the environment and guard against further damage?

ACTIVITY

1 In groups of two or three discuss the following issues:
   a) What are the arguments against continuing to use fossil fuels?
   b) What renewable sources of energy are the best option for the UK?
   c) Why will it be difficult to introduce these methods in the near future?
   d) What is the most feasible option for generating energy over the next 20 years?

CONCEPT 2

Our use of the environment has negative consequences

This concept section looks at some of the environmental problems humans have created. You will learn about:

- The effects of industrialisation.
- The effects of URBANISATION.
- GLOBAL WARMING and climate change.
- The problems created by pollution of the air, the oceans and the land.
- The loss of BIO-DIVERSITY.
- The effects of mass tourism on the environment.

All the issues described in the bullet points above are linked, and are the result of human activities over the last 300 years. Two social and technological revolutions have played a major part in changing the environment and these are explored below.

> The following are ideas and terms that you will need to know from this concept section:
>
> *urbanisation • loss of bio-diversity • global warming • climate change • industrialisation • pollution • tourism*

1 Industrialisation

As populations have increased across the world, and scientific knowledge has grown, the world has become industrialised. This means that the demand for energy and resources has been increasing steadily as people make advances in industry, transport and domestic lifestyles. The more things we make, the more resources we use. The major sources of energy are still non-renewable fossil fuels.

Over the last 100 years the use of these fossil fuels has increased seventeen-fold. The heaviest users until the last few decades were the MEDCs in the Western hemisphere: America, Europe and Russia.

Recently countries in the Eastern hemisphere, Japan, China, Malaysia and India have developed huge industries, still using mainly fossil fuels. Other countries such as Brazil and Mexico in Central and South America are also major industrial powers.

The use of resources as raw materials and fuel is continuing to increase across the world.

2 Urbanisation

Industrialisation brings other changes in the way people live. As industrialisation continues to grow across the world, so does urbanisation. This is people moving from the countryside to live and work in the city.

Industrialisation and urbanisation go together. If a country wants to become wealthy, it must industrialise, and this means it needs cities for the workers to live in.

People want to move to cities because they hope to live a better life, working in industry rather than in agriculture, earning and spending more money so that they can enjoy the products of industry and the lifestyle of MEDCs.

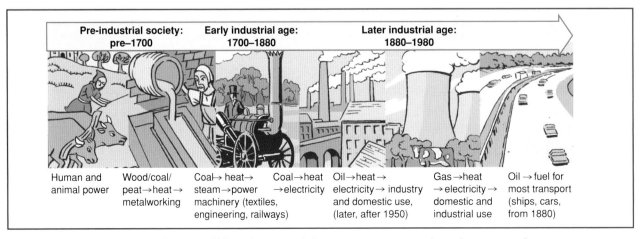

Pre-industrial society: pre–1700	Early industrial age: 1700–1880		Later industrial age: 1880–1980			
Human and animal power	Wood/coal/ peat→heat → metalworking	Coal→ heat→ steam→power machinery (textiles, engineering, railways)	Coal→heat →electricity	Oil→heat → electricity → industry and domestic use, (later, after 1950)	Gas →heat → electricity → domestic and industrial use	Oil → fuel for most transport (ships, cars, from 1880)

Energy sources throughout the ages. What do most of these energy sources have in common?

Urbanisation is the method that countries use to modernise the economy. Producing food is essential, but in many LEDCs it is done very inefficiently by farmers growing just enough food for their families. In MEDCs farming is mechanised, done on an industrial scale, and only needs a few people to produce huge quantities of crops and livestock.

So, in 2009, countries that 50 years ago were mostly made up of farming families in small villages now have cities with millions of inhabitants.

The article below describes the rapid development of China.

> The most dramatic industrialisation/urbanisation programme in the world is being developed by China. This has moved into the modern era at a blistering pace over the last 30 years. China will soon overtake Japan as Asia's No 1 economic power, and it may soon take over from the United States as the dominant global economy. The products of Chinese industry have flooded the markets of most countries over the last ten years.
>
> Chinese industry is largely dependent on fossil fuels and has recently overtaken the USA as the world's biggest polluter of the atmosphere. Along with this growth in industry, urbanisation has moved with similar speed. Already there are 160 cities in China with *inner-city* populations of over one million.
>
> The Chinese Minister of Civil Affairs, Doje Cering, said that over the next 20 years, about 12 million people from China's rural areas (mostly small farmers) will move to urban areas *each year*. This will mean that the equivalent of 20 new megacities will have to be built in the next 20 years.
>
> China consumes nearly half the world's cement. It commissions a new power station about every four days and last year built as much power generating capacity as the entire output of France. Three nuclear power plants are being built in China and 500 coal-fired power plants are going to be built in the next decade. It plans to build 97 regional airports in the next decade.

Hamish Macrae, 'The dragon awakens: China, how did it happen?', Independent, 10 May 2008.

China is not the only country with rapidly growing industries and the huge cities which go with industrialisation. The figures below are for *urban areas* (for example, the London figure here is for Greater London, not the inner city).

RANK	POPULATION	CITY	COUNTRY
1	12,778,721	Mumbai	India
2	12,207,254	Karachi	Pakistan
3	11,055,365	Delhi	India
4	10,840,516	Shanghai	China
5	10,375,688	Moscow	Russia
6	10,147,972	Seoul	South Korea
7	10,136,978	São Paulo	Brazil
8	10,121,565	Istanbul	Turkey
9	8,866,160	Lima	Peru
10	8,548,639	Mexico City	Mexico
11	8,407,479	Jakarta	Indonesia
12	8,158,957	New York	United States of America
13	8,124,310	Tokyo	Japan
14	7,741,274	Beijing	China
15	7,620,971	Bogotá	Colombia
16	7,438,376	Cairo	Egypt
17	7,404,515	Tehran	Iran
18	7,318,636	Ar-Riyad	Saudi Arabia
19	7,287,555	London	England

There are at least 20 more urban areas with populations of over 4 million.

ACTIVITIES

1 Identify which of these cities are in countries with developed economies, and which are in countries which are less developed and still developing.
2 Pick one of the developing countries on the list and find out what are the main products of that country, plus the environmental problems that country is facing.

The environmental effects of industrialisation and urbanisation

The growing world population, rapid industrialisation and expanding urbanisation of the twenty-first century have created many environmental problems. These problems have two major features:

- We are creating waste and pollution by using the Earth's resources, and this is damaging life on the planet.
- We are consuming and depleting many of the natural resources we need to survive.

Both these problems are getting worse as the population grows and we demand more resources.

In this section there are a series of examples of the negative consequences of our use of the environment.

1 Global warming and climate change

Many people describe this as the biggest problem the world currently faces. We examine why people think it is happening and what the likely effects of these changes are.

'Climate change is the single most important issue we face as a global community.'

Tony Blair, Prime Minister of the UK at the time, April 2004.

ACTIVITIES

Work in small groups and, after discussion:
1 Make a list of any changes or extremes of weather you have experienced or heard of in the last few years (such as floods, gales, droughts).
2 Explain what effects these extreme weather events have on the people involved.

By now, most people are aware of global warming. In the last five years it has been accepted by almost all scientists and politicians that the world is getting hotter, as more 'greenhouse gases' (carbon dioxide, methane, nitrous oxide, ozone and CFCs) are introduced into the atmosphere in increasing quantities:

- Carbon dioxide and nitrous oxide gases are produced by burning fossil fuels.
- Methane gas is produced by plants and animals, as well as by waste that we generate.
- Ozone and CFCs gases are produced by industrial processes.

The introduction of these gases has changed the atmosphere, which has led to the warming of the planet.

Climate change is the result of global warming. The Intergovernmental Panel on Climate Change (IPCC) predicts that average global temperatures will rise by somewhere between 1.4 and 5.8°C during the twenty-first century. This may not seem to be much, but when this happens weather patterns will change drastically. This, in turn, will affect animal and plant life.

Changes in global temperatures have taken place for millions of years, and some scientists argue that the current changes are just part of this pattern. However, most scientists are alarmed by how quickly this is happening and predict that these changes will cause global problems in the near future. They say this warming is taking place partly because of the increase in emissions of greenhouse gases.

Temperature figures from the past (gained by analysing very old Arctic ice that is drilled from frozen ice plates) and more recent records show that the average global temperature is rising. The chart below gives an indication of this sudden rise.

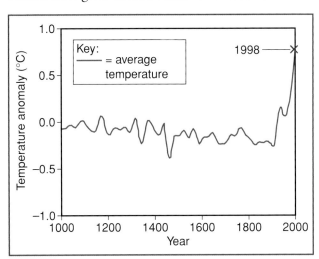

Reconstruction of temperatures for the past millennium averaged over the northern hemisphere.

The result of these changes in the average world temperature does not mean that everywhere is getting hotter. This will happen in some places, but it could also result in some places getting colder, wetter, drier, and more likely to experience extreme weather such as hurricanes and droughts. In other words, the effects of global warming on weather are unpredictable.

Does everyone agree that climate change is taking place?

Most scientists accept that the climate is changing, that we produce more greenhouse gases than we used to, that global warming is taking place. But not *all* scientists believe that this situation is a serious threat to the planet. They argue that:

- Climate changes have taken place before and people have adapted.
- The increased heat will create water vapour and clouds which will cool the planet down.
- More carbon dioxide will encourage plant growth, and these will absorb the excess CO_2.
- The oceans will be able to absorb more CO_2 (they already absorb a huge amount).
- Climate change does not have to be bad; many people will benefit from warmer weather and more or less rainfall.

So why should we worry?

The vast majority of scientists do think that this change in climate is a serious problem. Why?

Increasing CO_2 emissions

The most developed countries produce the most CO_2. The USA used to be the world's largest producer. However, other countries such as India and China now have growing populations and are becoming industrialised rapidly. China may now be producing more CO_2 than the USA. Despite attempts to use alternative sources of energy, the burning of fossil fuels is increasing. As a result, emissions of CO_2 and other greenhouse gases such as methane are also increasing. These increases can be measured scientifically and are not seriously disputed. We know this results in a thicker layer of CO_2 in the atmosphere.

There is a great deal of evidence of changes in climate.

a) Melting polar ice

Arctic sea ice is on average 1.8 m (6 ft) thick now, compared to 3 m (10 ft) thick in the 1970s. In 2005, NASA satellite imagery suggested that Arctic glacier ice is shrinking at the edges by 2.9 per cent per decade. Recent observations indicate that the Arctic is melting even faster than predicted.

Also, the Greenland Ice Sheet – with an ice volume of about 2.9 million cubic kilometres – is shrinking at a fast pace and 'could contribute much more than previously estimated to global sea level rise during the twenty-first century', the WWF (the World Wildlife Fund) said in April 2005.

b) Rising sea levels

Sea levels are rising as melted glacier ice enters the ocean. Two small islets in the Pacific Ocean have already disappeared in Kiribati and many low-lying islands are losing coastal land at a rate of up to 25 m (82 ft) each year from rising sea levels. If Arctic and Antarctic ice masses melt completely, average sea levels will rise by 6 m, which will flood many coastal areas across the world, and most major port cities such as London, New York, Sydney will be partly submerged.

c) Melting glaciers

Scientists now report ice and glaciers melting in all the world's major mountain ranges, including the Rocky Mountains, the Andes, the Alps and the

Himalayas. This will eventually reduce the amount of water that is released in spring. Ski resorts in Europe have recently had to reduce the ski season by five weeks. In Scotland, two ski areas have closed because of limited snow in the last five years. This means there are less jobs available to people living in the local area.

MOUNTAIN GLACIERS ARE SHRINKING THREE TIMES FASTER THAN THEY WERE IN THE 1980s, SCIENTISTS HAVE ANNOUNCED

The World Glacier Monitoring Service, which continuously studies a sample of 30 glaciers around the world, says the acceleration is down to climate change.

Richard Black, BBC News website, 29 January 2007.

d) Heatwaves

In May 2003, a record heatwave in India, with the temperature reaching 49°C (117° Fahrenheit), claimed more than 1,600 lives. In societies without air conditioning, there is no ready escape from the dangerous heat. But any society unaccustomed to high temperatures can be disrupted by a heatwave. In August 2003, record high temperatures across Europe claimed a startling 35,000 lives. In 2008, forest fires in Australia and California burned for weeks, forcing millions to evacuate and causing damage to property costing billions of dollars.

e) Falling crop yields

Crop yields have fallen as temperatures have climbed and rainfall levels have dropped in key food-producing countries such as the USA and India. Depressed world grain harvests over the last three years have left the world with a grain shortfall of some 92 million tonnes.

Global warming may cause world crop decline

Global warming could send world agriculture into serious decline by 2080 with productivity collapsing in some developing countries while it improves in a few rich nations, a study reported on Wednesday.

India, Pakistan, most of Africa and most of Latin America would be hit hardest, said economist William Cline, the study's author. The United States, most of Europe, Russia and Canada would probably see agricultural gains if climate change continues on its current course, the study found.

Overall, the world's agricultural productivity was forecast to decline by between 3 per cent and 16 per cent by 2080, according to the study published by the Washington-based Center for Global Development and the Peterson Institute for International Economics.

Among developed countries, Australia's outlook was bleakest with predicted declines in crop yields ranging between 16 per cent and 27 per cent. In the developing world, fast-growing India's declines were forecast between 29 per cent and 38 per cent while Sudan and Senegal both had predicted crop declines of more than 50 per cent, essentially a collapse of agricultural productivity.

Deborah Zabarenko, Reuters, 12 September 2007.

ACTIVITY

1 Take three of the examples of climate change listed on pages 61–63, and explain the effects of these changes on humans and on the environment. Use an internet search engine to investigate recent climate crises. For example, you could set your answer out like this:

Environmental change	Effect on the environment	Effect on people
Sea levels rise	Flooding of land and cities	Loss of homes, less food, social disruption, need to rebuild
More hurricanes		
Droughts		

f) Droughts

Occasional droughts are common in southern Africa, but the number of food emergencies in Africa each year has almost tripled since the 1980s. Across sub-Saharan Africa, one in three people is under-nourished.

> ### One third of the planet will be desert by the year 2100, say climate experts in the most dire warning yet of the effects of global warming
>
> Last year in Kenya's Rift Valley, the rains never came; large swathes of the Horn of Africa stayed brown. From Ethiopia and Eritrea, through Somalia and down into Tanzania, 11 million people were at risk of hunger.

Michael McCarthy, Independent Online, *4 October 2006.*

g) Floods

Britain has experienced serious flooding during the twenty-first century.

> ### A twenty-first-century catastrophe
>
> This weather is different from anything that has gone before. The floods it has caused, which have left more than a third of a million people without drinking water, nearly 50,000 people without power, thousands more people homeless and caused more than £2bn worth of damage – and are still not over – have no precedent in modern British history.

Michael McCarthy, Independent Online, *24 July 2007.*

Floods have also affected the rest of the world:

- In 2005, floods caused by Hurricane Katrina left New Orleans under water and made millions homeless.
- In August 2008, millions of people in Bihar, India and Nepal have been made homeless as the Kosi river burst its banks.

- Bangladesh has suffered from floods for many years, but over the last decade rainfall has been heavier and these floods have been more severe, lasted longer and extended over more land. In 2004, a third of Bangladesh was affected and three million people were marooned.

h) Hurricanes

Researchers found that average hurricane numbers jumped sharply during the twentieth century, from 3.5 per year in the first 30 years to 8.4 in the earliest years of the twenty-first century.

In 2004, the Caribbean islands and Florida experienced four major hurricanes over a two-month period. Two of these hurricanes were the most powerful for 30 years, and four major hurricanes in one year is double the average for the area.

Several extreme hurricanes made 2005 a landmark year. Katrina has been the deadliest for the USA so far. Hurricane Rita was the most intense hurricane to ever enter the Gulf of Mexico. Wilma was the most intense hurricane ever recorded in the Atlantic Basin.

Conclusion

Scientists and meteorologists believe that all these changes in climate and weather patterns are caused by global warming, which seems to be having increasingly serious effects.

The examples of climate change discussed above are more than descriptions of human disasters, they will affect the lives of everyone. Predicted effects include the following:

- Climate changes will take place, but no one is sure what they will be. Some areas will become hotter, others colder.
- Sea levels are going to rise as ice melts at the poles. This could mean that within this century many major cities near the sea will be flooded. London, New York and Hong Kong are all at risk. Large areas of land will disappear, as has already happened in Bangladesh. This will be a challenge for even wealthy countries – the New Orleans floods in 2005 showed that even the richest countries struggle with these natural crises – and poor countries are likely to be even less able to cope.

- Some places will get less rain and some will get more. Extreme weather such as floods, droughts and hurricanes will become more common. In a crisis like a flood, the countries that are poorer will suffer most because they do not have the resources to cope with a large-scale problem.
- Climate change will force large numbers of people to migrate to places in order to survive.
- Many countries that already have water shortages will be even drier – Sub-Saharan Africa is already largely dry, as are parts of America, Spain, the Middle East, Turkey, China and Australia. The most scarce resource in the latter part of the twenty-first century is likely to be fresh water, not oil.

We currently use about 70 per cent of our water supply in agriculture. But the World Water Council believes that by 2020 we shall need 17 per cent more water than is available if we are to feed the world. Today, one person in five across the world has no access to safe drinking water, and one in two lacks safe sanitation. Human health suffers: malaria, dengue ('breakbone') fever, yellow fever, cholera and rodent-borne viruses are also appearing across the world with increased frequency. These diseases are transmitted by insects, animals or unclean water.

- Changes in climate will affect plant life, which will in turn affect food production. In some areas, crops will fail; in others, new crops will thrive. The most extreme prediction is that there will be world food shortages by the middle of the twenty-first century.
- Animals, birds, fish and insects will all be affected by climate change, either dying out because they have lost their habitat, or by moving to new areas, threatening other species. In milder weather, many insects and pests will survive the winter, and become a threat to food crops. Already, mosquitoes are spreading to countries where there are no predators to control them. This could lead to the spread of diseases in places where people have no immunity.

The future
Global warming and climate change is taking place. How much hotter the world becomes depends on the amount of greenhouse gases we continue to produce and whether global warming can be reversed. Scientists disagree about how much the climate will change, but most say the speed of change is quicker than earlier estimates.

2 The pollution of the oceans
What does the sea do for us apart from providing food? For years, because the sea is so vast, people have assumed that our bits of waste and rubbish would be literally 'a drop in the ocean', easily carried away and cleaned up magically by the action of seawater. 'The solution to pollution is dilution' was the theory. This was human behaviour for most of our history. But now we know that even the sea can be damaged and unable to repair itself.

Case Study
The pollution of the oceans

This case study will look at:

- What we are putting into the oceans.
- What effect this is having on the water, animals, plants and humans.

What are we putting into the oceans?
We treat the oceans like an open sewer, dumping huge amounts of waste in them every day. We use drains and outflow pipes, and often rivers to dispose of this waste, and much of it eventually ends up in the sea.

This pollution includes human sewage and domestic wastewater, factory outflows of acids and poisonous metals, engine oil from roadside drains and garages, farm chemicals leaking from the land, nuclear waste from power plants, and oil from wells, refineries and tankers. The daily flow of materials into the sea also includes a million plastic items such as bags, nets, and bits of packaging. Some of this pollution is accidental, but many factories and sewage systems still legally dump waste in the sea.

The oceans break up, disperse, or dissolve large quantities of waste. But there are limits, and these have been reached in many areas of the oceans. In recent years, the sheer volume and toxicity (the degree to which a substance is poisonous to an environment) of the waste we are dumping into the sea has increased so much that it is causing damage to the oceans. Some of this damage may be irreparable.

The table below lists the main types of marine pollution:

TYPE OF MARINE POLLUTION	% OF TOTAL	EXAMPLES	PICTURE
Run-off from land, industry, domestic waste	44	• Sewage • Agricultural waste (fertilisers, dung, etc.) • Industrial waste (acids, oil, chemicals, etc.) • Food and drink (brewing waste, bad meat and vegetables)	 Industrial pollution pouring into the sea.
Atmosphere	33	• Windblown dust and gases from factories, fires and vehicles	 Forest fires not only kill trees and wildlife, they also produce carbon dioxide and acid rain – threatening pollution of the atmosphere for wide areas of the world.
Marine transport	12	• Oil leaks • Other cargo spills (chemicals, containers of food) • Pleasure boating (fuel spills, dumping rubbish)	 An oil tanker in the Gulf of Mexico. Note the oil spill around the tanker.
Dumping at sea	10	• Sewage sludge • Ships' rubbish thrown overboard • Dredging • Bilge water discharges • Rubbish disposal by barges	 Barge in the Thames loaded with rubbish heading out to sea.
Off-shore production	1	Waste from oil and gas extraction	 Oil rig burning off gas.

TYPE OF POLLUTION	HOW DOES THE UK DO?
Disposing of hazardous waste at sea	The UK is the only country in the world that continues to burn hazardous waste at sea – on average, 90,000 tonnes of PESTICIDES, solvents, metals and plastics are incinerated at sea by the UK every year.
Disposing of radioactive waste at sea	Since the 1950s, radioactive waste from Sellafield nuclear plant has been discharged into the Irish sea, which is now thought to be one of the most radioactive stretches of water in the world. Spray from the Irish Sea turns into radioactive dust and can be found on beaches and in people's homes. Increased rates of cancer have been reported on the east coast of Ireland and west coast of England.
Discharging raw sewage into the sea	A staggering 3.8 billion litres of sewage are produced every day in the UK, of which 24 per cent is discharged untreated, compared to West Germany and Denmark, which have no untreated sewage discharges. Many beaches, particularly on the south and west coasts of England, are regarded as unfit for safe bathing, and marine life is often contaminated.

The pollution of the sea is a worldwide problem, and most countries contribute to it in one way or another. Many countries have no other affordable way to dispose of sewage and other waste. Industries that have not modernised remain major polluters of land, sea and air. Many industries in LEDCs and the developing world are still at this stage. However, Britain is a wealthy country, but it is still a major polluter of the seas around the UK, as the table above shows.

Oceans turn to acid

The world's oceans are sacrificing themselves to try to stave off global warming. Their waters have absorbed about half of the CO_2 produced by humans over the past two centuries. Without this moderating effect, climate change would have been much more severe and rapid. But in the process, the seas have become more acidic, which threatens their very life. Research warns that this could kill off their coral reefs, shellfish and plankton, on which all marine life depends.

As the water absorbs carbon dioxide it forms carbonic acid. The acid then absorbs calcium carbonate, which sea creatures use to make the protective shells they need to survive. The results are incalculable because shelled creatures ranging from clams and corals to plankton form the base of the entire food chain of the oceans.

Adapted from the Independent, *1 August 2004.*

ACTIVITIES

1 From the information on pages 64–67, draw a diagram or picture that shows how the oceans are being polluted. Indicate which are the heaviest forms of pollution.
2 Read the newspaper article on this page. Then look at an atlas and explain why you think the North Atlantic is the 'most acidic' ocean.
3 What does the sea do for us apart from providing food?

What effect do different types of sea pollution have?

Run-off from the land: Agricultural waste, oil and dust from roads, industrial waste and domestic waste often find their way into the sea:

• Some agricultural waste (manure from animals and rotting vegetation) contains nutrients (nitrates and phosphates) from FERTILISERS. Too much of this causes algae to grow rapidly, which destroys other marine life. These are sometimes called red, brown or green tides. One effect of this is the death of coral around the world.
• Dust from roads; oil, diesel and petrol; and heavy metals from brake linings and car parts are all toxic to water life, and can get into our fresh water systems.
• Industrial waste can be toxic to sea and water life, and these chemicals may enter our bodies and cause illness if we eat polluted fish.

Sewage: Human excrement, which contains both nutrients and toxic material, is often dumped in the sea in huge quantities (for example, nine million tonnes of it are dumped off the coast of New York and New Jersey every year). This kills nearly every living thing for miles. In Europe, things are little better, and, along with untreated sewage, other materials flushed down the toilet end up in the sea or on beaches. This harms marine life, and also causes health problems for humans. Surfers and swimmers are particularly at risk because they breathe in a fine spray from the surface water – the most toxic part of the sea.

Oil spills and discharges: Although oil spills from tanker accidents do damage sea life and birds, the evidence is that the sea can cope with crude oil quite well over time. However, some ships are responsible for even more dangerous discharges into the sea, as they pump out BALLAST, which may contain toxins, or dump untreated rubbish (such as food waste and sewage) into the sea.

Chemicals and airborne gases and particles: More than half of the oxygen we breathe comes from the ocean. However, pollution is now reducing the oceans' ability to produce oxygen. In many large cities, the air quality regularly reaches such high toxic levels that the authorities advise the population to stay indoors. This polluted air is partly absorbed by the sea, where it reduces the oceans' ability to produce oxygen.

Many chemicals such as DDTA and PCBs end up in the fat of many sea predators such as bears, seals, whales and sharks. These chemicals are known to be harmful to marine life and are also a threat to human health. They seem to affect the hormones of animals so they cannot breed. If these effects are widespread, the marine ecosystem will be permanently changed and a major food source will disappear or be contaminated.

Other waste dumped into the sea: Until recently, most waste material that ended up in the sea disintegrated or decomposed. However, most plastic waste stays intact: bottles, polystyrene packaging, ropes and nets, plastic bags and toys all end up floating around for years. This debris has the additional effect of making many coastal areas unattractive and unhealthy for human beings. Many beaches across the world are polluted by sewage and urban wastewater.

ACTIVITY

1 Work in groups to devise and create a display that explains why pollution of the seas is bad for all living things including human beings. The display should tell the story in pictures and be understood without the use of words, or with no more than 20 words.

Many beaches across the world are polluted by sewage, urban wastewater and domestic rubbish.

How pollution affects both wealth and health.

Summary of Case Study

1 Humans have used the sea as a place to dump waste for thousands of years. For a long time, the small population and limited technology meant that it was not an environmental problem except in very localised coastal areas.

2 Nowadays, the volume and toxicity of the waste being dumped in the sea is causing problems across the world. These are threatening sea life and creating an ecological crisis.

3 There are many different ways in which pollution enters the oceans, but the greatest threats are from industrial, agricultural and human waste pouring into the sea from the land, and pollution that is airborne such as gases and solid particles.

4 This pollution is damaging to both marine life and humans. Even more so, the increase or decrease of species and micro-organisms is changing the whole marine ecosystem in ways that scientists cannot predict.

5 The outcome of these changes will adversely affect both the food supply and human health across the world.

3 Pollution on land

Landfills

Population growth and the material goods and wealth created by industrialisation have had a damaging side effect. We produce a huge amount of waste that has to be got rid of somewhere. Put simply, we create a great deal of waste because we have so much stuff. If electronic equipment gets out-of-date we dump it. If we buy a new washing machine it comes with several kilos of cardboard and plastic to be disposed of. Food comes in glossy printed boxes, and we throw the food away if it goes past its sell-by date. And most of this 'rubbish' goes into a wheelie bin. Then what happens to it?

The answer for much household waste is that it is dumped in a landfill site, often a disused quarry or mine – creating a huge rubbish bin. Space available for landfill sites is becoming less and less available. Nobody wants a rubbish tip near their home. The UK fills about 300 million square metres of land with waste every year: that's the same as filling a Premiership football ground 30,000 times over. This is leaving a dangerous legacy for the next generation, as vast areas of land are being left contaminated and unusable. Much of this waste will sit in the same place for years without decomposing – while most food stuffs decompose in a few months, a single plastic bag can last for 300 years, and a plastic bottle can last for 1,000 years.

Apart from looking messy and smelling bad, landfills create serious problems for the environment:

- Groundwater, often the source of our drinking water, can be contaminated.
- A toxic chemical mixture called 'leachate' is formed when hazardous materials, such as paint, thinners, cleaning liquids are dumped, mix with rainwater and trickle to the bottom of the landfill. This makes the soil below the site toxic, and unusable for growing crops or building on.
- Decomposing organic material generates methane, which is both explosive and a greenhouse gas. CO_2 is also produced in large quantities.
- Landfill sites provide a breeding ground for insects and vermin.

Rubbish is regularly dumped as a cheap way of dealing with it. How would you feel if you lived in this area?

Plastic waste doesn't go away. It's dumped onto the land and stays there.

Soil pollution from farms

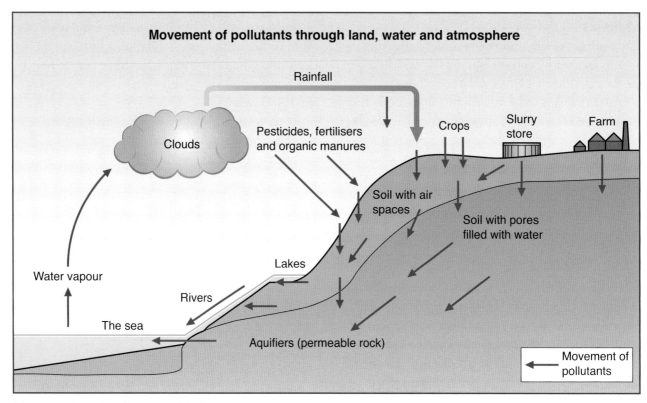

Movement of pollutants through land, water and atmosphere

Rainfall

Clouds

Pesticides, fertilisers and organic manures

Crops

Slurry store

Farm

Soil with air spaces

Soil with pores filled with water

Water vapour

Lakes

Rivers

The sea

Aquifers (permeable rock)

Movement of pollutants

Waste produced by farms, which includes pesticides, fertilisers, animal carcasses, sewage sludge, can easily enter the water system.

Industrial waste

Is this waste toxic? Do we know how it affects the land or people's health?

4 The threat to bio-diversity

What is bio-diversity?

Bio-diversity is shorthand for the biological diversity of living organisms and the ecological complexes of which they are part. It is the total range of all plant and animal species in the world. There are currently at least ten million species of animals and plants worldwide.

There is much concern about the effect of human actions on bio-diversity. We know that species of animals and plants are being lost forever on a daily basis. This section examines the problems we encounter when we exploit natural resources to such an extent that we endanger the survival of whole species of living creatures. It examines the problems this causes through looking at a case study of the oceans – examining the threats to many fish species and other sea life.

1 Make a list of species that you believe are endangered and give reasons why they are under threat of extinction.
2 What effects could the extinction of these species have on an ecosystem?

How important is bio-diversity to humanity?

We all depend on the natural world to provide us with food, clothing and other necessities. About 3,000 plant species are used worldwide as a food source. However, just 20 of these plants provide more than 80 per cent of our food at the present time. We need the other plants to help keep our food plants healthy and to make them resistant to pests and climate changes.

We use a small number of animal species to provide our food – but we need huge numbers of these animals. For example, in the year 2000, the amount of fish and shellfish caught totalled 87.3 million tonnes, of which 70 per cent was for human consumption.

In addition to food, many of our drugs and raw materials for manufacturing also originate from either plants or animals. Many industrial materials, such as fibres, resins, dyes, waxes, pesticides, lubricants and perfumes derive from plant or animal sources. Trees provide us with more than 3.8 million cubic metres of wood annually for use as fuel, timber or pulp.

Additionally, plants and animals are essential to our enjoyment of the planet's beauty.

What are the threats to bio-diversity?

Loss of habitats

The greatest threat is the loss of the natural habitats of plants and animals so that they have nowhere suitable left to live. This happens for various reasons, some of which are:

• Cutting down large areas of forests for timber or plantations.
• Allowing domestic animals to overgraze and damage the land.
• Draining wetlands for use by humans.
• Damaging heathlands and coral reefs with industrial and leisure activities.

Pollution is another threat to habitats. Pesticides, sewage, oil, combustion emissions and acid rain contaminate soils, fresh water sources, the oceans and the air. This results in animals and plants dying out in certain areas. Climate change will have even bigger effects on habitats, and these cannot be predicted.

Over-exploitation

Major human exploitation has pushed some species of animals to the verge of extinction. Examples include the tiger, giant panda, black rhinoceros, cod and several whale species. Between 1979 and 1989, the African elephant population was halved because of ivory poaching. Other species have been relentlessly persecuted as vermin, despite the fact they were causing no problems. For example, for centuries in Britain, red kites were believed to be 'lamb-killers' and were killed, in spite of their lack of strength for such a task.

The situation now

Resulting from this range of human threats, rates of extinction are now thought to be thousands of times greater than in the recent past. Humans now have the technology to make massive changes to the environment. For example, tropical forests are being destroyed at the rate of 0.8 to 2.0 per cent per annum, driving some of the estimated five million species that live there into extinction. We know that 484 species of animal and 654 plants have become extinct since 1600.

It is estimated that over the last 20 years in Britain alone, ten species of farmland birds are under threat because of modern farming methods.

Case Study
Bio-diversity: The threat to fish and marine life

Fish is an important part of the human diet in many parts of the world. Fish provides protein and essential vitamins and minerals. It is particularly valuable as food in developing countries such as Bangladesh, Ghana, North Korea and Indonesia, where it provides half the protein consumed. In the developed world, the demand for fish has grown, and consumption of fish by the rising populations of Asia has increased ten-fold since 1970.

The chart below shows how the total world sea fish catch has increased steadily since 1950. By the year 2000, the world's fishing fleets were catching five times the amount of fish they had taken 50 years ago.

However, in the twenty-first century, the total harvest of fish has stopped increasing. Overall it has dropped a little. This is because the world's fish stocks have been almost fully exploited.

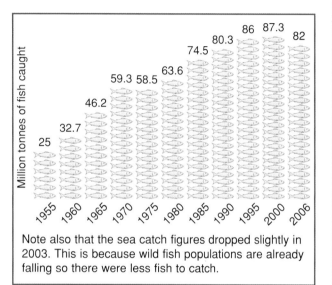

Note also that the sea catch figures dropped slightly in 2003. This is because wild fish populations are already falling so there were less fish to catch.

Total world sea fish catch data from 1950 to 2003.

What does fully exploited mean?

This means that the fish numbers have dropped to a level where the species might die out.

Look at the chart below to see how the current level of fishing is a threat to the survival of many species of fish.

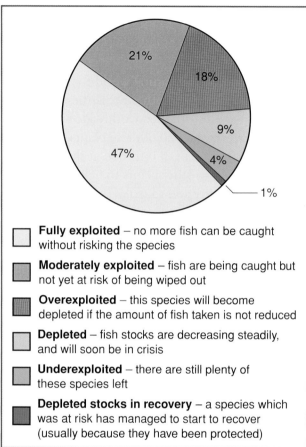

☐ **Fully exploited** – no more fish can be caught without risking the species

☐ **Moderately exploited** – fish are being caught but not yet at risk of being wiped out

☐ **Overexploited** – this species will become depleted if the amount of fish taken is not reduced

☐ **Depleted** – fish stocks are decreasing steadily, and will soon be in crisis

☐ **Underexploited** – there are still plenty of these species left

☐ **Depleted stocks in recovery** – a species which was at risk has managed to start to recover (usually because they have been protected)

State of the world fish stocks. Is there a problem here?

A huge catch of pollock on the deck of a factory trawler.

1 Use the information in the charts on page 72 to write a newspaper article, explaining why it is important to reduce the amount of fish taken from world oceans.

Fishing methods

Fishing has changed since the 1950s. Until then, boats with small nets sailed out and hoped to catch a few tonnes of fish, returning to sell the fish while it was still fresh. Their nets were quite small, and the mesh was set to catch good-sized fish and let the rest escape. When the net was hauled in, small or unwanted fish were thrown back. There was some waste, but not much.

By the mid-twentieth century, fishing boats were huge factory ships. They caught thousands of tonnes of fish, which they froze, and continued fishing. The nets were much bigger – sometimes 4 kilometres (2.5 miles) long – and the fish were detected electronically with great accuracy. These ships could catch everything in the area, including the young fish which had not yet started to breed.

What is 'by-catch'?

The growing demand for fish has created a dangerous form of fishing, an approach that results in much fish being killed needlessly. This is the problem of 'BY-CATCH'.

Fishing on a large scale is not careful. Bottom trawlers pull a huge weighted net along the seabed.

Sometimes two boats work together to pull a net 5 kilometres (three miles) long between them, catching everything in a wide area. Other nets scrape the seabed and scoop up fish eggs and young sea creatures indiscriminately. These are dumped as they cannot be sold, but it means millions of sea inhabitants never mature and breed.

Other fishing methods, such as nets, traps and hooked lines, also catch a wide variety of fish. This means that, as well as the 'target' species of fish caught, any number of 'non-target' species may also be hauled in. This accidental catch of other species is referred to as 'by-catch'.

By-catch is not limited to fish species. All types of marine life including whales, dolphins, porpoises, fur seals, albatrosses and turtles are killed as by-catch.

2 Give two reasons why people want to catch more fish.
3 Explain how this huge increase in fish catches has been made possible.
4 Why is it a problem for future fish stocks if many young fish are caught?
5 Explain in your own words what 'over-exploitation' of species means.

The picture below shows a porpoise that was killed by being trapped in a fishing net. The fisheries with the highest levels of by-catch are shrimp fisheries – often over 80 per cent of a catch comprises marine species other than shrimp.

A porpoise killed by fishing, washed up in South Devon, January 2004.

Globally, it is estimated that a quarter of what is caught is killed and dumped. That means about 20 million tonnes of unwanted fish are thrown back into the sea every year. Most of these will be dead or will die.

Why should we be concerned?

Fishing has a huge impact on the marine (sea) FOOD CHAIN. Fishing is like hunting, and we already understand that if you kill off the animals that breed, the whole species will die out. For example, buffalo and wild boars have been killed off in many parts of the world by hunting and killing the animals capable of breeding.

Over-fishing has meant that there are so few fish of some species that they cannot breed enough to renew themselves. So one result is that fish like cod, which used to be plentiful and cheap, are now rare and expensive. The species becomes depleted and, finally, unsustainable.

But the problem does not end with some fish disappearing or becoming more expensive for customers.

Bio-diversity and the marine ecosystem

The fish we take out of the ocean in huge numbers is also the food for other species. In order to survive, these marine creatures have to move away or change their eating habits. This in turn affects the whole balance of the marine ecology in ways that are still not understood by scientists.

What ecologists fear is that once this food chain is broken, the health of all the ocean's life, fish, plants and animals may be permanently damaged, and the ocean itself may not perform its other vital role: as the most effective mechanism for cleaning and purifying the planet.

Summary of Case Study

1 Life in the sea is an important source of food across the world. In some countries, it is the main source of protein.

2 Fish stocks across the world are falling; in some places, the seas are almost empty of life. Some species have become extinct and others are close to extinction.

3 The main cause of this depletion is a growing world population and the rise of technologies that are able to locate fish accurately and scoop them up in vast quantities.

4 Despite dwindling amounts of fish, much sea life is wasted as a result of by-catch.

5 When the number of a fish species falls below a certain figure, the whole species may become unsustainable, as it cannot breed fast enough to replace losses.

6 The loss of part of the food chain will have major knock-on effects on other species of plant and animal life in the area. These effects are unpredictable and may cause massive problems for linked ecologies.

5 Tourism

We will consider two questions:

- How important is leisure and tourism to the world economy?
- Why is leisure and tourism an environmental issue?

Tourism and the world economy

Leisure and tourism are not exactly the same thing, but the two worlds overlap. Tourism is the movement of people around the world for pleasure, and involves travel and temporary accommodation. Leisure activities include tourism, but also sports like golf and football, going out locally to pubs, clubs, restaurants, cinemas and so on.

Leisure and tourism are big business. In fact, it is the world's biggest industry. It is impossible to get an accurate figure, but the annual turnover is heading towards $4 trillion ($4 thousand billion).

- This is about eight per cent of total world trade.
- In Britain, ten per cent of the population is involved directly or indirectly in the tourist and leisure industry.
- The Caribbean islands get 50 per cent of their income from tourism. Some countries are almost entirely dependent on tourism, for example, the Maldives.

Tourism is growing rapidly. Most tourists are from rich countries such as the USA, western European countries and Japan. But as other countries grow richer, their people join the tourist population because people in richer countries have more leisure time, more disposable income, and because travel costs, particularly air travel, have become relatively cheap.

Many poor countries (LEDCs) see tourism as the quickest way of improving their economy so that they can modernise their SOCIETY and bring advantages to their people.

ACTIVITIES

1 Choose a popular holiday resort (UK or abroad). Make a list of all the jobs at that resort that are dependent on tourism.
2 What would happen to the economy if the tourists stopped coming?
3 Using the diagram below as a starting point, explain the advantages that travel and tourism can bring to an area or COMMUNITY. Use examples from your own experience, or research examples to illustrate your points.

Why is leisure and tourism an environmental issue?

A large number of people moving around the world and staying away from home for a while brings about many environmental changes. The reasons for these changes can be broken down into the following factors:

1 Transport (air travel, traffic and roads, parking).

2 Accommodation (hotels, food and drink supplies, sewage disposal) and use of resources (water supplies, use of electrical power).

3 Leisure activities (swimming pools, shops, eating and drinking facilities) and changes in land use (golf courses, safari parks, skiing, amusement parks, marinas).

4 Changes in lifestyle of local people.

1 Transport

Mass transport is essential for tourism to get people to their destination. Airports, roads, docks and rail terminals have to be built or extended. The growth in traffic, especially road and air, means more air pollution. Aircraft and increased road transport (hire cars, taxis, coaches) produce carbon dioxide and other pollutants in huge quantities. Roads and airports take up land and change the ecology of an area. Building roads and airports itself causes major pollution.

2 Accommodation and use of resources

Much tourism is centred in coastal areas. The classic desirable holiday image is a tropical beach scene, idyllic and peaceful. Many tourists want to

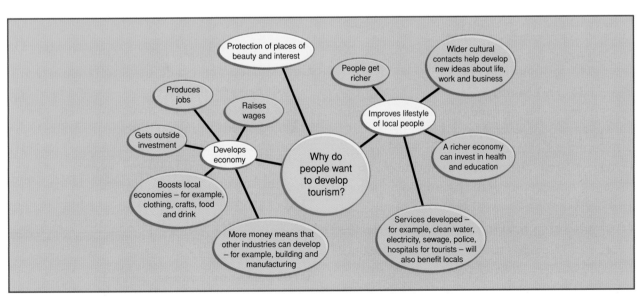

The benefits of tourism.

go to areas such as the Costas in Spain, the Caribbean, Goa and the Greek islands. Thailand and the Seychelles, which are new to mass tourism and were undeveloped until very recently, are becoming popular.

Tourists usually want attractive, clean, comfortable places to stay. This involves building modern hotels and resorts, usually in the most attractive areas. Often the local people have to move out. The building work itself often creates pollution from cement dust and machinery.

Tourists want water for showers, pools and golf courses. They want electricity for lifts, air conditioning and DVD players. They want modern plumbing and waste disposal. Consequently, power and water for tourists becomes a priority, but may leave local people short of electricity, or may drain limited water supplies.

- One large hotel in Egypt uses as much electricity as 3,600 local families.
- One tourist in Spain uses 880 litres (194 gallons) of water a day, compared with 250 litres (55 gallons) used by a local.
- Sewage disposal is a complex thing and the simplest way of disposing of a large increase in sewage is dumping dangerous waste into the sea a few miles from the tourist area.
- Building hotels, apartments, shops, clubs all uses local resources. Coral reefs are blown up to be used as a building material for coastal developments throughout the Indian Ocean, the Arabian/Persian Gulf and the Red Sea. Recently, whole beaches were stolen overnight in Jamaica to be used as building sand.

3 Leisure activities and changes in land use

Mountains and countryside

Second only to beaches and coastlines, mountains are the most popular of tourist destinations, accounting for 15 to 20 per cent of world tourism. People walk over them, climb them and ski on them. Some examples of the pressures on the local area that can arise are given below:

- The number of trekkers visiting the Everest region of Nepal has risen from none in 1960 to 25,000 in 2005. Now Nepal is building a road on the Annapurna trail, to make trekking easier for rich tourists, but in the process wildlife and

the unspoiled beauty of the mountains is destroyed.
- There were 628 ascents of Everest in 2007. Twelve per cent of the trail network has been damaged and there is an estimated 17 tonnes of rubbish per kilometre (0.6 miles) of trail. Four out of five local HOUSEHOLDS derive some income from tourism.
- Up to 700,000 skiers use Switzerland's mountain slopes on any one day during peak season. Ecological damage inflicted by the ski industry includes:
  – Changing the environment by the removal of forests, levelling of land and carving of pathways.
  – The production of artificial snow, which uses up vast quantities of water and energy, and can deposit artificial additives in snow. As a result of this, snow on many mountains has become unstable and avalanches are much more likely, which means artificial barriers have to be built. Most wildlife has left the area.
- In Britain, the most popular area for walkers is the Peak District National Park. There has been a steady increase in visits over the last 40 years as the area becomes more accessible to cars and coaches. The resulting traffic during holiday periods means that the air in some areas of the park is more polluted than the air in central London. The people who walk or ride bikes or horses have eroded footpaths. Last year there were about 22 million visitors to the park and most travelled by car.

Lower lands and plains

Golf courses: There are 29,000 golf courses across the world, which use large areas of land and need millions of litres of water. Some, in dry areas such as Dubai, need 2.5 million litres (0.55 million gallons) a day, as well as fertilisers and pesticides. The USA has about 23,000 golf courses – far and away the largest number in the world. What is more, a great many of them are located in the Western United States, an area classed by the World Water Assessment Programme as under 'severe water stress'.

Safari parks and national parks: In Kenya and Tanzania, the big attraction for tourists are the wildlife reserves of East Africa. Preserving an area

A golf course in Dubai. In a dry area such as this, the major expense is for water to keep the course green.

and its wildlife seems a good thing for the environment, and in many ways it is. The species are protected from poachers and the land is left to renew itself. But there are downsides:

- The Masai, the original inhabitants of the area, were forced off the land by the governments of Tanzania so that the land could become a 'protected area'. This is destroying their life and culture. Their only hope of work is in the tourist industry.
- Roads and hotels have been built. Heavy four-wheel-drive trucks churn up the land as they carry tourists around to look at wild animals.
- Studies in Kenya's Masai Mara National Park found that cheetahs were so disturbed by the volume of tourists that they frequently failed to mate, feed or raise their young. The animals do not seem to have been protected. A 2001 report by Kenya's Regional Centre for Mapping of

African safari buses. Wildlife find these daily intrusions very stressful. This is not the best way to see wildlife.

Resources for Development said wildlife in the park had declined by over 58 per cent in the past 20 years.

4 Changes in lifestyle of local people

Tourism not only changes the environment, it changes the way people live. Tourism brings jobs, and these jobs are very different from traditional work such as farming and fishing, which used to be the way of life in the area. People often give up the traditional work to take on new jobs, possibly because the pay is better, or because the work is more exciting as it is new and involves meeting new people. This can have the positive effect of helping people widen their horizons, learning new skills and developing new ambitions.

So, farming and fishing decline, and cooking and service jobs become the new life. As an area grows, local people are displaced by hotels, shops, restaurants and bars built where they used to live. The peaceful beauty of the place, which originally attracted the tourists, may be lost, and instead the area becomes a 'resort', which tries to provide the tourists with their 'home comforts'.

When the wealth of tourism comes to a country, its landscape changes and the people have to adapt to a new way of life. Some of the effects are good: more wealth, better INFRASTRUCTURE, new employment opportunities for the people, the land and sites of interest and beauty are protected and developed.

Some of the effects are bad: beaches and tourist areas are often closed to local people, hotels and roads destroy the beauty of the natural environment, and the area is polluted by sewage and traffic fumes.

Moreover, the culture is changed and the people are influenced by affluent cultures that bring with them bars, drugs and the lure of easy money. Thailand has become a centre for sex tourism; some Masai tribesmen have become dancers in hotel cabarets; crime, especially theft, has increased in countries where it was almost unknown. It is not hard to see why. The contrast between the lifestyles of the tourists and the locals is often extreme. In a community where earning enough to provide food and shelter is the goal of most people, the temptation of money, expensive clothing and technology casually lying around must be hard to resist.

These changes in culture and values alter social life, which has an impact on the environment. For example, increasing crime may lead to the separation of tourists from the local population by gates and fences. Money from tourism may mean that the priority for land use is hotels, roads, airports and areas for tourist recreation rather than for agriculture and the local community.

So should tourism be banned for the sake of the environment?

This is a very difficult question. Tourism is what many people want. It is one of the most effective ways of boosting an economy. Many countries including Spain, the Caribbean islands, Thailand and Greece have been able to modernise and provide good services to their people because of a tourist boom. Tourism provides jobs and helps economies develop. People in more affluent countries see 'leisure' and 'holidays' as being a reward and a break from the stresses of working.

At the same time, tourism is responsible for many environmental problems, from pollution of the sea and air to the destruction of wildlife and areas of natural beauty. Many places are watching their environment and the culture that goes with it deteriorate. The effects of pollution and

uncontrolled building have made many beautiful places ugly. The inflow of tourists has often resulted in increases in crime, disorder, and violence.

Summary

This section has given a range of examples of how human activities have had negative effects on the environment:

- Industrialisation has polluted the atmosphere, the sea and fresh water and the land.
- Growing populations and urbanisation have added to all forms of pollution, and increased demand for natural resources.
- Consuming natural resources has resulted in loss of bio-diversity, and shortages of essential materials.
- Mass tourism has damaged environments and increased the level of pollution in tourist areas, often making tourist areas less socially desirable and destroying their beauty.

These are not the only environmental problems. Other examples include: warfare and fighting, resulting in the destruction of habitats and crops; sickness and starvation caused by pollution; and changes in weather patterns that have produced droughts, forest fires and floods, hurricanes and tidal waves.

This section has made grim reading, so the next two sections investigate what we can do to resolve these problems.

Natural beauty – the clear sea in Corfu.

The new Corfu, Kavos, 2003.

CONCEPT 3

Individuals and groups have different attitudes and values and make different responses to environmental issues

In this concept section you will learn:

- How difficult it is to protect the environment.
- How different groups want different things from the environment.
- How the government's environmental policies are influenced by these groups.

The following are ideas and terms that you will need to know from this concept section:

environmental pressure groups • government policy • global responsibility

Difficulties in protecting the environment: Different people, different interests

Most people recognise that there are many environmental problems that need to be solved. These can be grouped into three basic environmental issues:

- **The over-use of world resources:** This will lead to shortages or the loss of materials needed to support human life and activities. Such materials include: fossil fuels, fresh water, basic food (grain, vegetables, fruit), fish, and timber.
- **The creation of pollution and waste:** Domestic, industrial, transport and agricultural waste is polluting the atmosphere, seas, fresh water and the land.
- **Major changes to the global environment:** Such as global warming, climate change, rising sea levels, and extreme weather such as droughts, floods, and frequent hurricanes.

Although some of these problems can be eased by individuals, businesses and industries changing the way they live and work, the only way to make a real improvement to the global environment is for every country in the world to work together to solve the problems. This means that protecting the environment is a GLOBAL RESPONSIBILITY.

However, people across the world have different priorities:

- **An individual** may want to stop climate change, but also want to go on driving a fast, comfortable car, flying to faraway places, keeping the house warm in winter, and using kilowatts of electricity to run computers, TVs, sound equipment, washing machines, dryers, and so on.
- **Industries** are trying to make money. So they will go on making what people will buy even though the processes produce chemical waste, toxic gases, and pollute fresh water.
- **Farmers** grow crops and raise animals, but the chemicals, fertilisers and animal waste often get released into the air or end up in streams and rivers.
- **People in many LEDCs** are struggling to survive, so they have to cut down trees for fuel, and burn scrubland to feed animals, even though they are creating deserts. They often have to use the same water for drinking, washing, and disposing of their waste.
- **Governments** of most countries have conflicting priorities when dealing with environmental issues. On the one hand they want to improve the economy, which means they want to exploit their resources and support industry and trade to make the country richer. But they also want to preserve the lives and health of the people in the country for the future, so they have to try to preserve the natural environment, reduce pollution, and maintain their resources so that future generations will be safe.

An example of a conflict of interest

On pages 45–48 we explained that the rainforest ecosystem is under threat. When we look closely at this problem we can see that several groups have very different interests and attitudes to the rainforest:

1 **The Brazilian government:** They are trying to cope with a big increase in population, and to develop a stronger economy. They are hoping to reduce the country's NATIONAL DEBT. They want to provide work, and to do this they need money for training, to invest in new industries, and to modernise the country. They are in favour of logging and mining because this will

provide wealth to be invested. They want to build roads to open up the land for farming and settlements for the Brazilian people, and want to produce electricity to allow modernisation of the area. They want to reduce poverty and to provide growth in the economy. They also try to save as much of the rainforest as they can, because they recognise the value of maintaining the ecosystem, but deforestation is still taking place.

2 **Commercial companies involved in logging, mining, road building, etc.:** Companies want to make profits from the raw materials and the rainforest environment, and develop their business. To get logs out of the area, roads need to be built, and large parts of the forest are destroyed. This is part of a growing economy, providing jobs and more wealth for both the workers and the owners. Once roads are built, people will start to build settlements, while other businesses will move in to make money by using the raw materials and providing services for the workers.

3 **The growing population of farmers:** Many people moving into the rainforest land will be hoping for a better life with more room to live and a means of providing for their families. In order to make land suitable for farming they often burn the trees and scrub to clear the land, so that crops can be grown and cattle can be raised. This process is called 'slash and burn'. Richer farmers are cutting and burning more forest, planting huge areas with cash crops, such as palm oil plants, or raising cattle which produces much wealth for them and their countries.

Despite this wasteful destruction of plant life, the ability to farm and be more self-sufficient has been a massive benefit to the growing populations of Brazil, Venezuela, Indonesia and other countries where rainforests grow.

4 **The original inhabitants of the forest (the Amazonian tribes such as the Kayapo):** These tribes have lived in the rainforest and learned how to use its resources without damaging the forest or overusing its materials. The native Amazonians live by a process called 'shifting cultivation': they live in one area and farm it, moving on when the land is no longer cultivable. When the nutrients in the soil have been used up by growing the crops, that area will no longer grow enough food and the farmers have to move on. This does not harm the forest, which quickly recovers. They see the rainforest as home, often as part of their family. They want to see the rainforest kept in its original state.

5 **Scientists, environmental researchers, meteorologists, medical researchers:** These people want to discover what effects deforestation will have on local and global living conditions. Some will want to do research on plants and animal life, often for medical purposes. Others will be very concerned about the effects of rainforest depletion on weather and climate change. They are trying to assess how the ecosystem is changing and how this will affect the environment in the future. Most of this group are agreed on one thing: that losing more rainforest will have very bad consequences for the ecology of the whole world.

ACTIVITY

1 Get into teams of five. Each person in the team plays the part of one of the five groups of rainforest users described on this page and prepares a presentation for the rest of the team. This should have the following elements:
- A description of how you are using the rainforest.
- An explanation of why you think it is right to use it in this way.
- An opinion of the other groups' attitudes to the forest.

At the end of your session, make a summary of the attitudes and values of each group.

How do groups influence a government's policies?

Governments have to decide on their policies and what they are going to do. In democratic countries, where the government needs the support of the people, it has to try to balance the interests of different groups before it makes a decision.

A few years ago, people who worried about damage to the environment, such as rainforests being cut down, global warming, whale hunting, and road building were seen as cranks by the majority of the population. In the USA they were known as 'tree-huggers' and were unpopular because they got in the way of progress, jobs and profits.

However, in the twenty-first century, as we learn more, environmental issues are at the top of the list of urgent social and economic problems across most of the developed world. 'Going Green', 'environmentally friendly', 'carbon footprints', 'sustainability' and 'conservation' are the buzz words now. What governments do about these issues affects everyone, so there are many groups who want to influence them.

1 Scientists, and environmental researchers

When scientists, environmentalists, medical researchers, the voting public and usually the media are able to convince the government that there is a problem, the government may act and bring in measures to deal with it.

An example of a group of scientists who have come together to try to influence the government is the Union of Concerned Scientists. This organisation operates in the USA and produces publications full of scientific data. This information is often used by the media to challenge the US government's policies. The group is influential because its members' high level of knowledge and expertise makes it hard to challenge them. It encourages the public to use the internet to tell the government what they think.

In Britain, the work of similar groups carrying out medical research or analysing drinking water, air quality and land pollution has convinced the government to come up with policies that start to deal with existing environmental problems. For example, in the UK, the government has:

• Set up an initiative called Local Agenda 21 (LA21). All local authorities are required to encourage local partnerships between communities, businesses and the local authority in order to do something about the global issues of climate change and sustainable development.

This has resulted in recycling schemes, reductions in town-centre traffic pollution and more efficient cleaning and waste disposal.
• Stopped the sale of leaded petrol to protect people's health.
• Increased the price of fuel to try to reduce carbon pollution by discouraging people from using private cars so much.
• Set up inspections of industrial sites to reduce pollution and toxic waste. Industries risk fines if they are heavy polluters.
• Educated the public about environmental issues, such as global warming, through the media and education. (This course is a part of your environmental education.)
• Made plans to replace some fossil fuels with renewable energy sources.

This research has had a big impact over the last ten years – everyone is now aware of environmental problems, and most have accepted that it is vital to make big changes in the way we live.

However, the government has to try to maintain the economy, so it cannot make really big changes overnight. We rely on industry, road transport, and fossil fuels at the moment, and there is no quick fix.

ACTIVITY

1 Use your local area as a case study to research the following:
• What has your local authority done to encourage recycling of waste?
• What has your local authority done to reduce traffic congestion and pollution in your town or city centre?
• What other measures have your local authority taken to protect the environment?
• Is there anything else that you think should be done to protect the local environment?

2 Industry and large business organisations

The work of most large industries is exploiting resources. Whether it's building, making vehicles, or growing food, resources are used up, and waste and pollution are produced. But our way of life depends on industry and commerce, and we have accepted that there are going to be environmental costs.

Recently, many laws have been passed to try to make businesses reduce pollution and make products that are less damaging to the environment. This tends to cost more money and companies often say that they can't afford to make the changes. Such companies can often speak directly to government ministers. They do research and deliver reports to the government about what they are able to do, how much green policies will cost, how long it will take to set them up, and what they are willing to do. Because the government relies on them to keep the economy going, they have a lot of power, and often governments make deals with them to keep them happy.

Business goes green
You have only to see advertisements from big companies, such as BP, Tesco and any car maker, to realise that 'going green' and 'eco-friendly' have become new selling points. Preserving the environment has become an accepted way of thinking and acting for many people, and big business has recently realised that the public are not happy about the environmental damage that is the result of their activities. And, of course, even billionaire businessmen don't want to destroy the planet (see further details on pages 5–6).

> Our strategy at Tesco falls into three parts. First, greening Tesco itself. Second, helping to turn the supply chain green. And third, helping our customers by making green choices easier and more affordable.

Sir Terry Leahy, Tesco chief executive, 3 September 2008.

3 Occupational groups
These are groups such as fishermen or lorry drivers who are going to be affected by policies such as raising fuel costs to reduce carbon emissions, or stopping fishing for an endangered species of fish. They are often concerned about losing their jobs. They often use public protests as a way of getting attention. They depend on the media to get publicity for their problems, and public support to put more pressure on the government.

> Hundreds of lorry drivers caused traffic chaos today as they descended on London in the largest ever protest over fuel duty.

Daily Mail, 27 May 2008.

These protests sometimes have an impact and the government changes its policy slightly – for example, delaying some measures for a year or so – but it rarely abandons a policy, and often the protests are completely ignored.

In May 2008, hundreds of lorry drivers headed towards central London to protest about the rising cost of fuel.

However, if the media are able to whip up wider support from the public, and the protest is joined by other groups, the government will be put under more pressure. The public objected to plans to increase road tax, so they supported the lorry drivers' protest. The government said it would consider not increasing road tax for one year.

4 Local environmental pressure groups

Environmental pressure groups are often started by groups of ordinary citizens who have a concern about a local issue. These groups are usually very dedicated because the issue is their main concern. These groups have basically the same objectives:

- To raise public awareness about the environmental issue.
- To get enough public support to force the people responsible to change things.
- To put pressure on the government to change a policy or to intervene to stop something happening.

This is part of a protest against building a third runway at Heathrow. As well as local residents, you can see that Greenpeace are involved.

Airports

Resident groups protest about new runways being built at airports such as Manchester and Heathrow. Often they are most concerned about noise, increased road traffic, and local pollution. Recently these groups have been joined by other groups who want to reduce all air traffic because of the worldwide pollution caused by aircraft.

Roads

There are always protests about new road building, because it destroys farmland and beautiful countryside, produces noise and pollution, or because of the argument that 'the more roads you build, the more cars will fill them'.

These protests usually get some publicity because protestors disrupt traffic by building road blocks, stop work by sitting in front of bulldozers or chain themselves to trees or buildings they want to preserve. The media bring publicity, and the protestors hope to build support in this way.

These protests often succeed in delaying the work, but most of the time the project is simply continued later on (unless the government fears that it will lose an election over the issue!).

Clashes of environmental interests

There is often a clash of environmental interests. Protests about the siting of wind farms usually oppose them because they are an eyesore or because they are dangerous for birds. But at the same time, wind farms are part of the solution to pollution by fossil fuels.

The government is unlikely to change its policies on renewable resources, as they are already acting in response to what other groups want.

ACTIVITY

1 For this activity you will need to do some research. In your own area:
   a) Name one local environmental pressure group.
   b) What issue(s) are they trying to do something about?
   c) What have the group done to raise awareness about the issue, or to bring about changes in the area?

5 International environmental pressure groups

Two examples of international environmental pressure groups are Friends of the Earth and Greenpeace.

Friends of the Earth

Friends of the Earth is one of the UK's leading pressure groups. It was set up in 1971 as the first environmental pressure group in the UK to campaign to protect the environment. The group was an early campaigner against acid rain, ozone depletion and climate change. It has built up a reputation for providing reliable and objective information based on sound research. This means that it often gives information to journalists and policy-makers, and is frequently asked to give evidence on environmental threats to committees in the House of Commons and the House of Lords.

But it doesn't just supply information, it also exposes environmental abuse and offers constructive solutions to current problems.

Examples of Friends of the Earth in action

The group's latest high-profile campaign is called 'the Big Ask', which has been a series of events and a steady stream of information about the problems and risks of climate change. This has been a major influence in persuading the government to make a real commitment to dealing with climate change, which resulted in a real political success: on 28 October 2008, MPs voted in favour of a Climate Change Law that will cut greenhouse gases by 80 per cent by 2050.

Protesters getting publicity for a cause by providing a spectacle which the media will show to the world.

Junked cars. Friends of the Earth use powerful images to show how 'our throwaway culture is risking people's health and squandering the world's natural resources'.

The group's methods of spreading knowledge include:

- Running campaigns to raise awareness of the issues. For example: on 1 May 2006, they presented the 'Big Ask Live' concert; and on 4 July 2007, they launched 'the Big Ask Online' march so people could lobby their MP using video messages.
- Appearing in the media, producing materials for journalists, and concentrating on getting publicity for their ideas by presenting well-thought out arguments that might influence the government.
- Collecting funds by appealing to people's sympathies through the media and posters that vividly highlight environmental problems.
- Supporting and producing materials for schools and for local organisations that are fighting for an environmental issue.
- Taking part in demonstrations that relate to environmental concerns and keeping their name in the public eye.

Apart from climate change, Friends of the Earth are also running campaigns to protect bio-diversity, make global trade fairer, make transport more efficient and less polluting, and deal with waste by reducing the amount we produce and disposing of it safely.

Global responsibility

Friends of the Earth's work is international, because they recognise that environmental issues have to be solved by everyone in the world working together; pollution of the atmosphere and oceans affects the whole world, and there is no way that one country can change that. So Friends of the Earth is now the largest international network of environmental groups in the world, active in 66 countries worldwide and trying to co-ordinate environmental policies across the world.

Greenpeace

Another international campaigning group that operates on a global scale is Greenpeace. Greenpeace is the best-known environmental pressure group in the UK, and probably across the globe. It operates all over the world and it attracts headlines for many of its campaigns.

Greenpeace campaigns about all the issues mentioned in this chapter, as well as many others. In 2004, its environmental campaigns included: ocean pollution and over-fishing, deforestation, nuclear safety, climate change, toxic chemicals, waste disposal and genetically modified (GM) crops.

Greenpeace is focused on environmental issues, but is also involved in campaigns to bring about global equality, fair trade and world peace.

Why is Greenpeace so well known?

The short answer is that its methods of getting publicity (and through this, getting attention from the public) are very effective. It has realised that to get ordinary people involved in these issues, it needs spectacular publicity. So, rather than write articles, it tries to attract press attention with actions that are unusual, possibly risky, and which can be photographed and filmed. This is called 'direct action'.

The media themselves want dramatic stories, and Greenpeace provides them. The press, in describing these events, will also have to discuss the issue, and this is what Greenpeace wants. For example, in recent years, Greenpeace activists have tried to stop whaling by sailing dangerously close to whaling ships and filming horrific sights of whales being killed. In this way, they got good pictures and videos, which the media used, and which reflected badly on the whalers, whilst the activists gained some support from admirers.

Greenpeace is well known because its actions have caught the public's imagination and helped to make the issues involved seem urgent and real. Its publicity operates on all levels: a very detailed website gives accessible information; its campaign posters are distinctive and attractive; it provides schools and other institutions with materials that explain the issues clearly; and it concentrates on gaining support, particularly from young people.

Greenpeace campaigns

Climate change: 'We want you to take part in an energy revolution. To go from a world powered by nuclear and fossil fuels to one running on renewable energy.'

Greenpeace activists being thrown off a Lithuanian trawler during a protest to stop bottom trawling (see pages 73–74 for further details of 'by-catch').

Defend our oceans: 'The Greenpeace Defending our Oceans campaign sets out to protect and preserve our oceans now and for the future by protecting large areas of the global oceans from exploitation and controllable human pressure.'

Protect ancient forests: 'Throughout the world, ancient forests are in crisis. Many of the plants and animals that live in these forests face extinction. And many of the people and cultures who depend on these forests for their way of life are also under threat. But the news is not all bad. There is a last chance to protect these forests and the life they support.'

Demand peace and disarmament: 'Make no mistake; nuclear weapons are a problem today. There are approximately 30,000 nuclear weapons in the world, belonging to nine countries: USA, Russian Federation, UK, France, China, Israel, India, Pakistan and North Korea. We have campaigned against both nuclear weapons and nuclear power. Observing and recording test zones, supplying scientific data and measurements on human and environmental impacts and by conducting direct non-violent actions to call attention to the problem.'

Greenpeace working to stop coal being used to make electricity.

Say no to genetic engineering: 'While scientific progress on molecular biology has a great potential to increase our understanding of nature and provide new medical tools, it should not be used as justification to turn the environment into a giant genetic experiment by commercial interests. The biodiversity and environmental integrity of the world's food supply is too important to our survival to be put at risk. Genetically Modified Organisms (GMOs) should not be released into the environment as there is not adequate scientific understanding of their impact on the environment and human health.'

Eliminate toxic chemicals: 'Toxic chemicals in our environment threaten our rivers and lakes, our air, land, and oceans, and ultimately ourselves and our future. Greenpeace are pressuring companies to identify the toxic material they produce and find ways of using less dangerous materials. It works on identifying the most dangerous dumping of industrial waste and making this public.'

End the nuclear age: 'Greenpeace has always fought – and will continue to fight – vigorously against nuclear power because it is an unacceptable risk to the environment and to humanity. The only solution is to halt the expansion of all nuclear power, and for the shutdown of existing plants.'

Summary

The pressure groups described in this chapter, and others, do have an impact on the attitudes of the general public, and on the government. Their biggest contribution is getting information across to the public. What the public know about many environmental issues is largely the result of the efforts of these groups in getting publicity in the media.

The government is made up of individuals who are also being informed about environmental risks, and, once the public become concerned, the governments in democracies have to act to satisfy their demands.

The years of campaigning have made environmental awareness part of most people's thinking. Without this understanding, there would be little concern until the state of the planet became so bad that no one could ignore it. Thanks to the work of environmental groups, we have more time on our side to deal with problems.

ACTIVITY

1 Use the internet to find information to prepare a presentation about a campaign by any pressure group. Research the following:
   a) What methods were used to influence people's behaviour, attitudes and values?
   b) Did the campaign bring about any changes in attitude, behaviour or government policy?

CONCEPT 4

Environmental problems can be solved in different ways

In this concept section you will learn:

- About methods and strategies of reducing or solving the environmental problems we have discussed earlier in the chapter.
- About how effective these methods and strategies have been.
- About the meaning and importance of sustainable development, conservation, carbon footprint, recycling, government action, international agreements, national parks.

The following are ideas and terms that you will need to know from this concept section:

sustainable development • *conservation* • *carbon footprint* • *recycling* • *government action* • *international agreements* • *National Parks*

Most of this chapter has been about the many global environmental issues that should concern us. Most scientists believe that the planet itself will survive, but there is no guarantee that human beings will. If we damage our environment seriously enough, many life forms will not survive, and that could include human beings.

At the moment, this seems a remote possibility – populations are growing, many people live longer than ever before, and some of the world's population live in great comfort. But the case studies have shown us that we face some major problems in the near future. The examples in this chapter are not the only environmental problems we face; you can probably think of others.

The previous concept section looked at the ways in which various groups have attempted to make people aware of the environmental problems we face. These groups have shown us the risks for the future, and suggested and promoted ways of treating the environment. This concept section will go back to some of the issues we have covered, and examine what is being done to try to solve or at least reduce some of the environmental problems.

Who is going to protect the environment?

There are many organisations and groups that attempt to protect the environment and ensure that the effects of environmental depletion and damage are reduced:

- **Governments of countries:** These introduce policies, laws and invest money to protect threatened environments.
- **Large political organisations:** These include the EU and the UN – the UN Environment Programme (UNEP) is the focal point for environmental action and co-ordination within the UN system. Such organisations try to get international agreements between countries to work together to protect the environment.
- **Large multinational industries:** Examples are oil companies, power industries, the car industry, the fishing industry and many others who are starting to realise that, in the long term, protecting the environment is as important as making a profit.
- **Individuals:** By changing the way they live and use the environment, and by putting pressure on governments, industries and communities, individuals can help to make major changes to the environment.

When you look at the above list, you can see that it's not going to be easy to get agreement and to change years of tradition. But some significant changes have taken place.

Political influences on environmental problems

Example 1: Saving the rainforest

Stewardship

The original inhabitants of the rainforests (such as the Yanomani) have helped to show the way. They were able to live in the forest, use its resources and keep it healthy and thriving. This approach is sometimes called 'stewardship', where the people who use the land understand what it needs to survive in the future and treat it with respect.

The whole world depends on the rainforests to produce oxygen, reduce carbon dioxide emissions, and sustain bio-diversity. One suggestion is to pay the rainforest's owners and the people who live in them to save and maintain the trees. This will both help the planet, and help reduce poverty in developing countries. This has not been agreed yet, but it could be a solution to the rainforest crisis.

Rainforest conservation: ARPA

In 2002, the government of Brazil, the World Bank, the Global Environmental Facility (GEF) and environmental organisations such as WWF got together to try to safeguard a part of the tropical rainforest. This large and ambitious initiative is known as the Amazon Region Protected Area (ARPA).

ARPA is a system of 80 reserves and parks, an area roughly the size of California, which is intended to keep this bit of the Amazonian environment intact.

In 2007, Simao Jatene, the governor of the northern Brazilian state of Para, designated an area as a unique conservation region – the biggest of its kind in the world. The area covered by the new state law is 63,320 square miles – 10,000 square miles bigger than England.

The land is next to rainforests that are already protected within Brazil and in the neighbouring countries of Guyana, Suriname and French Guiana. In total, the protection zones form an immense green corridor known as the Guyana Shield, which includes some of the richest wildlife habitats on earth and makes up 25 per cent of the Earth's humid tropical rainforest. Almost 90 per cent of it is still in its pure natural state.

Sustainable development

What is 'SUSTAINABLE DEVELOPMENT'? Sustainable means something that can be kept going in the future. Development means making changes that improve a situation.

In rainforests, sustainable development means making use of its resources, in a way that does not strip it bare and ensures that the ecosystem is not damaged.

Under the Para conservation agreement, about one third will be totally protected against any agricultural, industrial or domestic development. 'Traditional communities will be living in these protected areas. They will be allowed to use the forest in a sustainable way but this will not involve the clear-cutting of the forest,' the governor said through an interpreter.

Human activity such as road-building, logging, agriculture, and mining in the rest of the protected region will be allowed, but strictly controlled. Destructive, non-sustainable activities will be either banned or limited to a few small areas, the governor said. 'If anyone tries to do this illegally, it will be detected by satellites; they will be stopped and punished.'

Adapted from the Independent Online, 'Saving the rainforest: At last, action on the Amazon', 4 December 2006.

The trouble is that these major changes will not be easily carried through. It is not just big business that is causing deforestation; much of the pressure comes from local people struggling to survive and the governments of rainforest countries who need to trade to build their economies.

Restoring the rainforest

In 2008, Haiti was hit by four powerful storms that caused flash floods and landslides. This killed hundreds of people and created thousands of refugees. Haiti used to be covered by rainforest, but it has nearly all been cut down to make charcoal to be used as cooking fuel. Once the forest is gone the soil gets washed away and

Flooded houses in mudslides in Haiti, 2008.

mudslides sweep through the valleys. The Haitians are trying to stabilise the land by growing new trees and vegetation to rebuild the ecosystem.

In other rainforests, governments and timber industries are trying to replace what they cut down by planting new trees, but these take a long time to grow and will not regrow the forests for hundreds of years.

How successful have these measures been?
It's too early to tell. Despite the efforts of conservationists, rainforest losses in the twenty-first century have been increasing, as the growing of oil palms and the hunt for mineral wealth has intensified. Greenpeace estimates that all rainforest will be gone by 2080.

In 2008, Brazil's Environment Minister, Marina Silva, a staunch defender of the Amazon rainforest, resigned from her post, saying that her efforts to protect the rainforest were being ignored by the government. Other rainforests are disappearing even more quickly. According to FAO (Food and Agriculture Organisation of the UN), Vietnam lost a staggering 51 per cent of its primary forests between 2000 and 2005, while Cambodia lost 29 per cent between 2000 and 2005.

The attempts to conserve a huge national park in the Amazonian forest (ARPA) may not be enough to make a difference to the global crisis even if it is successful, because the pressure to use the forests to help economic development is growing stronger.

The idea of giving money to conserve the rainforests may succeed better, but this will need the agreement of many countries, both from the countries who give the money, and from the rainforest nations to stop clearing the trees in exchange for financial aid.

Investigation
1 Investigate ARPA or the Guyana Shield on the internet and find out what exactly they have done in the Amazon region.
2 Use the internet to discover other approaches to 'sustainable development'. Try using a search engine to look for: 'environmental stewardship' or 'environmental protection schemes'. As a result of your research, describe two other methods or projects designed to maintain the environment.

Example 2: Dealing with global warming
Most governments across the world recognise that unless the world can reduce carbon emissions drastically over the next few years, the average temperature across the world will increase by at least four degrees. This may not sound much, but it's enough to guarantee major rises in sea levels, droughts, floods and hurricanes across the world.

A sign of how seriously this is taken is that many countries have adopted measures to try to reduce greenhouse emissions. Some of the methods include:

United Nations: The Kyoto Protocol
The Kyoto Protocol is an international agreement linked to the United Nations Framework Convention on Climate Change. The Kyoto Protocol sets binding targets for 37 industrialised countries and the European community for reducing greenhouse gas (GHG) emissions. These amount to an average of five per cent against 1990 levels over the five-year period, 2008–12.

A protocol is a binding agreement on the people who sign up, to do what it says.

How much difference will the Protocol make?
- Anything helps, but most climate scientists say that the targets set in the Kyoto Protocol are merely scratching the surface of the problem. The agreement aims to reduce emissions from industrialised nations only by around five per cent, but many climate scientists warn that in order to avoid the worst consequences of global warming, emissions need to be cut by 60 per cent across the board.
- The USA and Australia did not sign up. The USA is the largest carbon polluter of the developed nations. In December 2008, George Bush's emissions committee said they would not sign up to an emissions limit. Under President Obama it may do so, but in 2009 it is not clear if and when this will happen.
- China and India have both signed the Protocol, but they are developing rapidly and they have actually *increased* their carbon emissions over the last ten years. China is now as big a polluter as the USA.
- It is not clear how the agreement will be enforced. What will happen if a country misses the target?

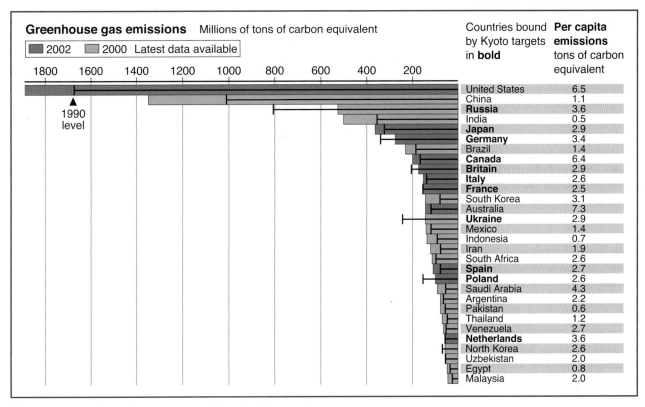

Greenhouse gas emissions Millions of tons of carbon equivalent

■ 2002 ■ 2000 Latest data available

Countries bound by Kyoto targets in **bold**	**Per capita emissions** tons of carbon equivalent
United States	6.5
China	1.1
Russia	3.6
India	0.5
Japan	2.9
Germany	3.4
Brazil	1.4
Canada	6.4
Britain	2.9
Italy	2.6
France	2.5
South Korea	3.1
Australia	7.3
Ukraine	2.9
Mexico	1.4
Indonesia	0.7
Iran	1.9
South Africa	2.6
Spain	2.7
Poland	2.6
Saudi Arabia	4.3
Argentina	2.2
Pakistan	0.6
Thailand	1.2
Venezuela	2.7
Netherlands	3.6
North Korea	2.6
Uzbekistan	2.0
Egypt	0.8
Malaysia	2.0

Chart showing the major carbon polluters in the world.

The European Commission (a part of the EU)

The European Commission set up the European Emissions Trading Scheme to try to force companies to cut down their carbon emissions.

How is the scheme supposed to work?

Hundreds of polluting companies, including power generators, oil producers and car makers, have a limit placed on their direct emissions from fuel use by the European Commission.

Companies that produce more pollution than allowed must buy permits from cleaner rivals. In time, the amount of carbon emission allowed is reduced and the price of carbon permits rises to the point where firms would rather invest in reducing their emissions.

How well has it worked?

Not well up to 2007. European governments gave out too many permits to their companies, which then put them up for sale. It hasn't put any pressure on these companies so far.

UK government policies

The British government has taken the problem of greenhouse gas emissions seriously. In December 2008, the Government Climate Committee proposed that the UK should reduce its carbon emissions by 20 per cent in ten years and by 80 per cent by 2050. The reduction would come about by changing the way electricity is produced, and by redesigning buildings and cars.

- The government plans to produce 30 per cent of electricity using renewable resources by 2020. Most of this will be produced by off-shore wind turbines. We have already discussed the problems of building off-shore wind turbines (page 53), but, out of the renewable resources options available, this is the one most people accept, rather than nuclear power stations, or hydropower schemes using wave or tidal power.
- By 2020 the government plans to power 40 per cent of new cars with electricity rather than fossil fuels. To bring this about, the government has started changing people's attitudes to using fossil fuels by increasing taxes on vehicles that produce the most CO_2, and by increasing the cost of petrol and diesel.

These targets will be technically difficult and expensive to achieve, but the government has already made some moves to bring them about. People are starting to change their behaviour and attitudes, partly through knowing more, and partly through government policies.

UK government campaigns and media influence

The biggest change that the government has seen so far is that people are much more aware of the need to reduce their 'carbon footprint' (i.e. the amount of CO_2 that is produced as a result of the way they live).

This has been brought home by endless references in the media, and by the increased cost of power and travel. Some of this coverage is prompted by government statements and initiatives, but much of it shows a growing recognition that environmental problems are a vital concern.

The government continues to run campaigns telling people how to live economically, by insulating houses, using low energy bulbs, turning off lights and not using standby modes on electrical equipment. To back this up they have given financial help to poorer households to improve their energy efficiency.

How effective will these agreements and policies be?

The effectiveness of these government agreements and policies depends on three things.

1 Will we be able to produce enough electrical power using renewable resources?

This will be expensive. The government will have to find a lot of money to pay for off-shore wind farms, and in 2009 this is not easy. It will mean that the cost of power to the public and industry is likely to rise.

It will also be technically difficult to build these off-shore wind farms, and we will still have to rely on nuclear and fossil fuels to supply the remainder of the electricity needed. The cheapest fuel for power stations is still coal, so any emissions from fossil fuel power stations will have to be cleaned up. This is also expensive.

2 Can emissions be reduced by electric cars, car tax and petrol duty?

If electric cars can be efficient enough to replace traditional cars this will make a big difference. At the moment, this is new technology and it will take time to get these on the roads. There will still be a lot of petrol and diesel vehicles on the road in 2020. If public transport was more convenient and flexible, and cheaper than using cars, people would use it more and emissions would be cut.

Demand for air transport is growing and this cannot be powered by non-fossil fuels yet, so emissions from aircraft would still rise.

3 Will the reductions in emissions be enough to control global warming?

This depends on whether the estimates of the pace of global warming are accurate. Some experts think that global warming is taking place faster than we thought. The melting of Arctic ice shelves and glaciers is more rapid than most predictions; this will affect ocean currents, which will in turn affect air currents, and these control climate changes.

The process of global warming is not an exact science, and changes in vegetation and melting ice will have a knock-on effect. For example, warmer weather will produce more methane and CO_2 from vegetation.

Global warming is a global issue

Dealing with global warming and climate change is an international issue. Measures by one or a group of countries will not resolve the problem of greenhouse gas emissions. The developed economies will have to take the lead because they have the wealth and technology to make an impact. Their lead is essential if they are to persuade developing countries to change their way of life. Developing countries are trying to reach the affluence of the developed world, and don't see why they should not get there using the resources in the same way as the developed world did.

The poorer countries will suffer the most in any climate change. They are already dealing with the disastrous effects of drought, flooding and hurricanes, which have increased in intensity over the last two decades. They are more likely to be victims, and these countries have fewer resources to mount rescue and recovery operations. They have no surpluses of food and water, and no money to provide care for the injured, starving and refugees.

Therefore, any useful measures taken by the developed world to reduce carbon emissions are vital. Even if they are late and not drastic enough to guarantee stopping global warming processes, they need to be put in place to show the way to make changes. Breakthroughs in science and technology are taking place constantly, and, under the pressure of the changes we know will take place soon, the efforts of developed countries will have some impact on global warming.

How environmental pressure groups influence individuals and governments

Dealing with threats to bio-diversity

Environmental organisations, such as the World Wildlife Fund (WWF), Greenpeace and Friends of the Earth play a large part in raising awareness about threats to bio-diversity. In particular, they focus on saving endangered species.

The WWF have run campaigns to try to safeguard threatened species such as giant pandas, tigers, gorillas, polar bears, whales and many other species. The threats come from two main sources: the animals' habitats are often threatened by modern developments; and the animals themselves (such as tigers and rhinos) are hunted for the value of their body parts or because the animals are seen as being a threat to domestic animals or local crops.

The methods of such organisations are based on making the public aware of the threats to these animals by using posters and media coverage. They then try to arouse enough sympathy to collect funds to put pressure on governments in the affected areas to strengthen protection against poachers, or to preserve and improve habitats.

Do the campaigns work?

Some are very successful in gaining public sympathy, because most animals appeal emotionally to much of the public. When a campaign is successful, the public can force governments to act. Public approval is important to them, and for some issues governments may act to show that they listening to the people.

The WWF and Greenpeace campaign to save the whale was very successful in persuading many countries to stop whaling. Only Japan and Iceland continue to hunt whales at the moment and pressure is constantly put on them by world disapproval.

Other campaigns to preserve the natural environment have been less successful because the government has decided on a policy that they are not going to change. Examples of this are road building projects, or protests about building something that will boost the economy, such as a new power station.

Saving depleted fish stocks.

Saving endangered fish species like cod and tuna doesn't have the same emotional appeal as saving the whales. Therefore, other methods have to be used to appeal to the public. Fish is an important part of world food supplies, and fishing is a major industry.

It is common sense that there should be some way of controlling the amount of fish and marine life taken from the sea to ensure that the species can be replenished (sustained). Otherwise both food and jobs disappear. However, it is difficult to persuade people to give up their food and jobs today, in exchange for the long-term good.

This means that, somehow, the whole of the world's fishing industries must be regulated. International laws have to be agreed and enforced. The UN Convention on the Law of the Seas (UNCLOS) has tried to set out rules to conserve fish and to settle disputes. But these laws and rules are extremely difficult to enforce:

• Oceans are huge, far too big to patrol and observe.
• Countries regard their coastal waters as their own territory. The fish in these waters are seen as their property. Sometimes countries claim that their culture depends on being able to take various kinds of marine life (for example, Iceland and whaling).

- Most of the oceans are international waters, which means that there are no legal controls, and no one has clear legal responsibility for what goes on.
- The growing populations of LEDCs and the rising wealth of MEDCs raises the demand for seafood year on year.
- The whole scheme depends on fishermen being honest about sticking to their QUOTA.

However, there is a positive side to this problem:

- Most governments recognise that unless they protect fish stocks, their own country will suffer.
- Fishermen also recognise that they risk losing their jobs in the future if they do not follow their quotas.
- Satellite technology and tracking devices make it easier to identify and punish 'rogue' fishing vessels.
- More people are becoming aware of endangered marine species, especially whales, thanks to 'Save the Whale' campaigns. Many people now support maritime laws and restrictions on many types of fishing, notably fishing that endangers dolphins and sharks. The publicity has also encouraged some people to adjust their lifestyle and eating habits.
- Some commercial organisations have environmental policies that limit and control the species and origins of the seafood they sell.
- Fish farming (AQUACULTURE) is on the increase, which may replace depleted stocks of some marine species.

Has this solved the problem?

Despite these efforts, over-fishing and marine species depletion is continuing. International bodies such as the International Whaling Commission (IWC), the Food and Agriculture Organisation of the UNITED NATIONS (FAO), and many others are still very worried that many oceans and their inhabitants are in crisis.

Where it does work, for example, in European countries where catches are inspected before they are landed, it has resulted in by-catch (see pages 73–74) being dumped back in the sea, often dead or injured.

(see pages 73–74)

ACTIVITIES

1 Devise a publicity campaign to make people aware of the risks to marine species and to encourage them to do something about them.

2 In groups, try to work out a way of controlling international fishing. Describe what should be done and assess the chances of your scheme working. What problems would have to be overcome?

The role of big industrial and commercial organisations

The main purpose of industrial and commercial organisations is to make money. To do this they have to provide goods and services that people want. They also have to operate in ways that governments and international political organisations, like the EU and the UN, say they should.

Much of what they use and produce is the cause of the environmental problems this chapter has discussed.

If they go on operating as they did in the past, problems will get worse. This has recently been recognised by governments and much of the world's population, and so they have come under pressure to deal with these problems. They have to change their way of working and their products.

However, this will be difficult. They have spent years and vast amounts of money setting up and running their operations. Changing their approach to the environment will cost them billions more, and will involve completely different techniques and technologies. Nonetheless, there are some powerful pressures forcing them to change:

- Many of the resources they need are running out. They are getting more expensive and harder to find.
- Governments and other powerful groups are putting them under pressure to stop polluting the environment. If they continue they can be fined or put out of business.
- The technology exists to detect most sources of environmental damage; they can no longer evade detection.

- The public, their customers, are more aware of the dangers of environmental destruction and pollution and how they behave in this area will affect their sales.
- The people who run the industries will be affected by environmental damage just like everyone else.

How have big industrial and commercial organisations changed?

You can't have failed to notice that half the products advertised now claim to be environmentally friendly. Almost every product bought by households, ranging from cleaning products to cars, is described as being good for the environment, or at least not as bad for the environment as they used to be. Terms such as 'green', 'eco-friendly', 'ethically sourced', 'free from pollutants', 'safe for plants and animals', 'made from sustainable timber' and so on are now part of advertising language.

Not only that, in an attempt to improve their public relations, large companies often take out adverts which simply say that they are doing no harm to the environment. This may simply be a selling tactic, but it shows that such companies have accepted that there is a problem to be solved and that they must play their part.

However, these kinds of adverts are sometimes called 'greenwash', which means that they are seen as attempts to sound green. The companies are still trying to sell the same products but using the environmental selling point to reach their customers. Car manufacturers offer 'eco-models', but at the same time they continue to make big-

The world's first environmentally friendly 'green' gas station has been built in Los Angeles.

engined 4x4 vehicles to be used for shopping and school runs. Makers of luxury cars, like Jaguar and BMW, have put pressure on the EU to allow them to continue to build them, despite the amount of pollution they produce.

Oil companies have started to get involved in developing other forms of renewable energy to produce electricity, but still continue to drill for oil in Arctic areas, and make plans to extract oil from oil sand in Canada, despite the fact that these will cause more pollution.

But there are signs that things are changing:

- New cars produce less pollution and use less fuel. Once the selling point was speed and luxury, now it is economy and low emissions.
- Many companies are developing new products like solar cells, wind turbines and machines to make use of wave and tidal power to make electricity.

Do you think the car industry can ever become truly environmentally friendly?

- Government inspections of industrial sites to check on pollution and waste disposal have pushed companies to clean up their production methods.
- Increasing costs of fuel and power and dwindling resources have put pressure on manufacturers to move away from polluting and wasteful products, because they know people will not want them or be able to afford them.

ACTIVITIES

1 Choose a sample of adverts from TV and from magazines. Make a list of products which are being sold as 'environmentally friendly'.
2 Identify the images, words and phrases that are used to get this idea across.
3 Design an advertisement for a 4x4 vehicle, a patio heater, or a luxury holiday, which uses saving the environment as a selling point.

The role of individuals in reducing or solving environmental problems

Individuals can have two roles in dealing with environmental issues:

- Identifying the problems, and finding strategies to put them right.
- Learning and understanding about environmental problems and changing their own behaviour to reduce or solve the problems.

Identifying the problem and doing something about it

Environmental pressure groups are formed by individuals who recognise a problem and who decide to do something about it. This was how Greenpeace and Friends of the Earth started. These two organisations are internationally famous, but there are many other smaller groups who have changed the behaviour of local authorities, industries, and individuals.

The National Parks

In the UK, we owe our National Parks to different groups of individuals who demanded freedom to roam the countryside.

In the early twentieth century most people lived in dirty industrial towns. These were unhealthy places to live, and many people wanted to get out into clean air, beautiful landscapes, breathe clean air and get some healthy exercise. This wasn't so easy to do; most of the land was owned by rich individuals who wanted to keep the people out.

Thousands of nature lovers and groups such as the Ramblers Association, the Youth Hostels Association (YHA) and the Council for the Preservation for Rural England (CPRE) got together in the 1930s. For 20 years they pressured the government into making the parks open to the nation and to preserving their natural state forever. One method of getting attention was to arrange a mass trespass into the Peak District in 1931. This caught the imagination of the people and the government started to see the value of having healthier, happier citizens. The steady pressure over the next 15 years worked and, at the end of the Second World War, National Parks became a reality.

They have been popular ever since and are the major natural tourist areas in the UK. Unfortunately, that is the problem. They are so popular that they are being damaged by the numbers of people who visit, mainly in cars. Now they are called 'honeypots' because they attract so many people. The beauty of the parks is being destroyed by litter, traffic congestion and pollution, footpath erosion resulting from overuse, and conflict with farmers and local people.

Now, organisations such as the Ramblers Association and the CPRE are trying to limit the damage. They are trying to place restrictions on the amount of traffic in the area by encouraging people to use public transport; controlling the numbers entering the park on any day; trying to get funding to repair paths and walls; and trying to stop the new development of tourist attractions.

Beaches and coastlines

The quality of seawater around some of Britain's beaches was at one time so poor that in 1999 the European Commission threatened legal action to force Britain to clean them up. Ten per cent of British beaches failed to meet acceptable safety standards. In 2008, several Scottish beaches were contaminated by sewage pushed by storms from nearby sewage outlets.

Problems were not only untreated sewage getting into the sea, but also toxic materials from industry, agricultural waste, and litter such as plastic bottles and dumped food packaging. Local councils were put under pressure, and local groups formed to do something about this problem.

One of the most famous is Surfers Against Sewage (SAS). SAS was founded in 1990 by a group of surfers in Cornwall, who were 'sick of getting sick' through repeated ear, nose, throat and gastric infections after going in the sea. They decided to take action to stop the sewage pollution at their local surfing beaches. They campaigned for clean, safe recreational waters, free from sewage effluents, toxic chemicals, marine litter and nuclear waste. This became a national campaign after the surfers gained media publicity by well-supported events, featuring a six-foot inflatable poo, polluted wetsuits and a sense of humour.

As a result of these successful protests, SAS have gained support and widened their targets to take on a broader range of water issues. Current campaigns include 'Sewage and Sickness', 'Safer Shipping', 'No To Toxics', 'Climate Chaos' and 'Marine Litter'.

These SAS campaigns have had a considerable impact on the sewage problem and the UK has now started to reduce the amount of untreated sewage pollution. Many local authorities have made big efforts to cut down on litter, by regularly cleaning beaches and fining people who drop rubbish.

Changing behaviour

Carbon footprint

A CARBON FOOTPRINT is the measure of the impact that human activities have on the environment in terms of the amount of greenhouse gas produced by them, which is measured in units of carbon dioxide.

So, an individual's carbon footprint is made up from:

1 The amount of fuel you burn in travelling or heating your house.

2 The amount of emissions used producing things you own.

3 The emissions produced to provide the electricity you use.

4 The emissions produced as a result of disposing of waste you create.

Surfers Against Sewage pose next to a symbol of their problem!

In the last few years most people have heard about a carbon footprint, and understand roughly what it means. As we know, the big producers of greenhouse gases are industry and agriculture, but how we live as individuals adds up to a big proportion of the total carbon dioxide produced. How much individuals produce depends on who you are, where you live – and above all – how you live.

On average, each of us in Britain has a carbon footprint of about nine tonnes. That compares with about 20 tonnes for each American and around 18 tonnes for each Australian. But the Swiss and the Swedes – with higher standards of living than us – manage to keep theirs down to about six tonnes. People living in less developed economies produce a lot less. The average Chinese carbon footprint is about three tonnes, the average Indian one about one tonne and the average Ethiopian about a tenth of a tonne.

As we explained earlier in the chapter (pages 91–92), government taxes can help to reduce our carbon footprint by making it too expensive to drive. A better way of reducing car use would be to set up a good public transport system that was cheaper than travelling by car and as convenient. At the moment many people live in areas with poor or non-existent public transport and have to use their private cars or taxis.

The cost of electricity and gas in homes also pushes people into using less, but has already caused difficulties for people on low incomes, and is a health risk to many older people with low pensions.

It's in our hands!

Whatever the government does, the environment will only be protected if individuals are willing to change their attitudes and behaviour. We have to recognise what we are doing to the environment, demand less resources, and reduce our individual pollution. Ways of reducing our carbon footprint are in our hands:

a) We can recycle more; this saves resources and the environmental cost of producing materials that will end up in a landfill, or be burnt.

b) We can make our homes more efficient by insulating them, using energy efficient bulbs, turning off lights and not using standby mode on electrical goods, i.e. by not wasting power.

c) We can buy local goods (less air miles) and avoid buying things with needless packaging.

d) We can travel less, especially by air. This will be hard for many people, who have to travel for work, or family commitments, and also because we have grown used to the idea that holidays abroad are essential for our happiness.

e) We can look at how the environment is damaged and realise that it is our business to protect it; we can't just expect the government to sort it out.

ACTIVITY

1 Research a local environmental issue that has resulted in some kind of protest.
   a) Explain what the issue was (what was happening and why did people object?).
   b) Describe what action was taken.
   c) Describe the outcome.
   d) Explain why the outcome turned out the way it did.

Conclusion

This chapter has produced a bleak picture of the future for our planet. Although we have created some serious environmental problems that will have to be sorted out, there are some optimistic facts:

• The environment has gone through massive temperature changes in the past. The planet has been hotter – there is evidence that 50 million years ago there were no polar regions and the Arctic area had palm trees – and colder – there is evidence that 30 million years ago the planet was almost entirely covered in ice. Life survived.

• We have much greater scientific understanding of why this happens and greater technology to deal with it.

• We are already starting to do something about it.

This chapter has explored how we are trying to reverse global warming and other environmental problems. But perhaps we should also accept that there will be climate change and prepare to adapt to changes that are likely to take place. Pages 99 to 100 consider some of the things we could do to prepare for the future.

Prepare to deal with extreme weather

Hurricanes

Hurricanes can be predicted to some extent. For example, hurricanes have a season in the Caribbean (August–November) and they follow a similar path, so it would be possible to build houses that can resist the power of the wind and rain. Evacuation to safe places, rescue services and emergency services following natural disasters can be on permanent worldwide readiness. Recovery operations can be planned, even rehearsed.

So far we have done little about this, and the slow and inefficient response to the flooding of New Orleans after Hurricane Katrina shows that even the richest countries have a long way to go before they are prepared adequately.

Floods

In the UK, we know which places might flood so we can prepare flood defences and build in order to hold out water. Once an area has flooded, we know it could happen again. The floods in Boscastle, Cornwall, in 2004, and the flooding of the West Country in 2007, were predictable, and it is possible to plan for both flood defence and recovery operations. London already has a flood barrier crossing the Thames.

Prepare for changes in the environment

Some of these emergency plans are starting to happen, but the work needs to be extensive and world-wide which so far it is not. If countries simply look after their own interests, global inequality could lead to international CONFLICT.

The devastation caused by the Tsunami (tidal wave) in the Indian Ocean on 26 December 2004 to Indonesia, Thailand, Sri Lanka and other countries was not the result of climate change. However, many scientists believe that environmental disasters of this enormous scale are likely to become more common as climate change develops. The aid that was sent was extensive and generous, but it was not available when it was most needed (immediately after the Tsunami struck). This underlines the importance of planning ahead to cope with the unexpected events that are likely to happen in the future.

After the flood in Boscastle, Cornwall, 2004.

Hurricane damage can be limited by good building design.

Much of the UK was hit by flooding in June 2007. Tewkesbury in Gloucestershire, shown here, was one of the worst hit areas.

Some measures need to be taken immediately to prepare for changes in the environment:

- Begin to plan how to develop and introduce new species of plants that can thrive in warmer/wetter/drier weather in different zones of the world.
- Make preparations to combat diseases that may come into an area after climate change, for example, malaria in the UK. Have anti-malaria medication ready.
- Prepare people for environmental changes before they happen through the media and education. Allow people time to adjust.
- Give experts time and money to research and find responses to predictable changes.
- Ensure that emergency water and food supplies and disaster relief are prepared, and that delivery and distribution is planned.
- Set up worldwide organisations and funds to identify and help areas and countries in distress.
- Make plans to cope with the large-scale migrations that are likely to occur if climate change leads to famine, or if areas of the planet become uninhabitable.

In different parts of the world some of these measures are being put into action. Research into developing plant species which can survive extreme weather, and into combating diseases which may become epidemic or pandemic in the future, has become a priority for the UN and many governments.

The skills for organising disaster relief are steadily being improved, but are not yet efficient enough to cope with large scale international shortages and migrations. Planning for world climate change has begun in some areas, for example in the move to renewable energy sources, but the situation will obviously have to be dealt with on a global level. Some countries are unwilling to co-operate fully with others because of political disagreements, national pride, and the massive costs of preparing for a world crisis.

Although scientists are sure that world climate change will be taking place rapidly over the next 50 years, governments are reluctant to act and spend money until the effects are on their doorstep. However, when we look at the widespread changes in attitude to protecting the environment that have taken place over the last ten years, we can see there is a much greater chance that important global preparations will take place.

CONFLICT AND CO-OPERATION

INTRODUCTION

This chapter will help you understand more fully the meaning of conflict and co-operation. It is based on four concepts:

1. There are basic rights, freedoms and responsibilities for all individuals
2. There are many different causes of conflict
3. Conflicts can have many different effects
4. Different methods can be used to resolve conflict and work towards co-operation.

Conflict and co-operation can occur on different scales and in different contexts:

• personal or individual
• local or community
• national (within a country)
• international or global (involving other countries or the whole world).

ACTIVITY

1 List the different types of conflict shown in the picture above and, in groups, brainstorm the ideas and feelings you associate with conflict.

What is conflict?

CONFLICT is the struggle between two or more opposing forces, ideas or interests. It can involve disagreement, quarrels and fighting. For many people, 'conflict' means 'violence'. In the activity below, the ideas and feelings you came up with may have been centred around images of violence – beatings, killings, guns, war, etc. However, although conflict is inevitable when people have different VALUES, ATTITUDES or BELIEFS, it is important to understand that not all conflict results in violence. Conflict only explodes into violence if it is not dealt with constructively. Violence is a LEARNED RESPONSE to conflict, so, if violence can be learned, other responses are possible and can be learned as well.

At the root of all conflict is the attempt by people to achieve MUTUALLY EXCLUSIVE goals. A simple example would be a brother and sister arguing because they want to watch different TV programmes at the same time. How many ways of resolving this conflict can you think of?

Conflict affects everybody at some time in their lives. It may affect you in your FAMILY, at school, at work or in your social life. Man has been in conflict with his fellow man since time began. Competing for food was probably the cause of the earliest conflict between individuals. Soon after, when Early Man started living in groups (see pages 4–5), the conflict simply occurred on a larger scale.

Types of conflict

Conflicts can occur at different levels.

• Personal or individual: examples include bullying (see pages 117–120), arguments at work, etc.
• Local or COMMUNITY: these are conflicts on a small scale. Examples include territorial clashes between rival gangs.

- National: these will be conflicts on a larger scale as they affect far more people. They might involve various interests within the country, or the whole country. The controversies over gay marriages and female priests in the UK are examples of the former, while the Civil Rights Movement in the USA (see pages 121–131) is an example of the latter.
- International or global: these might involve disputes between different countries, so examples of this would be the two World Wars. The development of weapons of mass destruction (WMDs) has meant that human conflict on an international level, if not managed carefully, has the potential to destroy the world we live in. There could also be conflicts over issues affecting the whole world, such as DEFORESTATION, GLOBAL WARMING and POLLUTION (see Environmental issues chapter).

Causes of conflict

A cause of conflict is what makes it happen, i.e. a reason for it. Some causes of conflict are long term (going back many years) and some short term (more recent or immediate). These causes are often linked.

Causes of small-scale conflict

The causes of conflict can be put into the following categories:

- Religious: disagreements about beliefs and practices.
- Political: disputes regarding power and control.
- Economic: disagreements about ownership of wealth, territory and property.
- Social: cultural clashes (differences regarding values, attitudes and behaviour).
- MORAL: arguments about what is right or wrong.

Some small-scale conflicts, such as divorce, might have more than one cause (see Source A).

Source A

Cause	Example: divorce
Religious	If partners are of different religions, it may cause tension on important decisions.
Political	Family 'politics' may mean one partner is overpowering.
Economic	Debt and financial worries can cause tension and are often a cause of divorce.
Social	Partners from different backgrounds – upbringing, class, culture – may have irreconcilable differences in their values.
Moral	One partner considers the other's behaviour wrong, e.g. adultery.

ACTIVITIES

1 In pairs, using the causes listed in Source A, decide what was the cause of each of the conflicts described in the newspaper headlines below.

A MUSLIM STUDENT IN DISPUTE WITH SCHOOL OVER RIGHT TO WEAR HIJAB

Firemen on strike over pay and conditions

PENSIONERS CLAIM THEY HAVE BEEN CHEATED OVER PENSIONS

Villagers up in arms about traveller camp – say crime and litter will increase

MOTHER TAKES HOSPITAL TO COURT TO ALLOW HER SICK BABY THE RIGHT TO LIFE

2 Choose another small-scale conflict – for example, someone taking their employer to court for unfair dismissal – and create a table similar to that in Source A. You may not be able to fill in all of the different causes, depending on what conflict you choose to use.

Causes of large-scale conflict

Causes of conflict at a national and international level can be split into the same categories as those for small-scale conflict (see left). The following case study on the Palestine–Israeli conflict illustrates this.

Case Study
The Palestine–Israeli conflict

Over 2,000 years ago Jews and Arabs lived together in Palestine. However, when the Romans conquered the land they forced most of the Jews to flee to Europe and elsewhere. This was called the Diaspora. This meant that the Jewish people had no country to call their own. They were made to feel unwelcome in most of Europe, which had become Christian and hostile to Jews. PERSECUTION continued into the nineteenth and twentieth centuries (see pages 154–159).

So, at the end of the nineteenth century, a campaign was launched in Europe to establish a homeland controlled and run by Jews. Supporters of a homeland were known as Zionists.

At the beginning of the twentieth century, some Jews began to return to Palestine, their original home.

In 1948, the United Nations (UN) decided that Palestine should be divided into two states – one for Palestinians and one for the Jews (named Israel). The Palestinians could not accept the loss of their land and conflict has ensued since then. The diagram below suggests some causes of this conflict.

ACTIVITY

1 a) In groups decide what type of cause of the Palestine–Israeli conflict is suggested in each speech bubble below. Some bubbles may suggest more than one cause. Record the results of your discussion in a table like the one on page 102.

b) Discuss which bubbles are Israeli and which are Palestinian supporters. Give reasons.

c) Can one cause be said to be more important than another? Explain your views.

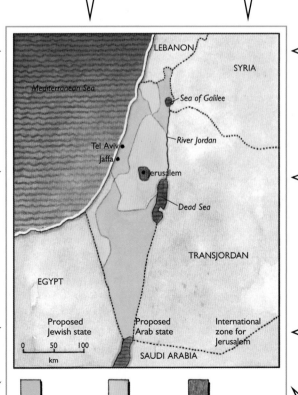

1. By the end of the nineteenth century we were fed up of being treated as outsiders. We suffered discrimination and persecution in Europe and, in the middle of the twentieth century, the Holocaust made it clear we had no future in Europe.

10. We want to be independent so that we can create our own wealth.

9. The British government made a clear commitment in 1917 that it would help us establish our own country in our promised land.

8. In our holy book, the Torah, it makes it clear that we are God's chosen people and that this land is rightly our land – it is the 'promised land'.

2. In 1916 the British government made a clear commitment to support our cause: independence for us from the oppression of the Turks (the old Ottoman Empire). It was this commitment that won us over to support the British in the First World War.

7. We have a right to our country. We have lived here continuously for thousands of years. At first we had no problem with a few refugees. But when they came in larger numbers, intent on taking over our land, we had to resist.

3. The UN's proposal to partition Palestine in 1948 was not a perfect plan – but it was a start. We have simply built on this. We shall never give in to terrorists who are our enemy.

6. The UN's proposal to partition Palestine was unfair. The US president, who depended on the Jewish vote in the US for his election, dictated it. We shall never surrender while our land is occupied and we live as refugees.

4. Jerusalem is our holy city. They have no right to take it from us.

5. Jerusalem is our holy city. It belongs to us.

The UN partition plan. What problems might you expect in a state which is divided into three parts?

Map labels: LEBANON, SYRIA, Mediterranean Sea, Sea of Galilee, River Jordan, Tel Aviv, Jaffa, Jerusalem, Dead Sea, TRANSJORDAN, EGYPT, SAUDI ARABIA, Proposed Jewish state, Proposed Arab state, International zone for Jerusalem, 0 50 100 km

Effects of conflict

Effects of conflict are what happens because of the conflict, i.e. the results of it. The consequences of conflict can also be short term or long term and be classified in the same way as the causes.

- Religious: growing hatred between faiths.
- Political: shift in power.
- Economic: cost of conflict, re-building, etc.
- Social: destruction, displacement, deaths, etc.
- Moral: decline of values, e.g. addiction.

They can affect individuals, groups, communities or states. A short-term effect of most wars is death and destruction, whilst a long-term effect might be lasting hatred. Sometimes an effect of a conflict can also be a cause of prolonging that conflict or starting another one. For example, the Treaty of Versailles, which was the peace settlement following the First World War, caused resentment in Germany and became one of the long-term causes of the Second World War. In the same way, American and British involvement in Iraq and Afghanistan has led to the wider clash between the Western, Christian world and ISLAM. The result of this has been the escalation of suicide bombing and terrorist activities across the world.

The conflict in Northern Ireland makes an excellent case study of the effects of national conflict.

Case Study
Conflict in Northern Ireland

In 1801, the Act of Union joined England and Ireland and led the Irish to demand Home Rule. This meant they wanted to run the home affairs of Ireland themselves. This was not granted, so at the beginning of the twentieth century many of the Irish began to demand independence. A COMPROMISE solution was reached in 1921. A Catholic REPUBLIC was established with its capital in Dublin, while Protestant Ulster (Northern Ireland) remained part of the UK.

In the 1960s, the Catholic minority in Ulster complained of DISCRIMINATION while an IRA bombing campaign started in support of a united Ireland. The Protestants feared being ruled by a Catholic majority so their MILITANT extremists retaliated with violence. In

1998, the Good Friday agreement was signed. This has provided Northern Ireland's divided SOCIETY with a political framework to resolve its differences.

The conflict had a number of different effects – as can be seen in Source A.

Source A

Effect of conflict	Example: conflict in Northern Ireland
Religious	Some Roman Catholics and Protestants are reluctant to live and work together. Most schools remain segregated.
Political	Direct rule from England.
Economic	Lack of investment in Belfast because of bombing of businesses. Increase in taxation to pay for army in Northern Ireland.
Social	Communities destroyed by bombing, for example, in Omagh, Enniskillen. Young people turning to drugs because of fear and disillusionment.
Moral	Condemnation of British government by other nations. Loss of support for IRA because of bombing campaigns on mainland Britain.

ACTIVITIES

1 Copy and complete the table below about the effects of a small-scale conflict. Remember, effects can become causes of further conflict.

Effect of conflict	Example: divorce
Religious	'Until death us do part.' The difficulty of remarriage in some religions.
Political	
Economic	
Social	
Moral	

2 Choose one effect of divorce and suggest what this, in turn, might cause.

CONCEPT 1

There are basic rights, freedoms and responsibilities for all individuals

In this concept section the focus will be on:

- The basic rights and freedoms of individuals in different kinds of society.
- The different responsibilities that result from the rights and freedoms.
- A case study of human rights involving dictatorship and democracy.

The following are ideas and terms that you will need to know from this concept section:

UN Declaration of Human Rights • power • responsibilities • authority • Amnesty International

Rights and responsibilities

On pages 4–5 you have read about how early humans had rights, freedoms and responsibilities. Early humans had the right to collect fruit and berries and hunt animals. Humans joined groups to improve their chances of survival. This gave them the right to expect help and support, but at the same time gave responsibilities also. Humans would now have a role to play in the group, and would be expected to accept certain norms, such as sharing food. Some of these norms became formal rules, especially when groups got larger and comprised whole tribes. These were the earliest societies, recognising human rights even before writing had been invented. These are the rights a person has as a human being. They are regarded by most societies as belonging to everyone.

Power and authority

Early groups also accepted that someone had to have the final say in decision making, to avoid argument and quarrelling. In other words, there had to be a leader to govern or rule the group. He or she would be given power and authority to control others, to make decisions and enforce the rules. He or she would be responsible for the welfare of the whole group.

Some societies progressed more than others, due to 'kinder' environments and technological developments (see pages 9–10). They became civilised, built cities and created empires. This meant that government became more complex. Written laws became necessary to protect the rights of the individual and to make it clear what their responsibilities were.

Examples of written laws

- The Ten Commandments (around 1000 BCE): laid down some of the earliest basic rules of behaviour.
- The Magna Carta (1215): set out the obligations of the King of England to treat his subjects according to the laws of the land.
- The US 'Declaration of Independence' (1776): laid down principles of freedom and equality.
- The 'Declaration of the Rights of Man' (1789): underlined that in return for obeying the laws of society man should have certain rights.
- Several Geneva Conventions (1864, 1929, 1949): set down rules about the rights of wounded soldiers and prisoners of war.

Different kinds of society

Today there are very different kinds of societies all over the world. They all have their own attitudes and approaches to rights, freedom and responsibilities. Here are some examples:

- Primitive tribal groups such as the Kayapo in Brazil, who follow a traditional way of life with elders making decisions (see page 80).
- Less developed societies that are under the control of a modern central government, but where local tribes are still the main political groups, e.g. the Democratic Republic of the Congo. Here decisions are made by tribes (who often fail to agree).
- Modern, industrialised countries run by a single party dictatorship, e.g. North Korea, China.
- Modern, industrialised countries that have a democratic government elected by the people, e.g. UK, France.

The UN Declaration of Human Rights

By the twentieth century there were many different types of societies all over the world with very different attitudes and approaches to rights, freedoms and responsibilities. Most of them had written laws (see box on page 105). Many referred to human rights, but unfortunately there was no clear, official and universal recognition of what these rights involved.

The events of the Second World War (1939–45), and in particular the Holocaust, revealed the need for change. In 1945, the UNITED NATIONS (UN) was set up to encourage peace and international co-operation (see page 145). On 3 December 1948, it issued the UNIVERSAL DECLARATION OF HUMAN RIGHTS (UDHR). This listed 30 rights that all individuals should have – based on life, freedom, equality and security. It included the right to food and water, shelter, education, work, travel and a fair trial. It banned torture and discrimination of any kind. Nearly every country in the world has signed the Declaration, which is now recognised as the single most important human rights document.

Source A

Extracts from the Universal Declaration of Human Rights

ARTICLE 1:

All human beings are born free and equal. They are endowed with reason and conscience and should act towards one another in a spirit of brotherhood.

ARTICLE 13:

1 Everyone has the right to freedom of movement and residence within the borders of each state.
2 Everyone has the right to leave any country, including his own, and to return to his country.

The UDHR, however, was only a statement and had to be put into practice.

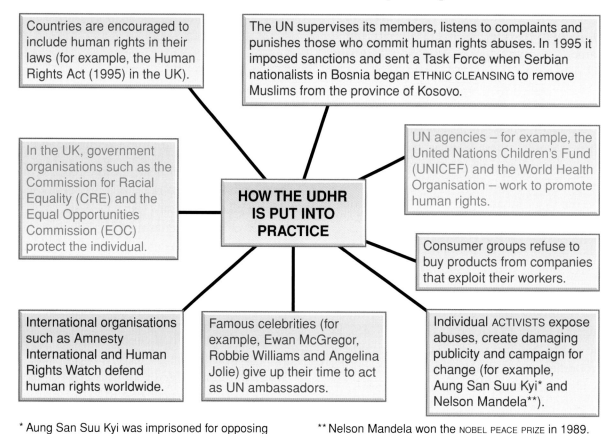

Countries are encouraged to include human rights in their laws (for example, the Human Rights Act (1995) in the UK).

The UN supervises its members, listens to complaints and punishes those who commit human rights abuses. In 1995 it imposed sanctions and sent a Task Force when Serbian nationalists in Bosnia began ETHNIC CLEANSING to remove Muslims from the province of Kosovo.

In the UK, government organisations such as the Commission for Racial Equality (CRE) and the Equal Opportunities Commission (EOC) protect the individual.

UN agencies – for example, the United Nations Children's Fund (UNICEF) and the World Health Organisation – work to promote human rights.

HOW THE UDHR IS PUT INTO PRACTICE

Consumer groups refuse to buy products from companies that exploit their workers.

International organisations such as Amnesty International and Human Rights Watch defend human rights worldwide.

Famous celebrities (for example, Ewan McGregor, Robbie Williams and Angelina Jolie) give up their time to act as UN ambassadors.

Individual ACTIVISTS expose abuses, create damaging publicity and campaign for change (for example, Aung San Suu Kyi* and Nelson Mandela**).

* Aung San Suu Kyi was imprisoned for opposing military dictatorship in Burma. She was awarded the Nobel Peace Prize in 1991.

** Nelson Mandela won the NOBEL PEACE PRIZE in 1989. He had spent 27 years in a South African prison for opposing apartheid.

Angelina Jolie is one of many celebrities who act as UN ambassadors.

Source A opposite illustrates how the Universal Declaration of Human Rights is put into practice. Below you will learn how one international organisation, Amnesty International, defends human rights across the globe.

Amnesty International (AI)

AMNESTY
INTERNATIONAL

'AMNESTY INTERNATIONAL's vision is of a world in which every person enjoys all of the human rights enshrined in the UDHR and other human rights standards.'

Statute (law) of Amnesty International, 2005.

Beginnings

Amnesty International was started in 1961 by a British lawyer, Peter Benenson, who appealed in a newspaper article for people to work independently and peacefully for the release of prisoners of conscience (those imprisoned for their religious or political beliefs).

Aims

This developed into a Western-based international organisation to prevent abuses of human rights and to demand justice for those whose rights have been violated. It deals with five key areas:

1 women's rights
2 children's rights
3 ending torture and execution
4 rights of REFUGEES
5 rights of prisoners of conscience.

Methods

Amnesty International acts independently and has nearly two million voluntary members and supporters worldwide. It works to mobilise public opinion, which then exerts pressure on those responsible for the abuse of human rights. It does this in many ways, including:

- producing reports based on thorough research involving visits and observations
- conducting publicity campaigns: for example, direct appeals (letters) and media work (leaflets, posters, videos, websites)
- diplomacy: trying to influence governments through dialogue and negotiation
- fund-raising: for example, appeals and benefit shows such as The Secret Policeman's Ball.

Results

Amnesty International was awarded the 1997 Nobel Peace Prize for its 'campaign against torture', but has received criticism for both anti-Western and pro-Western bias. It is often accused of one-sided reporting or failure to treat threats to security as an excuse for torture.

Unfortunately, despite the efforts of the UN, governments, organisations and individual activists, millions of people worldwide are deprived of their human rights. There are a number of reasons for this (see page 108).

ACTIVITIES

1 Read through this section on Amnesty International and choose one key area listed under 'Aims'. Write a newspaper report on the area, giving examples from your own research. Suggest what might be done to prevent abuse in this area in the future (Amnesty's website provides information to help you: www.amnesty.org.uk).
2 Find out as much as you can about the work of Aung San Suu Kyi or any other human rights activist.

Why are so many people still denied their human rights?

1 Many governments see the UN as a threat to their own independence. They resent interference with their own laws and customs. For example, some US states will not give up the death penalty.

2 Governments put political or economic interests before human rights. For example, worldwide dependence on oil has led to a blind eye being turned to abuses in oil-rich countries such as Saudi Arabia.

3 Dictators are against human rights because they are afraid of losing power. For example, President Mugabe of Zimbabwe announced that he was only accountable to God when it was revealed that he had denied his people a fair election in 2008.

4 Differing ideologies: communist governments believe in economic and social equality but put little value on political freedom. This was apparent before the 2008 Beijing Olympics, when protestors in Tibet, demonstrating while the Olympic flame was carried through their country, were dealt with very harshly by China. On the other hand, some capitalist countries like the USA might allow political freedom but do not regard it as their duty to provide free healthcare.

5 Culture clashes: some Muslims see the UDHR as being based on the ideas of Western civilisation. Sharia law differs from the laws of the Western world (see below). Sometimes legal attitudes to women do not conform with laws and attitudes in the West. In some countries like Iran, lashings, amputations and stonings are carried out for crimes such as adultery or blasphemy.

People's human rights have suffered in Zimbabwe because of the lack of a fair election in 2008.

Sharia law

Sharia law is ISLAM's legal system. It is based on the Qur'an as the word of God, the example of the life of the prophet Muhammad, and fatwas (the rulings of Islamic scholars). It differs from the laws of the Western world because it covers every aspect of the life of a Muslim while Western law confines itself largely to matters relating to crime, contract, civil relationships and individual rights. In the UK, some Muslim communities have established Sharia courts to deal with family or business disputes. The government has also allowed some Sharia practices, for example, allowing meat to be slaughtered according to Islamic practices.

6 The UN takes a long time to act as all countries have to agree. In the case of Rwanda in 1994, it acted too late to prevent the massacre of 800,000 Tutsi people by the Hutu majority.

7 Lack of information: countries with poor human rights records deny access to foreigners and censor the media.

8 Lack of money: Third World countries do not have the resources to provide food, schools, hospitals, etc.

9 War: when this occurs, abuse of human rights is inevitable. For example, civil war in Somalia in 1992 thwarted attempts at famine relief and six million people starved to death.

10 Rights often clash with each other, with some people's beliefs, and with the law. For example:

  a) One person's right to express an opinion might conflict with another's right to privacy.

  b) The strict enforcement of a uniform policy by a school might offend Muslims, whose faith demands that the head and body must be covered by the hijab.

  c) The wider interests of the community as a whole should be taken into account in the interests of preventing crime, protecting public health or safeguarding lives:

  • CCTV might infringe on our lives but it helps to prevent theft.

  • The ban on smoking in public places is in the interests of the health of non-smokers.

  • The fight against terrorism requires the acceptance of limitations on our actions, even to the extent of what we can carry on to planes.

  • China's One Child Policy in the 1980s might appear inhumane, but was undertaken to slow down overpopulation and prevent mass starvation.

Source B

Recent newspaper headlines

All frontline police officers to be given access to 50,000-volt stun guns

YOUNG CHILDREN NEED PLAY, NOT TARGETS

A DISGUSTING FEAST OF FILTH: An exhibition at the British Library explores different kinds of censorship

Jerry Springer the Opera portrays Christ as gay

GOVERNMENT WILL SPY ON EVERY CALL AND EMAIL

Headmaster's killer can't be deported in case we break his right to a 'family life'

Ethiopian army keeps food from rebel areas as millions starve

Student faces GBH charge for defending home from serial burglar

---

Source C

Surveillance in the UK

CCTV cameras in London (72,050)

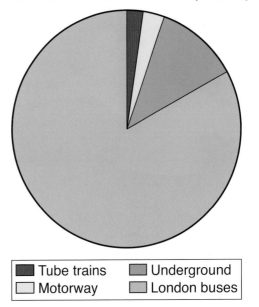

■ Tube trains   ■ Underground
□ Motorway   ■ London buses

• **4.2 million:** The number of CCTV cameras in the UK.

• **519,260:** Requests from police and other public bodies for personal communications data in 2007.

• **3,254:** The number of pieces of personal information stored about the average UK citizen per week.

ACTIVITIES

1 Study the information on this page. Choose one reason why people are denied their human rights and try to find more examples.

2 Study the information in Source C. Discuss with your group whether there should be so much surveillance of UK citizens.

3 Do you think we should have Sharia law alongside our traditional laws in the UK?

4 Look at all the headlines in Source B. How might each one involve a clash of human rights?

The different responsibilities that result from the rights and freedoms

In the UK the Human Rights Act (1998) was followed by the Data Protection Act (1998) and the Freedom of Information Act (2000). Together they were intended to bring in a new civil rights culture based upon a balance of rights and responsibilities. They identify the rights that individuals should enjoy. They also impose responsibilities on individuals, involving important considerations about balancing their rights with those of others. We must also recognise that there are occasions when the state can have a good reason to interfere with our rights.

It is not only individuals who have responsibilities – so do organisations and institutions. The table below illustrates what some of these responsibilities are and how they are both carried out and sometimes ignored.

Lindsay Lohan hiding from paparazzi. Do celebrities have a right to privacy or does fame make them public property?

Some responsibilities	Examples of good practice	Examples of bad practice
Individuals To treat others as they would like to be treated.	• A child helping their mother with housework.	• A football fan singing racist chants.
MULTI-NATIONAL COMPANIES To consider rights of workers and consumers.	• Body Shop – promotes human rights of child workers.	• Sports clothing companies exploiting child labour in the Far East.
Media To investigate and report abuse of human rights.	• John Pilger, an investigative journalist, has received awards for his campaigning work.	• Paparazzi who follow celebrities everywhere they go, hoping for revealing photos.
Religious leaders To provide moral leadership.	• Present-day Roman Catholic Pope promoting toleration worldwide.	• Medieval popes ordering the burning of heretics.
National governments To protect their citizens.	• UK Labour Government creating the NHS in 1948.	• Abuse of power by President Mugabe in Zimbabwe in 2008.
Local councils To look after the interests of local communities.	• Councils making adequate provision for the disabled.	• Councils wasting taxpayers' money on inefficient projects.
Schools Teaching children moral values – a sense of right and wrong.	• Involving students in the discussion of important issues in subjects such as Citizenship and Humanities.	• The indoctrination of young people in Nazi Germany (1934–45).

Dictatorship and democracy

In the last section we looked at how governments have a responsibility not to abuse their power and authority. There are many systems of government ranging from DEMOCRACY to DICTATORSHIP.

Democracy is the system most popular in the Western world. It was devised originally by the Ancient Greeks. The term is taken from two words: 'demos' (people) and 'kratos' (strength). It literally means 'rule by the people'. Greek city states were small enough to allow direct democracy whereby all male citizens (but not women or slaves) came together to vote on important issues.

In large modern states this is not possible, so representative democracy has been adopted. The voters elect representatives to rule on their behalf, usually for a fixed length of time. Those given authority accept that a balance has to be maintained between the power they hold and the rights and freedom of the people. This balance is not always easy to achieve, especially in times of national emergency, such as war. However, the people do have the opportunity at the next election to change their government.

In the UK our representatives are Members of Parliament (MPs). They usually belong to a political party, such as Labour, Conservative or Liberal Democrat. The party that has the most MPs after an election usually forms the government.

Democracy is the system most likely to safeguard the rights and freedoms of its citizens. Yet for most of history democracy has been the exception rather than the norm.

States and societies have either preferred, or been forced, to accept a very different type of government where an individual, group or party holds all the power without restrictions.

This is called dictatorship and it is the exact opposite of democracy. Nazi Germany under Hitler (see pages 154–159) and Communist China under Mao were examples of such rule. Usually dictators allow no opposition and demand complete obedience to the state: in other words, the system is totalitarian. The rulers are sometimes referred to as tyrants as they usually ignore human rights and are cruel and unjust. There is no balance between authority and the rights of the people in such a state. As they hold no fair elections the only way a dictatorship can be overturned is by force, either by revolution from within the country or through foreign intervention and war.

Strengths and weaknesses of political systems

Most modern countries are, or pretend to be, democracies. They claim that final power belongs to the people, who have full political rights and freedom.

However, this is misleading. Many states include minority communities of different race or religion. They are often poorly represented in the government and their interests ignored. US democracy before the Civil Rights Movement denied blacks equality (see pages 121–131). In the same way, Roman Catholics in Northern Ireland suffered at the hands of the Protestant majority who controlled power during the period of the Troubles (see page 104). Countries that are not used to democracy also find it difficult to adjust to its demands, as we will discover when we look at Afghanistan (see pages 113–116). It seems to be better suited to the Western world.

In some countries at certain times dictatorship has enjoyed greater success than democracy. When a society is under threat, either internally or from abroad, it can offer more decisive leadership as there is less need for discussion and agreement. Germany initially prospered and progressed more under Hitler than it had under the democratic Weimar Republic (see pages 154–159).

ACTIVITIES

1 Read page 112. What do you think is the greatest strength and the greatest weakness of democracy?
2 Why do you think dictatorships have most appeal when countries are struggling?

Dictatorship

Strengths	Weaknesses
1 People can identify with a leader who can become a cult figure, thus ensuring support, e.g. Stalin, Mao.	1 Sometimes there is no constitution to set the limits of what government can and can't do.
2 Absolute power is in the hands of a single person, group or party so that there is more likelihood of agreement.	2 There is no separation of powers: all three branches of government are under single control.
3 Efficient form of government in an emergency where quick action is called for, as there is no need for consultation.	3 There is no check on abuse of power or corruption.
	4 In case of personal dictatorship, too much power and responsibility rests on a single person.
	5 A cult of leadership can make it easy to deceive and exploit the people.
	6 There is no guarantee of political rights and freedom.
	7 Only government-approved candidates are allowed to stand for election, giving voters no real choice.
	8 Opposition is not allowed: often censorship, imprisonment and executions take place.

Democracy

Strengths	Weaknesses
1 Popular sovereignty: final authority belongs to the people. Unpopular governments can be removed at the next election.	1 In practice, the ideal of rule by the majority is not so easy to carry out in an indirect democracy.
2 Legitimate government, because it is based on the consent of the people.	2 Conflicting interests can't always be accommodated, e.g. increased public spending rules out tax cuts.
3 Government responsible to the people, so tends to rule for the benefit of the community as a whole.	3 There is always the possibility that government representing the majority might ignore or oppress minorities.
4 Constitution usually states how government must rule.	4 Elections often fail to produce a majority for one party, so there has to be a coalition government of more than one party. This can mean that decision making becomes difficult and slow.
5 All adults are usually citizens with full political rights and freedoms.	5 Voters are often apathetic: for example, in the USA only about one in two vote in presidential elections.
6 There are checks and balances: usually there are three branches of government (legislature, executive and judiciary), which are all separate.	

To compare the merits of democracy and dictatorship today it is necessary to look at the experience of a single country. Afghanistan makes a good case study as it has recently tried both forms of government, if only with limited success. It also is the focus of a wider struggle between the forces of Western democracies and Muslim conservatism. The USA claims it is trying to make the world safer by bringing democracy to some of the world's most wretched dictatorships.

Afghanistan and its neighbours.

Background

Afghanistan is a mountainous country in Central Asia. Throughout history it has been invaded by nomads and conquering armies. Its rulers have included Alexander the Great and Genghis Khan. In 1747, the people gained their independence and a modern kingdom was founded. However, because of the mixture of ETHNIC GROUPS which make up the population, national unity was difficult to achieve. Most of the people were poor farmers and herdsmen and nearly all Muslim.

The democratic experiment

In the early twentieth century, the monarchy followed a policy of Westernisation in an attempt to turn Afghanistan into a modern secular NATION state. There was a deliberate attempt to unite the various ethnic groups and to switch the people's loyalty from the tribal chiefs to the royal family.

Two written constitutions in 1923 and 1931 introduced the democratic idea of popular consent. The monarchy was no longer based on divine will or tribal decisions but on the will of the people. The rights and duties of the monarch and his subjects were listed and an elected National Assembly was introduced. All subjects, whether Muslim or not, were made equal; they were citizens of the state of Afghanistan. They were given the right to receive free education. Forced labour, slavery and torture were abolished and freedom of the press was granted. However, in spite of all these reforms, the king still retained absolute power.

The constitutions broke with the old ideas of tribal loyalties and the values of the Muslim community. Consequently, there were rebellions against the reforms as they interfered too much with tradition. Attempts to introduce Western dress and to free women from the veil met strong resistance. Museums and libraries, symbols of modernisation, were destroyed. Many reforms had to be withdrawn.

In spite of these setbacks, the state, and not the tribe, became increasingly the most important factor in the life of the individual. As the state increased its power it needed more civil servants and soldiers, so more people became dependent upon it. After the Second World War (1939–45), Afghanistan, like other developing nations, was forced to look for foreign aid and so became exposed to foreign influence. This led to a marked increase in the pace of modernisation. Roads and other INFRASTRUCTURES were built, and towns developed. A new educated urban MIDDLE CLASS emerged.

In 1964, in recognition of the growing changes in his country, the king accepted a new liberal constitution. Afghanistan became a constitutional monarchy, with the royal family no longer allowed to play a key role in running the country. Sovereignty now belonged to the nation through its representatives in parliament. The constitution guaranteed education, freedom of property, freedom of RELIGION, freedom of the press and of assembly.

CONFLICT AND CO-OPERATION

Women were allowed to vote and also run for office – a dramatic breakthrough for what had been such a conservative country.

Unfortunately, these changes failed to satisfy both the traditionalists and the modernists. Western values offended those brought up to believe in Islamist ideology, while the urbanised, educated middle class did not think the changes went far enough. The new constitution failed to achieve national unity. Afghanistan was finding it difficult to adjust to democracy.

In 1973, the monarchy was overthrown by a military coup and the Democratic Republic of Afghanistan was established. The country became unstable, lapsed into civil war and, as had often happened in the past, was invaded – this time by the Soviet Union in 1979. A communist government was set up, which meant the end of democracy. In response, the USA and other countries intervened in the name of freedom, forcing the Soviets to leave.

Various ethnic and political rivals now fought for control of the country. The Taliban emerged as the most powerful group and in 1996 set up an Islamic dictatorship under the leadership of Mullah Mohammed Omar.

The Taliban period

The name Taliban means 'students'. Most of the Taliban were former students in religious schools for Afghan refugees set up in the 1990s in Pakistan. The withdrawal of Soviet troops and the collapse of the communist government had led to a breakdown of law and order in Afghanistan. The traditional warlords were running the country, but decades of warfare had devastated its economy and left the people short of food, clothing and medical care. The sale of opium from the growth of poppy seeds was the major form of income. Against this background the Taliban appeared as a force for social order and started subduing the warlords. By 1996, popular support for the Taliban as well as assistance from Islamic groups abroad enabled them to gradually defeat their enemies. By 2001 they ruled over virtually the whole country.

The Taliban were fundamentalist Muslims and set up an Islamic theocracy. They were very popular at first because devout Muslims had resented the anti-religious policies of the previous communist government. They brought law and order, which

Source A

Taliban rules and punishments

1 Women banned from working.
2 Women banned from going out unless accompanied by a male relative.
3 Women not allowed to deal with a male shopkeeper, or be treated by a male doctor, or talk to men outside the home.
4 Women must wear a burqa (a long veil), which covers the wearer from head to toe.
5 All windows to be painted black to prevent women from being seen from outside.
6 Watching movies, TV, videos, the internet or listening to music prohibited.
7 Men must attend prayers in mosques five times a day.
8 Girls over eight years old not allowed to attend school.
9 Non-Muslims must wear a distinct badge or stitch a yellow cloth on to their dress for identification.
10 Amputation of hands for theft.
11 Stoning in public for having sex outside marriage.
12 Execution for anyone who converts to any religion other than Islam.

improved the lives of the ordinary people. Their rejection of the materialism of the Western world appealed to many of the more conservative Afghans, who also felt that democracy was not the answer to their problems. However, their determination to rule according to a strict and literal interpretation of Sharia law (see page 108) placed severe restrictions on the people, particularly women. The refusal to allow women to work meant that the country was short of teachers, nurses, doctors, etc., and the economy was affected. CAPITAL PUNISHMENTS were also introduced that involved violation of human rights. The Taliban were also intolerant of other religions. In 2001 they destroyed the two ancient Buddhas of Bamiyan, built in 554 BC. Non-Islamic art was banned and works in the National Museum of Art were smashed with sledgehammers.

There was soon widespread criticism of the new regime abroad and most countries refused to recognise the Taliban as the legitimate or lawful government of Afghanistan because of its dictatorship. The Western powers were further angered when Afghanistan became a haven for Islamic extremists, including Osama Bin Laden and his terrorist network, Al-Qaeda. When the Taliban refused to extradite him following his alleged orders to destroy the World Trade Center in New York on 11 September 2001, the USA and its allies started bombing Afghanistan. At the same time, the opposition forces within the country advanced towards the capital, Kabul. By December 2001, Taliban rule was over. The tribal ruler, Hamid Karsai, was appointed to head an interim government by the UN.

The war had intensified the abuse of human rights within Afghanistan as it was accompanied by the usual catalogue of destruction, injuries, torture, rape, deaths and ethnic massacres. The neglect of rules of health and hygiene meant that diseases such as malaria, smallpox and cholera, which had been eliminated in the 1980s, made a comeback. Food and water became very scarce. It was estimated that 30,000 children were surviving by begging or scavenging through garbage and war ruins, while three million people became refugees.

The Allied forces were not blameless during the conflict. Aerial bombing on one occasion caused many casualties amongst a wedding party, while the scandal of Camp X-Ray (see Source D on page 116) brought shame on the West. These events prove that during war a democratic country can no more guarantee to respect human rights than a dictatorship.

Afghanistan today

The fall of the Taliban did not end the suffering of the Afghans. The laws were relaxed and women were given far more freedom and rights, but stable government has still to be established. Fighting also continues as part of the war against terror. US and NATO forces are still bombing Taliban and Al-Qaeda strongholds. Consequently, human rights are still being abused. In 2008, Amnesty International condemned the use of 'human shields' by the Taliban and civilian deaths from Western air strikes.

In Britain, there is a growing disillusionment with the war. By 15 July 2009, the number of British soldiers killed in action reached 185 and a survey in the Independent in July 2009 revealed that over 50 per cent of people in the UK believed the war to be unwinnable. It seems likely that Afghanistan's problems cannot be solved by military means alone: the country needs reconstruction and economic development. The war has also highlighted the problems of trying to impose democracy on a fragmented, tribal and largely uneducated society unused to central government authority.

Troops locating Taliban fighters in the hills of Afghanistan.

The Taliban insist that Muslim women be fully covered at all times in public.

Source B

Taliban views of women

'Women just aren't as smart as men. They don't have the intelligence. We ... refuse to let women vote or participate in politics.'

Nur Mohammad, Governor of Herat,
Sunday Times, 24 March 1996.

'There are two places for a woman: one is the husband's bed and the other is the graveyard.'

Official quote from a Taliban minister.

Source C

In the hands of the Taliban

'I am given a radio to listen to the BBC World Service and am asked if there is anything else I need ... Everyone is bothered that I'm not eating and ask if there's something wrong with the food ... They constantly refer to me as their guest and say they are sad if I am sad. I can't believe it. The Taliban are trying to kill me with their kindness.'

Extracts from the diary of Yvonne Ridley, a Western journalist arrested for entering Afghanistan illegally (disguised in a burqa), from her book In The Hands of The Taliban, *2001*

Source D

Camp X-Ray

In January 2002, 20 prisoners from Afghanistan arrived at Camp X-Ray, a US military base at Guantánamo Bay, Cuba, to be interrogated about their links to Al-Qaeda. They were held without trial, shackled, kept in tiny cage-like cells, and there are also allegations of torture. The then US Defence Secretary, Donald Rumsfeld, defended the policy: 'There are among these prisoners, people who are willing to kill themselves and other people. Unlawful combatants do not have any rights under the Geneva Convention.'

ACTIVITIES

Read the case study on pages 113–116 and complete the following activities.

1 **a** In what ways was Afghanistan a democratic country by 1964?
   b What would the advantages of democracy be to the country?

2 The Taliban government that ruled in Afghanistan (1996–2001) was a dictatorship.
   a Why did they gain power?
   b What advantages did a dictatorship offer the Afghans at the time?
   c Why did the Taliban government meet so much opposition both at home and abroad?

4 **a** Read Source A (page 114) and briefly summarise the way the Taliban abused human rights.
   b What other factors made it difficult to protect human rights in Afghanistan during their rule?

5 Read Source C. Why do you think the experience of Yvonne Ridley differed so much from that of most women in Afghanistan?

6 What are the disadvantages of dictatorship as shown by Taliban rule?

7 Study Source D about the alleged abuse of human rights on behalf of a democratic government. Do you think the treatment of the prisoners was justified? Give reasons for your answer.

CONCEPTS 2 & 3

There are many different causes of conflict and many different effects

The specification looks at causes and effects of conflicts separately: here we have combined the two concepts so that we can consider causes and effects together.

In this section we will focus on:

- A range of causes and effects of conflict.
- A case study of the causes and effects of conflict at an individual/small group level.
- A case study of the cause and effects of national conflict.
- A case study of the causes and effects of an international conflict.

The following are ideas and terms that you will need to know from this section:

Concept 2: political, moral, economic, religious and social causes • long- and short-term causes

Concept 3: political, moral, economic, religious and social effects • long- and short-term effects

What are the causes and effects of individual and small group conflicts?

What is bullying?

Bullying is any BEHAVIOUR that deliberately upsets, threatens or hurts another person. It is a good example of conflict between individuals as well as conflict within the community where it is taking place, such as school or work. Like most small-scale conflicts it is caused by intolerance, INJUSTICE and CONFRONTATION (see page 102). It results in the basic rights and freedoms individuals have in society, such as peace, education and beliefs, being denied in some way.

There are different types of bullying. These are:

- physical – violence (for example, punching, kicking), stealing (for example, sweets or money)
- verbal – teasing, name-calling, racist or sexual remarks
- emotional – socially isolating people (for example, leaving people out, the 'silent treatment'), spreading rumours, dirty looks.

Types of bullying change with age: playground bullying, sexual HARASSMENT, gang attacks, date violence, assault, marital violence, child abuse, workplace harassment and abuse in care homes are all examples of bullying that can take place throughout different stages of life and in different communities.

Reasons for bullying

People become bullies for a variety of reasons. These can include:

- poor discipline at home – children are not taught what is right or wrong
- abuse or lack of love at home – bullies have often been bullied themselves
- a sense of failure at school or work – bullies take out their frustration on others
- a sense of power and success – bullies are often good at what they do and so do not want to stop
- PEER PRESSURE – some people join in simply because their friends do it or because they are afraid if they do not they will be bullied themselves
- neighbourhood culture – where violence and intimidation is a common way of behaviour.

Anyone can be bullied, but some are more likely victims than others:

- those who are different (in race, RELIGION, size or shape, ability)
- those who lack friends or are shy
- those who come from an over-protective family ENVIRONMENT.

Bullying today

Modern technology has brought many benefits but it has also helped the spread of bullying. Text messages, 'happy slapping', videos on social network sites, etc., have all contributed. Gangs use websites such as YouTube, MySpace and Bebo to glorify gang violence, for example by showing weapons in their videos to intimidate rival gangs or warn what might happen to them should they stray on to their territory. According to a recent report, one in six children aged 8 to 15 have viewed 'nasty, worrying and frightening' content on the internet. The messages that young people get influence their behaviour and they get a lot of those messages from the internet. They are susceptible to the message of following the crowd.

Source A

Holes

This source is an extract from a novel called *Holes* by Louis Sachar.

Stanley didn't have any friends at home. He was overweight and the kids often teased him about his size. Even his teachers sometimes made cruel comments without realising it.

A bully named Derrick Dunne also used to torment Stanley. The teachers never took Stanley's complaints seriously because Derrick was so much smaller than Stanley. Some teachers even seemed to find it amusing that a little kid like Derrick could pick on somebody as big as Stanley.

ACTIVITIES

1 What two surprising facts can you learn about bullies from Source A?

2 What do you think is meant by the following statements? How do they explain why some children become bullies?

   • Bullying is a way of refusing to become invisible.
   • Children fear, despise and refuse to tolerate non-conformity.
   • Power is the ability to make others suffer.

3 Look at Source B and discuss with your group whether children are more likely to inherit aggression than to acquire it from their upbringing and environment.

4 Look at Source C. Why do you think all the people mentioned were bullied? Suggest different reasons.

5 Think about mobile phones and the internet. How has modern TECHNOLOGY made the problem of bullying worse? Discuss what could be done to prevent this happening.

Source B

'Bully genes'

A recent study suggests that people who bully others are likely to have children who are also bullies. The aggression of a bully is likely to be inherited from 'bully GENES'. The findings suggest that a tendency to bully is about 60 per cent influenced by genes and 40 per cent by upbringing and environment.

Daily Telegraph, 1999

Source C

CHILDREN HAVING COSMETIC SURGERY TO ESCAPE SCHOOL BULLIES

Almost a third of girls under 16 said they would have surgery to improve their looks. For a 9-year-old boy in Scotland, the bullying was so intense he begged his parents for plastic surgery to remove a mole on his face.

Daily Mail, 28 August 2008

Choirboy Andrew Johnston, 13-year-old finalist on *Britain's Got Talent*, admits he was bullied at school.

BBC Breakfast News, 27 September 2008

ARMY INSTRUCTORS SUSPENDED

One corporal is said to have urinated on a recruit's boot. Another recruit said that his hand was so badly beaten that he could not salute properly.

The Times, 19 September 2008

POLICE SCOUR SOCIAL WEBSITES TO TACKLE YOUNG CRIMINALS

Twenty-six teenagers have died violently in London this year. One boy was beaten with a baseball bat and stabbed repeatedly after allegedly being lured into an ambush by a teenage girl. Some messages on a tribute website described the boy as a 'fallen soldier', while others carried death threats for the girl.

The Times, 18 September 2008

Effects of bullying

ACTIVITY

1 One of the main effects of conflict is that it denies certain rights and freedoms that all individuals are entitled to under the HUMAN RIGHTS ACT. This applies to small-scale conflict such as bullying, as well as to large-scale conflict. Look at the list below of some basic rights and freedoms for children, as outlined in the UN CONVENTION ON THE RIGHTS OF THE CHILD. Discuss which rights you think bullying denies and how it does this.

- Life
- Privacy
- Protection from being hurt, violence, abuse and neglect
- The best health possible and access to medical care
- Help from the government if you are poor or in need
- A good enough standard of living to develop properly
- Education
- Use your own language and practise your own CULTURE and religion
- Play and free time
- Protection from work that is bad for your health or education.

Bullying should be challenged because it has a harmful effect on its victims. Some of the main effects on victims are:

- security – they can be injured and property destroyed. Victims are sometimes tempted to carry knives or other weapons as a means of defence.
- well-being – their lives are made miserable; they can lose their SELF-ESTEEM and self-confidence; some blame themselves; some cannot sleep and become depressed; some commit suicide.
- educational progress – they cannot concentrate on their work and so their learning suffers; many are afraid to go to school and so play truant.

Bullying also affects the reputation of the community in which it takes place. For example, a school or workplace needs to be seen as effective and caring through policy and action. If it is not dealt with, bullying can provide a model for bad behaviour – if bullies are allowed to get away with it, others are encouraged to bully. Not doing anything can be taken as condoning bullying. It is therefore important that something should be done to stop bullying, wherever it occurs.

Bullying does not only have a profound effect on its victims but also on those who care for them. Some of the sources below and on page 120 illustrate this.

Source D

I'm the King of the Castle

In the novel *I'm the King of the Castle*, by Susan Hill, Charles Kingshaw and his mother are forced to move to live in an ugly, isolated Victorian house with Joseph Hooper and his son Edmund. To young Edmund, Charles is an intruder, a boy to be persecuted. On his arrival at his new home, Edmund passes him a note – 'I didn't want you to come here.' The rest of the novel concentrates on the bullying of Charles. This extract describes the tragic end to the story.

Kingshaw took all his clothes off by the stream and folded them in a pile. He shivered and the water was very cold, silky, against his body. For a second, he hesitated, part of his mind starting to come awake. And then he thought of everything, of what else would happen, he thought of the things that Hooper had done and what he was going to do ... and the wedding of his mother. He began to splash and stumble forwards, into the middle of the stream, where the water was deepest. When it had reached up to his thighs, he lay down slowly and put his face into it and breathed in a long careful breath.

It was Hooper who found him ... When he saw Kingshaw's body upside down in the water, he thought suddenly, it was because of me, and a spurt of triumph went through him.

Source E

Report of a court case in 2002

A schoolgirl broke into the house of an alleged bully and repeatedly stabbed her in the head. The victim, 14, woke up and screamed out to her mother, who rushed into the bedroom to see a figure standing over the bed, screaming, 'You have ruined my life.'

The mother intervened and pushed her daughter's attacker to the floor. The victim needed 14 stitches for wounds to her head.

Adapted from The Times, 2002

Source F

Suicide

A 13-year-old schoolgirl from South Wales took a fatal overdose to escape being bullied at her comprehensive school. Her treatment made her feel 'ugly and worthless'. She left a note saying that she wanted to die rather than walk through the school gates.

The Times, 2004

Source G

Confessions of a victim

My bullying went on for four years non-stop. I practically lost the faculty of speech and put on weight. My shyness became so severe it was almost a medical condition.

Sunday Telegraph, 1999

Source H

Crime statistics

Five deaths have occurred as a result of bullying and fighting in school in just over a decade:

- a 16-year-old boy who suffered brain damage during a playground fight in a Gateshead comprehensive in 1998
- a 15-year-old boy knifed in London in a lunch-break row
- a 12-year-old boy who died in another London playground fight
- a 14-year-old boy who was stabbed in the corridor of a Lincolnshire school.

Source I

Bully Cycle from *A Study in Child Development*

1 Students who are bullied frequently are more likely to develop depression or antisocial behaviour, which in turn makes them more likely to attract further bullying.

2 People who bully others are likely to have children who are also bullies.

Source J

He fought back, he kept smiling, he kept his head high and did not give up. He has not let you beat him. He has come out winning. He is a world champion. We are immensely proud of him.

Message to bullies from the father of Tom Daley, 15, (Britain's diving gold medal winner) to his tormentors who forced him to move schools, 22 July 2009.

ACTIVITIES

1 Study Source D on page 119. What effect did the events described have on the bully? How might this explain why bullying takes place?

2 How does the reaction of the victim of bullying in Source E differ from that in Sources F and G?

3 Using the sources and the information on pages 117–120 write a letter to a newspaper explaining why it is important to stop bullying from happening.

4 Draw a poster for your school to help prevent bullying.

The following case study considers the causes and effects of an example of national conflict – in this case, the struggle for civil rights in the USA.

Case Study
The struggle for civil rights in the USA in the 1950s and 1960s

1 Causes of the struggle

Source A

Extract from the American Declaration of Independence, 1776

All men are created equal. God gave all men life, freedom and the right to be happy.

ACTIVITIES

1 The UK CONSTITUTION holds the same values as those in Source A. In groups, discuss:
   • the ways in which we are all equal and free
   • the ways in which we are not all equal and free.

2 Read Sources A and B and the information on pages 121–123. List the causes of the conflict that developed between black and white Americans in the 1950s. Try to arrange these into long-term and short-term causes. What was the spark that ignited the conflict?

Source B

From a speech by Martin Luther King, Washington DC, 1963

I have a dream that one day this nation will rise up and live out the true meaning of its creed … that all men are created equal.

When we let freedom ring … we will be able to speed up that day when all of God's children, black men and white men, Jews and Gentiles, Protestants and Catholics, will be able to join hands and sing in the words of the old Negro spiritual, 'Free at last! Free at last! Thank God Almighty, we are free at last!'

Martin Luther King's speech in Source B was delivered almost 50 years ago. His campaign for civil rights helped make life much better for black Americans.

More than 200 years of discrimination was behind this campaign. In spite of the abolition of slavery in 1863 and amendments to the Constitution granting equal status, blacks in the southern states were deprived of their rights in the following ways:

• *politically* – STATE LAWS devised 'qualifications' for voting, which were carefully designed to exclude blacks. For example, they had to own property or be able to write
• *economically* – blacks were given the worst jobs with poor pay, or were unemployed. This inevitably meant they lived in the worst houses in the worst areas
• *socially* – some STATE GOVERNMENTS in the 1890s imposed complete racial segregation through the so-called 'Jim Crow' laws (see Source E on page 122), covering every area of life. For example, black people had their own schools, entrances to cinemas, waiting rooms at stations.

The government in Washington allowed this to happen, as it was reluctant to confront the southern politicians who strongly argued for individual states to govern themselves rather than central FEDERAL GOVERNMENT to impose laws to say how states should be run. The complex system of government and laws in the USA made intervention by central government difficult.

Source C

Michael Howard, Conservative politician

In 1963 I toured the USA. There was no official segregation but it was taken for granted that white people sat at the front and blacks at the back. In Mississippi, I deliberately sat at the back next to a black teacher. When we stopped, I suggested we got out for a cup of coffee. The teacher said, 'We can't have a cup of coffee together.' I said, 'That's ridiculous! If you can't come and have a coffee in a place reserved for whites, I'll come and have a coffee in a place where you can go!' He said, 'They'll put you in jail.' I couldn't believe that that happened in my lifetime.

The Times, 2001

ACTIVITIES

1 Read Source C on page 121 and the information on pages 121–123.
   a) What is segregation? Make a list of the ways blacks and whites were SEGREGATED.
   b) Apart from segregation, in what other ways were black Americans deprived of their civil rights?

2 Using the blue information box below, answer the following questions.
   a) Why did so many people join the KKK?
   b) What appeal would the uniform and ceremonial aspect have to these people?
   c) Why did the federal government fail to stop the KKK?

Source D

Extract from the KKK 'bible'
Are you a native born, white, gentile American? Do you believe in and will you faithfully strive for the eternal maintenance of white supremacy?

The Ku Klux Klan (KKK)

The original KKK was set up in 1866 to persecute black Americans recently freed from slavery. Apparently the name is derived from the Greek word *kyklos*, meaning circle. In the 1920s, WASP Americans (white, Anglo-Saxon, Protestants) felt threatened by non-WASP immigration. This led to a revival of the Klan. They not only attacked blacks but also Roman Catholics, Jews and all foreigners. By 1924 there were four million members, including judges, local officials, politicians, police officers and business people. Most supporters were ignorant, southern whites, who believed that they were defending the American way of life against all kinds of enemies. The rituals and uniform brought a sense of purpose and excitement to their lives. Some of their actions included LYNCHING blacks, burning crosses and firebombing homes and churches.

Source E

Jim Crow was a musical character in the theatre in the 1870s who dressed in rags and blacked up his face and made fun of black people. He came to represent the white view of blacks and his name was given to the segregation laws.

The Real History of Jim Crow.

'Him so werry scientific
Him go down to L below
And ebbery one who hear him
Dance & jump Jim Crow.'

(Moncrieff's Comic Songs)

Ku Klux Klan members. What influence might they have had on a child's socialisation?

Discrimination continues

Blacks in the northern states of the USA were also discriminated against. They were forced to live in GHETTOS, suffered segregation and persecution. In 1919, a black teenager was stoned to death in Chicago for swimming in a 'whites only' part of a lake. This incident set off a race riot that lasted a week.

During the Second World War (1939–45), many blacks joined the US forces and played a significant part in the Allied victory. After the war they expected change – they had been fighting for freedom abroad and so were no longer prepared to remain second-class citizens in their own country. Many left the south and moved to the industrial towns of the north. They hoped to share in the economic boom of the 1950s, but many failed to get jobs and were living below the poverty line. The unemployment rate for non-whites was always almost double the national rate. They were becoming disenchanted and impatient for change.

In December 1955, Rosa Parks was arrested for refusing to give up her seat on a bus in Montgomery, Alabama. Martin Luther King, a local Baptist preacher, organised a protest that involved a bus BOYCOTT by black people. This demand for integration (mixing) of the races on public transport was the beginning of the campaign for equal civil rights in the USA.

ACTIVITIES

1 Look at the graph in Source G. It shows that many more blacks than whites were illiterate. Discuss how this contributed to maintaining segregation.

2 Look at Source E opposite and the information above. Imagine you are a black teenager in Montgomery in 1955. Write a diary for one week describing your experiences. (You could mention cases of discrimination, segregation and persecution and explain how you might feel towards white Americans there.)

Source F

Civil right activist Rosa Parks

Rosa Parks got on a bus after work in a department store. Feeling tired she sat down in the black section. A few stops later when the bus was full, the driver told her to give up her seat to a white man. Her feet were hurting and feeling humiliated once too often she refused to get up. The police were called and she was arrested for defying the local bus segregation law. She was later fined $14.

Source G

A graph showing illiteracy as a percentage of the American population

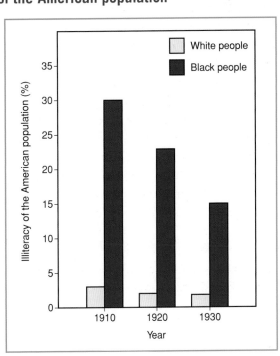

2 The struggle for civil rights

Supreme Court rulings

The Civil Rights Movement took off in the 1950s, but long before Martin Luther King there had been a campaign for equality for blacks. The National Association for the Advancement of Coloured People (NAACP) had been set up in 1905. Unfortunately, it had very little success until 1954, when the SUPREME COURT finally accepted that segregated schools were UNCONSTITUTIONAL and directed local authorities to desegregate them. In 1956, following Martin Luther King's bus boycott, the Supreme Court decided that the Alabama bus laws were illegal. In the same year, King was elected president of NAACP.

Many southern whites ignored these rulings. In September 1957, the State Governor used the NATIONAL GUARD to prevent nine black students from enrolling for the Central High School in Little Rock, Arkansas. The President of the USA had to send 1,000 federal paratroopers to ensure they got in. There was violence on a large scale as the white community fought to preserve its way of life.

It was obvious that the decisions of the Supreme Court were not enough. A civil rights law needed to be passed to ensure those decisions were carried out, and so in 1959 Martin Luther King decided to sacrifice his career as a preacher to concentrate on his work as a civil rights leader.

ACTIVITY

1 What do the events at Little Rock suggest about the strength of white opposition to the Civil Rights Movement? How do you think Elizabeth Eckford felt about white people? Use Source H in your answer.

Source H

Elizabeth Eckford at Little Rock Central High School, 1957. Elizabeth was one of the nine black students who were turned away by the National Guard.

CONFLICT AND CO-OPERATION

Peaceful protest

Martin Luther King believed in peaceful protest as the main way of resolving the conflict. Both his religious background and his admiration for the pacifist Indian leader Mahatma Gandhi made him opposed to violence.

He set up a training centre, which provided workshops for his followers, teaching them how to deal with the expected threats against them. Early action concentrated on sit-ins. Black students all over the south began to enter 'whites-only' lunch-counters. They would ask politely to be served and would not leave until served in an effort to end segregation. King often joined in and, like others, suffered attack by white on-lookers, arrest and imprisonment. The King household received threatening phone calls, 30–40 hate letters a day, and was even bombed.

Martin Luther King (1929–68) was the son of a Baptist minister who, after a good education, became a minister himself. He was convinced that non-violent resistance was the most powerful weapon available to oppressed people in their struggle for freedom.

His part in the Montgomery bus boycott made him a national hero. He often suffered for his beliefs. In 1968, he moved to Chicago to concentrate on helping the poor.

He remained committed to non-violence but became less hopeful of peaceful change after his experience of violence there.

He was shot dead on the balcony of a Memphis hotel by a white racist, James Earl Ray. This set off riots in cities across the USA.

> ### Source I
>
> #### The words of Martin Luther King, 1955
>
> We will not resort to violence. We will return hate with love. If we are arrested every day, if we are EXPLOITED every day, if we are trampled over every day, don't let anyone pull you so low as to hate them.
>
> In our protest, there will be no cross burnings. No white person will be taken from his home by a hooded Negro mob and brutally murdered. There will be no threats and intimidation. We will be guided by the highest principle of law and order.
>
> Our cause is right. If we are wrong, the Supreme Court is wrong, the Constitution of the USA is wrong, God Almighty is wrong.

In 1961, freedom rides were introduced to take the students on buses to wherever there was segregation. They met such violence and intimidation that federal troops were sent in to protect them. One bus was stopped and set on fire, while the KKK, carrying lead pipes, bats and bicycle chains, attacked another.

Source J

Children participating in a civil rights protest wait for a police van to take them to jail in Birmingham, Alabama.

Birmingham, Alabama

In 1963, the Movement focused on Birmingham, Alabama, the most segregated city in the USA. A Children's Crusade was organised – where thousands of children marched in the hope that they would grow up in a country where blacks and whites were equal. Millions of Americans saw on TV pictures of police brutality against the protestors. Powerful fire hoses were used to throw marchers against buildings and dogs were unleashed amongst them.

Newspapers also stirred the people's conscience. This created a backlash. Public opinion polls showed Americans increasingly sympathetic to the civil rights cause. President Kennedy commented, 'I can well understand why the Negroes of Birmingham are tired of being patient.'

March to Washington

In August 1963, a quarter of a million people, both black and white, took part in a march to Washington. It was there that King delivered his famous speech: 'I have a dream …' It was 100 years after the end of slavery in America. He told the crowd, 'We seek the freedom in 1963 promised us in 1863 … I have a dream that one day sons of slaves and sons of slave owners will be able to sit down together at the table of brotherhood.'

His words echoed around the world and a year later he was given the Nobel Peace Prize. His faith in non-violent resistance was partly rewarded. The black people had found their pride and a way to use it effectively. 'We got our heads up now,' one of them said, 'we won't bow down again, except before God.'

ACTIVITY

1 Look at Sources H–J (pages 124–126). How might newspaper and TV pictures of events at Little Rock and Birmingham have helped the Civil Rights Movement? In your answer, think about how the aim of the protestors contrasts to the reaction to them.

The Black Muslims

However, by this time, many blacks were becoming increasingly disillusioned with the slow pace of progress. Civil rights still seemed a long way off.

A new movement called the Black Muslims came to the forefront of the struggle. They broke away from King and challenged his policy of non-violence and the help of whites to achieve his aims. They wanted a blacks-only protest; some wanted blacks-only communities. In other words, they wanted separation. They believed in BLACK POWER and were led by Malcolm X.

Their SEPARATIST attitudes and aggressive speeches led the media to portray them as dangerous black racists in contrast to the peace-loving Martin Luther King. One of their most prominent members was Malcolm X.

Malcolm X (1925–65) was born Malcolm Little, the son of a preacher. Both of his parents were involved in the fight for black rights. He did well at school but on leaving turned to crime. He was jailed and there joined the Black Muslims and changed his name. When released, he became a Muslim preacher.

Later he broke with the Black Muslims and was converted to integration. He realised after visits to Mecca how many white Muslim 'brothers' he had and so became more forgiving towards whites. His home was bombed in 1965 and he was assassinated in 1968 by a Black Muslim.

Source K

Martin Luther King, 1963

We have waited more than 340 years for our constitutional and God-given rights. The nations of Asia and Africa are moving with jet-like speed towards gaining political independence, but we still creep at horse-and-buggy pace toward gaining a cup of coffee at a lunch-counter.

Source L

The words of Malcolm X

When a person places the proper value on freedom, there is nothing under the sun that he will not do to acquire that freedom … A man who believes in freedom will do anything under the sun to acquire … or preserve his freedom.

Source M

Malcolm X speaking in New York City, December 1964

I believe in the brotherhood of man, all men, but I don't believe in brotherhood with anybody who doesn't want brotherhood with me …
I'm not going to waste my time trying to treat somebody right who doesn't know how to return the treatment.

ACTIVITIES

1 In groups, discuss how the struggle for civil rights might have affected:
   a) a black student protester
   b) a white southern racist
   c) a white liberal (someone who believes in civil rights for all).

2 Read Sources K, L and M, and the short biographies of Martin Luther King (page 125) and Malcolm X (left).
   a) How were their views of the conflict and how to resolve it similar?
   b) How were they different?
   c) Which views most closely fit the six-step 'model' for problem solving on page 141? Give reasons.

PRESIDENT	DATE	ACTION
Harry S. Truman	1945–53	Wanted to end segregation but could not get his plans passed by a conservative CONGRESS.
Dwight D. Eisenhower	1953–61	Keen not to make an issue of civil rights because he knew it would upset many important people. Despite his lack of action, the Supreme Court declared separate schools and public facilities unconstitutional.
John F. Kennedy	1961–63	Promised a 'New Frontier' – a policy of social reform, which included equality and eliminating poverty for black people. But foreign affairs took up most of his time and little progress was made before his assassination in 1963.
Lyndon B. Johnson	1963–69	Introduced a programme called 'The Great Society' to help the disadvantaged, most of whom were black people. He did pass some important reforms, but the cost and distraction of the Vietnam War meant he could not increase spending on welfare and could not deal directly with the conditions in the black ghettos.

Source N

1954	Supreme Court declared segregated schools unconstitutional
1956	Alabama bus laws declared unconstitutional
1957	A sheriff in Mississippi beat a black man to death with a truncheon for no apparent reason. He was freed after 20 minutes of interrogation even though there were four witnesses to the murder
1959	Alabama still did not have a single integrated school
1961	Police in Jackson arrested a black woman for attempting to enter a toilet marked 'White Women'
1961	Whites tried to ban black music from local radio stations in Alabama
1964	George Wallace elected Governor of Alabama. He campaigned strongly as a firm believer in segregation
1964	The town of Selma, Alabama still kept blacks off the voting register for the most trivial reasons, for example, not dotting an 'i' on registration forms. The sheriff and two deputies beat up a black woman who tried to register
1964	Civil Rights Act
1965	Voting Rights Act
1968	Civil Rights Act
1981	A black teenager was lynched by a couple of white thugs in Mobile, Alabama. They chose the innocent victim at random
1991	Rodney King, a black car driver, was brutally beaten by white Los Angeles police officers. The incident, captured on video camera, led to the worst riots in US history: 55 people were killed, 2,383 injured and the damage caused amounted to $1 billion
2002	In Belle Glade a black unemployed handy man was apparently hanged for dating a white neighbour. The police (90 per cent white) insisted it was suicide even though the man was hanging 3 m (10 feet) up a tree. The president of the local branch of the NAACP commented 'They have not told us how he got up in that tree. They have shown no bark under his fingernails or on the souls of his shoes. It's as if he flew up there.'
2005	Hurricane Katrina led to the flooding of 80 per cent of New Orleans. The bodies of mainly black Americans rotted in the streets for days as members of the National Guard calmly looked on and ate their sandwiches. President George W. Bush was accused of 'not caring about black people'
2008	Barack Obama elected as the first black US President

Source O

Three different black people looking back on life in the 1950s

Segregation wasn't such a bad thing. You went to school, shopped and worked with black people. It was better than going into an integrated place and feeling all of those white people hating you.

Segregation wore you down. You felt you were worth less than the white man. You always got the worst schools, homes and jobs.

Over 30,000 black teachers lost their jobs when segregation ended. Many black-owned businesses and shops had to close. They could not compete with the fancy places run by whites that now had to let black people in.

The peaceful campaigning of black leaders like Martin Luther King in the 1950s and 1960s did produce some notable victories for the Civil Rights Movement and had political, economic and social effects on the lives of black people. However, progress was painfully slow because the presidents of the time found it difficult to act. The table on page 128 shows the complexity of resolving the conflict as most of the presidents were sympathetic but were not free to act as they might have wished.

Johnson did, however, introduce the following acts that addressed the inequalities the Civil Rights Movement had been fighting against.

- The 1964 Civil Rights Act made illegal all segregation and discrimination on grounds of race.
- In 1965, the Voting Rights Act ended intimidation of voters. The number of black voters rose dramatically, especially in the Deep South.
- In 1968, another Civil Rights Act made discrimination in housing illegal.

There was by now a marked improvement in the poverty statistics as non-whites moved into jobs formerly closed to them.

They also made great progress in government and politics. By 1975, over 3,000 black Americans held office; they occupied 18 seats in Congress and 278 in state governments; while 120 large towns and cities were run by non-white mayors.

Unfortunately, this progress was not maintained. Inner city ghettos still remain one of the biggest problems facing the US government, while many black people say that although they might be equal in law, in reality these laws are not always upheld and they are still discriminated against in employment and education.

Sources N–Q on pages 128–130 provide some more information on the results of the Civil Rights Movement.

ACTIVITIES

1 Give two reasons why the US presidents in the 1950s and 1960s found it difficult to give the black Americans their civil rights.

2 What can be learned from the table on page 128 about achieving conflict resolution on a national scale?

3 Study Source O and answer the following questions:
   a) Why did some people think that segregation was a good thing?
   b) Why would black people have such different views about segregation?

4 Study the table and Source N on page 128. What part was played in resolving the conflict between blacks and whites by:
   a) the American Constitution?
   b) the Supreme Court?
   c) US presidents?

5 Imagine a non-racist and a racist are arguing about segregation:

   Non-racist: 'Segregation is a cause and effect of the conflict.'

   Racist: 'Segregation is a way of resolving the conflict.'

   Explain these differences of opinion.

Source P

Martin Luther King talking at the time of the Vietnam War, 1965

We were taking the black young men who had been crippled by our society and sending them to guard the liberties in South East Asia, which they had not found in South West Georgia and in East Harlem … We can watch Negro and white boys on TV screens as they kill and die together for a nation that has been unable to seat them together in the same schools.

Source Q

Stokely Carmichael, one of the leaders of Black Power, speaking in 1969

Institutional racism keeps black people in dilapidated slum tenements, subject to the daily prey of exploitative landlords, merchants, loan sharks, etc.

International effects

In spite of disappointments at home, the Civil Rights Movement in the USA influenced similar movements elsewhere.

In South Africa, it inspired Nelson Mandela's stand against apartheid, which denied CITIZENSHIP to a vast majority of the population.

In Northern Ireland, Roman Catholic protestors copied the idea of peaceful marches in their struggle for civil rights in the 1960s. They, too, were often met by violence.

It could even be claimed that the struggle for equality for blacks has naturally developed into a struggle for equality for all persecuted minorities, including women. The WOMEN'S LIBERATION MOVEMENT sprang to life in the 1960s.

A civil rights protest in South Africa.

ACTIVITIES

1 Copy and complete the table below on the effects of the civil rights struggle. Indicate the ways the black people have benefited (+) and how things have remained the same or changed for the worse (–). Some examples have been done for you.

Effects	Short term	Long term
Political	+ Black people allowed to vote	+
	–	–
Economic	+	+
	– 30,000 teachers lost their job	–
Social	+	+
	–	– Ghettoes still remain

2 Study Sources N (page 128), P and Q (above). Discuss in groups whether you think the reforms of the 1950s and 1960s created a just and equal society in the USA.

3 Design the front page of a newspaper for 5 April 1968 – the day Martin Luther King was shot. It should contain mention of the assassination, his involvement in the Civil Rights Movement and the effect his death is likely to have on race relations in the USA.

4 What has been the significance of the Civil Rights Movement in the USA to the rest of the world?

The USA today

On 4 November 2008, Barack Obama was elected the first black American President, allowing a black family to move into the White House – the most desirable address into the country. This symbolised a moment of true racial progress. However, the privileged lives of the Obamas now serve as a reminder of the inequalities still existing in America (see Source R). Barack Obama himself had declared during his campaign to be President: 'In this country – of all countries – no child's destiny should be determined before he takes his first steps. No little girl's future should be confined to the neighbourhood she was born into.' This was a recognition of the challenge he faces in turning electoral promise into lasting social reform.

Source R

A list of the disadvantages facing a black woman growing up in the USA

- Over 70 per cent of black children are born to single mothers.

- A black baby girl is more likely to contract childhood diseases such as asthma and diabetes.

- She will be more prone to obesity (being overweight).

- She is much more likely to end up in an under-funded and under-staffed school, where her grades are likely to be significantly lower than those of white students of the same age.

- She can expect to live five years less than a white woman.

- Throughout her life she will be paid on average less than two-thirds of an average white man's wage.

- She is likely to face problems affording a house in a neighbourhood free of drug dealers.

Adapted from an article by Tony Allen Mills,
Sunday Times, 9 November 2008

Source S

Nelson Mandela, on President Obama's election

'Your victory has demonstrated that no person anywhere in the world should not dare to dream of wanting to change the world for a better place.'

Source T

He had a dream – now it's true

Sunday Times, 9 November, 2008

ACTIVITIES

1 Study Sources R–T above. Do you think Barack Obama's election as President (referred to in Sources S and T) will bring an end to the inequalities highlighted in Source R?

2 Look again at pages 125–127. Whose methods did Barack Obama follow most – those of Martin Luther King or those of Malcolm X? Give reasons for your answer.

What are the causes and effects of international conflict?

Case Study
The Vietnam War, 1963–75

1 Causes of the conflict

Background

In 1939, Vietnam, Laos and Cambodia were part of French Indo-China. They had been COLONISED by France in the nineteenth century. During the Second World War (1939–45), Japan occupied the area to gain control of valuable NATURAL RESOURCES such as rice, coal and rubber. The Japanese treated the people badly – millions starved to death. In response, organised RESISTANCE GROUPS were formed. One of them was the League for the Independence of Vietnam (or Vietminh). It was mainly communist and led by Ho Chi Minh. It carried out a GUERRILLA CAMPAIGN against the Japanese.

Source A

Two superpowers – USA and USSR – battle it out.

In August 1945, Japan surrendered. The Second World War was over, but the twentieth century's longest war soon began. It was to decide who should now rule Vietnam – the French or the Vietminh. The French tried to re-take Vietnam, but Ho Chi Minh would not let them. War broke out.

Source B

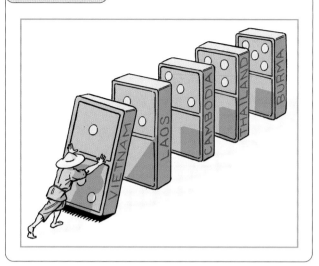

Source C

US President Eisenhower, 1954

You have a row of dominoes … You knock over the first one. What will happen to the last one is the certainty that it will go over very quickly. Asia has already lost some 450 million of its people to communist dictatorships. We simply can't afford greater losses.

This was the era of the Cold War. At the end of the Second World War, the USA and the Soviet Union had emerged as the two superpowers, soon both to possess nuclear weapons. They believed in very different ideologies, namely CAPITALISM and COMMUNISM. Both countries were very suspicious of each other and sought to establish their own spheres of influence. The state of tension and rivalry that existed between them is referred to as the Cold War as they avoided direct military confrontation. The USA decided on a policy of containment – to contain communism to the countries where it had already taken hold. They applied this policy in South East Asia, based on the 'domino theory' – the idea that countries were closely linked together and if one fell to communism, the others would follow (see Sources A, B and C).

ACTIVITY

1 Study Sources A, B and C above. How did the domino theory help to bring about America's involvement in the Vietnam War?

The USA gave nearly $3 million to help the French oppose the spread of communism. China, which had become communist in 1949, gave military supplies to the Vietminh. In 1954, the war came to an end with the decisive communist victory at Dien Bien Phu.

Peace talks

Peace talks were held at Geneva. According to the Geneva Agreement, Vietnam was split temporarily along the line of the 17th parallel. The North became a communist republic under Ho Chi Minh and the South a democratic republic under Ngo Dinh Diem. An election was to be held for the whole country in two years so that it could be united again.

The election was never held. Diem knew that many in the South were supporters of Ho Chi Minh and an election would turn all of Vietnam into a communist country. The USA also feared this and so supported Diem's government of South Vietnam despite the fact that it was corrupt and unpopular.

Civil war breaks out

In 1959, Ho Chi Minh issued orders to the communists in the South to rebel against Diem's government. They became known as the 'Vietcong' (Vietnamese communists). Civil war soon started with most of the peasants on the communist side.

US involvement increases

In 1961, John F. Kennedy became US President. He wanted to be seen as tough on communism. He realised American money and arms had not saved Diem, so he decided to send more advisers and military experts. In the meantime, Diem's government was becoming more and more unpopular. In November 1963, it was overthrown and Diem was shot dead. A few weeks later, Kennedy was also shot dead.

The next President, Lyndon B. Johnson decided to get even more involved. The US navy patrolled the coast of Vietnam. In August 1964, the North Vietnamese attacked a US destroyer in the Gulf of Tonkin. This gave Johnson the excuse to escalate the war.

Congress passed a law to allow the army to fight a full-scale war against the North (the Tonkin Resolution). It has been recently accepted that the Johnson government manipulated intelligence in this incident to go to war, that is, they made up the story of the attack on the US destroyer.

Ho Chi Minh was the son of a peasant. He came to Europe as a young man. He was first and foremost a NATIONALIST who wanted to get rid of the French from his country. He became a communist because the USSR promised to help all peoples struggling for independence from foreign rule.

Source D

South East Asia in 1954.

1 Look at page 133. What were the strengths and weaknesses of the Geneva Agreement (1954) as a means of resolving conflict?

2 Look at Sources A–E (pages 132–134) and explain why the USA was ready to get involved in Vietnam.

3 List three stages of US involvement, showing how it escalated.

4 'The USA were right to support the corrupt government of South Vietnam.' Discuss this statement.

5 Different countries had different reasons to become involved in the conflict in Vietnam. Copy the table below and fill in reasons why they wanted to become involved. Some examples have been done for you.

Reasons for going to war in Vietnam

	France	Japan	USA	Government South Vietnam	Government North Vietnam
Political		To build an empire			
Economic	To gain resources				
Social					To bring equality to the peasants
Moral			To maintain freedom		

Source E

The Tonkin Resolution, Johnson's message to US Congress, August 1964

- North Vietnam has broken the Geneva Agreement of 1954.

- The USA will continue to help all nations of South East Asia to defend their freedom from communism.

- The USA will promote the maintenance of international peace and security in South East Asia.

Investigation

The Tonkin incident never happened – the US government misled its people to provide an excuse for intervention in Vietnam. The British government has been accused of similar deception regarding Saddam Hussein's possession of WMDs (weapons of mass destruction) as the reason for invading Iraq in 2003 (Operation Iraqi Freedom). Research Operation Iraqi Freedom to find similarities between this and the Gulf of Tonkin incident as a cause of an international conflict.

2 Effects of the conflict

One hundred and fifty thousand US marines arrived in Vietnam in early 1965. By 1969, there were half a million. During the war, 200,000 South Vietnamese soldiers, one million North Vietnamese soldiers, over 50,000 US soldiers and 500,000 civilians were killed. The war destroyed 50 per cent of the country's forest cover and 20 per cent of agricultural land.

Vietcong tactics

1 Booby-traps – the Vietcong hid in a network of tunnels which ran for 320 km (200 miles) in South Vietnam. These tunnels were often heavily booby-trapped to avoid capture. Sharpened bamboo stakes were camouflaged in shallow pits. Trip wires tied to grenades were strung along paths or in shallow water.

2 Guerilla warfare – the Vietcong had no aircraft, no tanks and no artillery, but they were experienced guerrilla fighters. They avoided open battle in which US equipment and weaponry would be decisive. Instead, they attacked the enemy when they least expected it and then ran away to hide amongst the peasants. Many peasants actually helped them – working in the fields by day and joining in raids at night.

3 The Tet Offensive – in January 1968, during the Vietnamese New Year or Tet holiday, 70,000 Vietcong attacked 100 towns and cities in South Vietnam in a dramatic departure from the usual guerrilla warfare. They fought conventional battles in urban areas. The objective was to break the deadlock in Vietnam and convince the USA that they could not win the war. But the tactic failed – although the offensive only lasted a month, the Vietcong suffered heavy losses (45,000 killed). However, it did have the effect of turning the US media against the war. The photo below shows the bombing of Saigon.

US tactics

The USA had a variety of tactics in Vietnam to win the war but these tactics were not very successful.

1 'Operation Rolling Thunder' – a bombing campaign over North Vietnam to destroy supply routes along the Ho Chi Minh Trail, which ran through Laos and Cambodia. The USSR and China sent up to 6,000 tonnes of supplies along this route each day. Three times more bombs were dropped here by the US air force than were dropped in the whole of the Second World War. The worst bombs were cluster bombs, which exploded in the air and released up to 600 smaller bombs.

2 Search and destroy – the aim was to flush out the Vietcong hiding in the jungle. This was impossible as it was very difficult to distinguish between a member of the Vietcong and an ordinary peasant.

3 Strategic hamlets – they turned the peasants out of their homes and put them in squalid camps to prevent them helping the Vietcong.

4 'Winning hearts and minds' (WHAM) – the Americans hoped that the people of South Vietnam would join them in the war against the Vietcong. They were given farming advice and support, schools were built and children were inoculated. However, this tactic failed as the US army was accused of trying to tell the people how to run their own country.

5 Chemical warfare – as the enemy could not be seen, the Americans sprayed Agent Orange to defoliate the trees and destroy crops. Traces of it contaminated the water and caused cancer. Napalm (a bomb which exploded and showered victims with a petroleum jelly that burnt at 800°C) was used to clear undergrowth.

The bombing of Saigon, 1968.

ACTIVITIES

1 a) What advantages did the Americans have in pitched battles against the Vietcong?

b) What advantages did guerrilla warfare offer the Vietcong?

2 Why do you think the Americans failed to win over the 'hearts and minds' of the people of South Vietnam even though they fought on their side? Has the same thing happened recently after their involvement in Iraq and Afghanistan?

3 What impact did foreign intervention have on the Vietnam War?

South Vietnamese civilians training to be guerrillas.

Effects on views about war

The Vietnam War convinced the people involved and observers of the futility of war. It was a lesson that the use of modern weaponry and the intervention of superpowers is no guarantee of resolving conflict. Robert McNamara, the US Defence Secretary at the time and the man responsible for escalating the war has recently admitted that they were wrong. He said that the toughest issues relating to Vietnam had not been foreseen and believed that the same was true of the war in Iraq.

Effects on morale

American soldiers

At the end of the conflict, the morale of US troops was at an all time low. Most of them were DRAFTED and only served a year in Vietnam, which meant they were not professional soldiers and were inexperienced. They were not committed to the cause and could not see what the war had to do with them. There was tension between black and white soldiers. The blacks did not want to fight the white man's war (this was the time of

the Civil Rights Movement, see pages 121–131). The officers were regular soldiers and so were more committed. Three per cent were killed by their own troops for putting their lives at risk (this was known as 'fragging' as fragmented grenades were used).

The constant heat, rain and mosquitoes depressed many soldiers. They tried to escape the horrors of war by taking drugs such as marijuana or 'speed' to keep them alert in the jungle. They became very racist towards the Vietnamese, calling them 'gooks'. Between 1966–73 there were over half a million incidents of desertion.

Vietcong soldiers

Their morale was better as they were fighting for two causes (communism and NATIONALISM) and were backed by the peasants. But even they suffered as they lacked supplies and weapons, and spent a great deal of time in hiding underground.

At home in the USA

By 1967, US opinion began to turn against the war as horrifying images on TV shocked many people. They realised that the cost was too high in terms of men and money ($20 billion a year). The media took on an anti-war attitude and said that it was illegal and immoral. They informed the people that they had been misled and were not being told the truth about casualties.

Dramatic images such as the shooting of a Vietcong prisoner in the head (see photo below) made Americans feel ashamed. Revelations of torture under the supervision of the CIA, the mutilation of bodies and the collection of body parts as trophies were evidence of serious war crimes.

The final straw was a press report of the My Lai massacre of between 300–500 civilians by a US platoon led by Lieutenant Calley (March 1968). Calley was convicted of murder in 1971 and was sentenced to life imprisonment, but only served three and a half years.

These events illustrated the deterioration taking place in the behaviour of US troops and undermined the arguments about the need to save Vietnam from 'the evils of communism'. As one mother of an accused soldier said, 'I sent them [US army] a good boy, and they made him a murderer.'

The Saigon Chief of Police shoots a Vietcong prisoner during the Tet Offensive (see page 135).

Opposition to the war

Opposition came from many quarters: pacifists were against the war on moral and religious grounds; LIBERALS felt the people of Vietnam were fighting for freedom and their own country; while the great majority thought the war was not the USA's concern. Protests included DRAFT-DODGING and the burning of draft cards. Mohammad Ali was the most famous to refuse to fight – he explained, 'No Vietnamese called me a nigger.' Students went on protest marches (half a million marched to Washington in 1971). Martin Luther King denounced the sending of blacks to fight for a country that treated them so badly at home (see Source P on page 130). The film star Jane Fonda became known as 'Hanoi Jane' for her involvement in demonstrations. Ex-soldiers formed 'Vietnam Veterans Against the War'. Below are some anti-war slogans and extracts from anti-war songs.

ACTIVITIES

1 Work in a group of three. Each person in the group must take the part of one of the following:
   a) A US soldier.
   b) A Vietcong soldier.
   c) A member of the American public.
   Prepare a short play for the class as a discussion between these three people about why the USA should withdraw from the Vietnam War.

2 Design an anti-war poster for the Vietnam War or the war in Afghanistan – you could use the slogans in the picture above or make up your own slogan.

3 What part did the US media play in spreading opposition to the war?

After the war

The Vietnam War created doubts about American judgement, about the reputation of America, about American power and not only at home but throughout the world.

Henry Kissinger

The Vietnam War was the first war the USA had lost. Before the war Americans had great trust in their leaders and their government. After the exposure in the media of how they had been lied to, they lost their innocence. Americans began to feel other nations should determine their own destinies and that the USA should take a less active role in foreign policy.

For a period also the USA seemed to have lost its ability to provide decisive leadership of the Western world. Its allies in turn began to re-think their commitment to the USA. Not until recently and the wars against Iraq, in Afghanistan and against terrorism has the USA again taken the lead. However, the growing cost of these wars in both lives and money has led to further disillusionment.

Summary of the effects of the war

	SHORT-TERM EFFECTS	LONG-TERM EFFECTS
Political	The USA had lost its first war. Vietnam turned Johnson into the most unpopular US President in history. He did not stand for re-election. The domino theory was proved wrong. Vietnam, Laos and Cambodia became communist but not the rest of South East Asia, which remained unstable.	The Vietnam War played its part in ending the Cold War. The superpowers realised the danger of war and moved towards *DÉTENTE*. President Nixon visited China and the USSR, and the superpowers agreed to limit how many nuclear missiles they built. Americans lost interest in foreign affairs.
Social	Two million people were killed. Millions more were injured or lost their homes. Many American GIs deserted or became addicted to drugs. The war gave a boost to the Civil Rights Movement in the USA. Increase of racism: both between US soldiers and the Vietnamese, and between black and white soldiers in the US army.	Many mines and booby-traps are still in Vietnam, while the people continue to suffer from the effects of chemicals and defoliants. Two million people fled from Vietnam to escape famine and communism. These included 1 million 'boat people', who tried to sail away (many drowned). Many American GIs found it difficult to readjust to civilian life. They felt betrayed because they were often treated as war criminals rather than heroes. Half a million suffered from 'post-traumatic stress disorder'. This often led to alcoholism, drug addiction and divorce. Many found it difficult to find work. More have committed suicide since the war than were killed in the fighting.
Economic	The fighting cost the USA $120 billion, which meant that the US government was unable to spend money on much needed welfare reform so that poverty and racial inequalities continued.	Vietnam was united as a communist country, but a devastated one with its economy in ruins. From being a major exporter of rice, Vietnam was reduced to a country unable to feed itself.

ACTIVITY

1 Choose any two of the following and write about 300 words in a letter to a friend describing the social and economic effects of the war on:
   a) the Vietcong
   b) a South Vietnamese peasant
   c) a US marine.

Investigation

Carry out research about:

- mistreatment of prisoners at Abu Ghraib prison or at Camp X, Guantánamo Bay during the 2003–04 Iraq war
- protests against the war in Iraq in London.

Compare what you have found out with what you have learned about similar events relating to the Vietnam War.

3 Resolving the conflict

There are many ways of resolving international conflict, as we will see on pages 144–145. Not all of these methods were used in Vietnam. APPEASEMENT and SANCTIONS, for instance, were never considered as they were not practical. Negotiation was difficult because:

- communism and capitalism represent very different ideals
- the strong nationalism of the Vietnamese meant they were completely against the division of their country
- the interference of outside powers, each with their own agenda, complicated matters.

Nevertheless, listed below are some of the methods that were tried.

1 Force

Both sides used force – initially in the hope of a quick end to the conflict, but then as a means of continuing the conflict in the hope that the enemy would give in. All force achieved was an escalation of the war. The ensuing suffering also meant there was less likelihood of either side compromising with each other.

2 Deterrent

The possession of nuclear weapons by both the USA and the USSR prevented a full-scale war, but it also meant that both the USA and the USSR could only fight or support a limited war, which gave both sides less chance of winning.

3 Protest

The peace movement with its anti-war demonstrations played a major role in ending the conflict. When the American public turned against the war, the politicians were forced to negotiate.

4 International co-operation

In 1968, President Johnson decided to seek an end to the fighting and started peace talks. Each time the US government tried to involve the UN in talks the North Vietnamese refused to co-operate. They

By 1968, a large number of Americans were against the war and politicians began to look for a way out. This photo shows a student anti-Vietnam rally in Iowa, 5 November 1968. The demonstration was staged on the steps of the Iowa capitol building after a 5-km (3-mile) march under police supervision.

insisted that the US forces leave Vietnam first. Johnson's successor, Richard Nixon began the policy of Vietnamisation, which meant pulling troops out and leaving South Vietnam to defend itself.

Talks now began but it took five years of negotiations in Paris before an agreement was finally reached (January, 1973). The South Vietnamese had objected to the Vietcong being present while the USA and the North Vietnamese were reluctant to make any concessions. When a settlement was finally agreed, the US representative, Dr Henry Kissinger, and the Vietnamese delegate were awarded the Nobel Peace Prize between them. This was indeed a tremendous achievement when seen in the context of the Cold War. However, relations between East and West had been improving because of DÉTENTE. Neither side had wished to jeopardise this.

The war still dragged on for a further two years because the government of South Vietnam would not give up. They finally surrendered and in 1976 North and South Vietnam were united at last as an independent nation.

ACTIVITIES

1 Look at the table below. Was the USA right or wrong to get involved in the war in Vietnam? For each argument in column 1, put a tick in column 2 if you think it is an argument for US involvement. Put a tick in column 3 if you think it is an argument against.

Argument	For	Against
Use of force by North Vietnam against terms of 1954 Geneva Agreement.		
Only use of force can stop communism taking over in South Vietnam.		
Might lead to Third World War.		
Doing nothing will encourage the USSR and China elsewhere.		
Action will encourage the USSR and China to get involved.		
Talking is the only sensible way to resolve conflict.		
A democracy should not support an undemocratic government.		
Stability in South East Asia is vital to the West.		
If South Vietnam falls, other Asian states will follow (domino theory).		
The war is a civil war: foreign countries should not interfere.		

2 Do you think the countries involved in the Vietnam War acted to make a better world or acted in their best interests? Support your argument. Consider both noble motives (peace, support of communism or democracy) and selfish interests (control of resources, power).

3 Explain why the causes and effects of the Vietnam War made it difficult to resolve. For causes, you could include the number of countries involved, resources and superpower rivalry. For effects, mention the cost, suffering and hatred that the war produced.

4 In groups, imagine that you are members of the UN trying to end the conflict in Vietnam in 1968. Use the six-step problem solving method outlined on page 141. Write down what action you would take for each step.

5 Draw a spider diagram showing how the results of the war not only affected Vietnam but also other countries. Show how some results lead on to others.

6 The twentieth century was the bloodiest in all of history – 160 million human beings were killed in conflict. As a class, discuss how we can avoid similar bloodshed in this century.

7 Choose any national or international conflict you have studied and copy and fill in the boxes below to show how it had a range of causes and effects. It may not be possible to fill in all of the boxes.

A political cause	A political effect	An effect that is also a cause
A religious cause	A religious effect	An attempt to resolve conflict
An economic cause	An economic effect	A reason for failing to resolve the conflict
A moral cause	A moral effect	How the conflict ended
A social cause	A social effect	

CONCEPT 4

Different methods can be used to resolve conflict and work towards co-operation

There is a range of methods and strategies that can be used to resolve or prevent conflict. Some may be better than others in particular contexts. Each of us has a choice in the ways we respond to and manage conflict through developing negotiation and problem-solving skills.

In this concept section the focus will be on:

- A range of methods and strategies and their effectiveness in resolving/preventing conflict.

The following are ideas and terms that you will need to know from this concept section:

United Nations • negotiation • arbitration • pacifism • force • sanctions • protest • counselling

How can conflict be resolved?

ACTIVITIES

1 What do you think the message of Source A is?

2 Look at the six steps of problem solving below. How might this method have worked in resolving one of the conflicts studied on pages 103–104?

The resolution of a conflict requires the underlying causes to be addressed. There has to be some form of co-operation. This means acting or working together with others to achieve a common goal.

Talking to each other is a good starting point. A meeting allows both sides to put over their point of view and to NEGOTIATE. One way of resolving a conflict is the six-step solution.

Six-step problem solving
1 Identify each side's needs.
2 Define the problem.
3 Brainstorm solutions.
4 Evaluate solutions.
5 Decide on best solution and try it.
6 Check how things turn out.

Methods of resolving small-scale conflict

Sometimes it is necessary for an INTERMEDIARY or third party to become involved. For instance, a couple might try to save their marriage by going to a counsellor (an adviser); a dispute at work could be taken to an INDUSTRIAL TRIBUNAL.

The third party is, however, unlikely to succeed without some give and take on behalf of those involved in the conflict. In other words, MEDIATION has to lead to compromise.

In some disputes, there is no obvious third party to refer to, so it might be necessary to approach someone or some organisation that both sides respect, for example, the Church. In other instances, there are obvious places to go for ARBITRATION, for example, ACAS (Advisory, Conciliation and Arbitration Service). This is an organisation that hears both sides of an industrial dispute and decides the outcome. In 2009, for example, ACAS were involved in consultations between Vodafone and its staff over redundancies.

When all else fails, force or punishment might have to be used.

Source A

'THE TWO MULES'

CO-OPERATION
IS BETTER THAN CONFLICT

METHODS OF RESOLVING PERSONAL OR LOCAL CONFLICT

THIRD-PARTY INTERMEDIARY

Advantage – Neutral, unbiased, unemotional.

Disadvantage – Compromise still has to be reached.

Example – Marriage counsellor.

ARBITRATION

Advantage – Experienced professional decides outcome.

Disadvantage – Compromise might still be required, verdict might be ignored.

Example – ACAS.

NEGOTIATION

Advantage – Allows both sides to put across their point of view.

Disadvantage – Might inflame situation.

Example – Meeting between hostile neighbours.

PROTEST

Advantage – Gains publicity.

Disadvantage – Can upset those not involved in dispute.

Example – Stunts of Fathers 4 Justice.

FORCE

Advantage – Acts as a deterrent.

Disadvantage – Leads to bitterness.

Examples – Punishment (fines, imprisonment, etc.).

Case Study
Bullying – resolving conflict

Source A

Janet Clare was in her kitchen when she overheard her daughter and friends saying unpleasant things and telling stories, which showed they had been needling a particular girl. When the others had gone, she confronted her daughter. She said, 'I would feel horrible if people were saying those things about me. How would you feel?' Her daughter said nothing, just looked down at the table. But then, a few months later, she announced suddenly, 'I used to be a bully. But I stopped doing it because you said something.'

The Times, 2004

ACTIVITY

1 Look at Source A. This shows how a parent can help stop bullying. In groups, discuss how you as students can help stop bullying.

Not all scenarios are so easily resolved as in Source A, but both at school and at work attempts have been made to deal with the problem of bullying. The diagram below helps you understand different methods that could be used in school.

Most schools now have an official policy on bullying, although many do not like to admit that the problem exists. There is also the danger that highlighting or talking about bullying might encourage it.

1. Exclusion
Bullies are removed to special centres for problem children. Such centres are not popular with local residents.

2. Assertiveness training
Teaching students how to leave a bullying situation and get support from bystanders. Attempting to boost their SELF-ESTEEM.

3. Quality circles (qc)
This idea comes from industry where discussion circles are used. This encourages students to discuss and come up with their own solutions to bullying by:
- Identifying the problem.
- Analysing the problem – considering possible causes and establishing the extent of the problem by collecting data through surveys, interviews or observations.
- Developing a solution – such as improved supervision, a playground development plan to get rid of danger areas, drama to raise awareness, activities at lunchtime to avoid boredom (a known cause of bullying).
- Presenting the solution to the school management.
- Reviewing the solution – the solution is tried and evaluation takes place to see if it worked.

4. Student mediators
Training students in basic MEDIATION TECHNIQUES, such as listening to both sides, showing no bias, and asking the warring students to come up with their own solution to their argument. The 'peacemakers' then mediate, rather formally, over a school desk. The idea is that peer pressure can be used to reduce conflict and bullying rather than persuading bullied students to go to the teachers for help, as this risks further harassment for 'telling tales'.

7. Surveillance
The use of CCTV to catch and deter bullies.

6. Behaviour management
Students are taught to understand and control their emotions. Disruptive students are helped to channel their anger and aggression into positive relationships and more effective learning. Schools that teach this claim that students are less stressed, achieve better results, possess better INTERPERSONAL SKILLS and can 'manage conflicts'.

5. 'No blame' approach
Under this system no one is blamed or punished. Instead, with their teachers' help, the children work out solutions. This approach works on the idea that bullying is normal human behaviour. The bully is not labelled as a bully, but seen as simply a person whose behaviour needs to be changed. KIDSCAPE, the anti-bullying charity, believes that the method will produce a generation of violent louts which takes no responsibility for the consequences of its actions.

Some of the methods used by schools to resolve the problem of bullying. Which of the methods listed here do you think would be most effective?

ACTIVITIES

1 List all the methods 1–7 given in the diagram above in rank order according to how you think they would work. Give a mark out of 10 for each method.

2 Choose one of the methods 1–7 and list all its advantages and disadvantages.

Source A

Code of advice
The website Bully OnLine has the following advice for someone being bullied at work.
- Recognise that you are being bullied.
- Realise that it is not your fault.
- Tell the bully that his/her actions are unacceptable.
- Inform your manager/personnel department.
- Keep a diary of what happens.
- Keep copies of letters, memos, emails.
- Build a support network (friends, family).
- See your doctor if the bullying causes you stress.
- Record a formal grievance.

Bullying at work

In the past, victims of bullying at work have gone to industrial tribunals or court. But this involves asking people to go through a legal process that could be damaging to them emotionally.

Recently, some firms have set up harassment advice services. Staff are invited to ring a hotline if they feel they are being bullied. An adviser then organises a face-to-face meeting.

Some trade unions are also promoting the idea of independent OMBUDSMEN to handle unresolved complaints.

ACTIVITIES

1 Develop a code of advice, like the one in Source A on page 143, for a victim of bullying at school.

2 Design your own website for victims of bullying.

3 Having looked at all the evidence in this section (pages 142–144), explain why you think it is difficult to find a perfect solution to the problem of bullying.

City worker Helen Green suffered a nervous breakdown after years of being bullied in the workplace. A court later awarded her £800,000 compensation for the trauma she had endured.

Methods of resolving international conflict

Just like individuals or groups, nations also have to seek to end conflict, often using a variety of methods.

The Palestine–Israeli conflict (see page 103) has still not been resolved after nearly a century. In September 2008, at a concert in Tel Aviv, Sir Paul McCartney was again pleading to the crowd to 'Give peace a chance'. Terrorist activities (car bombing, kidnapping, etc.) on both sides continue and not just in the Middle East. Nine thousand Palestinians, including hundreds of children merely involved in stone-throwing, are held in Israeli jails.

The two sides still can't agree on where the border between them should lie, and can't even agree among themselves on whether to keep the talks going. There are HAWKS and DOVES on both sides.

Many Israelis are more worried about the nuclear threat from Iran. Outside powers – the USA and the EU – are unwilling to negotiate directly with Hamas, the militant group in Palestine. So, after all this time, there seems to be no end in sight.

Methods	Examples and comments
Appeasement	In 1939, the British Prime Minister, Neville Chamberlain, thought that he had guaranteed 'peace in our time' at Munich by getting Hitler to make a written promise not to seize more land. But his policy of APPEASEMENT (a form of PACIFISM) failed to prevent the Second World War.
Force	In Afghanistan, in 2002, and Iraq, in 2003–04, the US President, George Bush, preferred force as an instrument to ultimately end terrorism. This does not seem to have worked in the short term, but it might be too early to judge. Certainly, in the Second World War, the use of force was important in saving democracy from fascism.
Protest	Greenpeace activists scaled Big Ben as part of a non-violent protest against the war in Iraq. This protest was completely ignored by the governments involved. However, protest can work – for example, Gandhi's methods of peaceful demonstrations gained independence for India from the British Empire in 1947.
Sanctions	Sanctions against Iraq, Cuba and Libya by various Western governments have failed to make them change their ways. These sometimes make the country more determined while denying food and medicine to millions of innocent people. On the other hand, the use of sanctions against South Africa helped bring an end to APARTHEID.
Deterrent	Building up weapons as a deterrent is sometimes seen as making conflict less likely. For example, Pakistan and India have both developed nuclear weapons and know that if they went to war they could both completely destroy each other. This makes the decision to go to war less likely. However, increasing armaments failed to prevent the First World War (1914–18).
Improving links	In India and Pakistan, an agreement was made in 2004, after nearly 50 years of non-contact, to play test cricket against each other in an attempt to ease tension.
International co-operation	Undoubtedly the greatest attempt to resolve conflict in the last 50 years has been the setting up of the UN in 1945. The UN is an international organisation, which attempts to resolve conflict and problems throughout the world. It has achieved great success in many areas through its various agencies, but has failed to prevent or stop many modern wars.

ACTIVITY

1 a) List the methods of resolving conflict in Source B above and give each a rating out of 10 (with 10 being very effective and 1 being least effective).

  b) Discuss your ratings and the strengths and weaknesses of each method in groups.

  c) In your group, decide on which you think is the most and the least effective.

  d) Feed back to the class with your reasons and listen to the other groups' reasons for their choice.

  e) Take a class vote on which you think is the most effective and the least effective.

Investigation

Carry out an investigation into how the UN or one of its agencies attempts to resolve conflict.

The UN

Formed after the Second World War, the UN aims to:

- maintain international peace and security
- develop friendly relations among nations
- achieve international CO-OPERATION
- encourage respect for human rights and fundamental freedoms.

PREJUDICE AND PERSECUTION

INTRODUCTION

This chapter will help you understand more fully the meaning of prejudice and persecution. The chapter is based on four concepts:

1. There are different causes of prejudice.
2. There are different forms of prejudice and discrimination against individuals and groups.
3. There are different causes and effects of persecution.
4. Different methods can be used to reduce or resolve prejudice, discrimination and persecution.

In your work on culture and beliefs you will have learned about agents of SOCIALISATION, which help mould us as individuals by giving us our BELIEFS, VALUES and ATTITUDES. Prejudice is an attitude that can lead to PERSECUTION.

Prejudice and persecution can occur at different levels and in different contexts:

- A personal and individual level
- A local and community level
- A national level (within a country)
- An international level (involving other countries or the whole world).

Each of the concepts listed in the box above is covered in this chapter, but Concepts 1 and 2 are combined together to consider the different causes and forms of prejudice and DISCRIMINATION against individuals and groups. In the specification there are three case studies outlined for each of Concepts 2, 3 and 4. Here the single case study is used to cover three concepts in order to show clearly:

- The range of different forms of prejudice and discrimination.
- The way prejudice leads to discrimination.
- The attitudes and actions of the government of one state against individuals and groups leading to persecution.

- The causes and effects of persecution.
- The methods used to prevent prejudice and discrimination.

The intention of the unit is to help you understand why we should fight prejudice at the earliest opportunity before it leads to its logical conclusion of persecution on a horrendous scale.

ACTIVITY

1 List three advantages to SOCIETY of young people learning about the dangers of prejudice.

What are prejudice and persecution?

Prejudice

Prejudice is an attitude about a person or group that is formed without having all the facts – that is, pre-judging someone. It usually involves disliking someone because of their class, GENDER, ETHNICITY, age, SEXUALITY, RELIGION, etc., rather than because of their personality.

Prejudiced attitudes are learned. We are not born with them. We develop them through socialisation (involving family, peers, school, media, etc.) (see pages 17–18). For example, children in Nazi Germany were taught to hate Jews (anti-Semitism) (see pages 154–159).

Discrimination

Prejudice often influences our behaviour and leads to discrimination. Discrimination is treating someone differently, usually less well, because they belong to a particular group.

Moreover, governments can also be guilty of SYSTEMATIC DISCRIMINATION against certain groups so they are treated unequally in law. A good example of this is the Jim Crow laws in the southern states of the USA (see page 122).

A

B

C

D

E

F

1 a) Study the drawings on the left and match the captions below to the pictures.

i) By law, organisations do not have to provide a prayer room. But if you request use of a quiet place that is available and are refused, this could amount to discrimination.

ii) 'I can't even go out for a night on the tiles – just because pubs, clubs and venues don't think about their disabled customers.'

iii) 1.8 million people between the ages of 55 and 64 have experienced AGEISM in their job.

iv) In 2004, a black woman was turned away from a hotel in Chorley. She was suspicious and asked a friend to phone them. The friend was told there were three free rooms.

v) Every year, in England and Wales alone, around 1,000 women take legal action against their employer claiming they were sacked because of their pregnancy.

vi) Private members' clubs, such as golf clubs, can choose to be men-only or have men-only areas – such as the clubhouse – as they are exempt from the Sexual Discrimination Act.

b) What do we learn from these examples about discrimination in Britain?

c) What have all the victims of discrimination got in common?

d) What attitude is held towards each of the victims of discrimination?

PREJUDICE AND PERSECUTION

There are different forms of prejudice and discrimination. Activity 1 on page 147 should have started you thinking about some of these such as disability, gender, religion, age and ethnicity.

Many women, for example, have experienced a glass ceiling – a barrier that prevents them from gaining promotion to top jobs (see Source A).

Source A

Women face a ceiling of reinforced concrete rather than glass in their efforts to advance in politics and business. New research reveals that there were fewer women MPs, Cabinet members, senior police officers, judges, NHS executives, etc., than a year ago. So things are changing for women at the top at a snail's pace.

Susan Thompson of the Equality and Human Rights Commission, quoted in The Times, *4 September 2008.*

ACTIVITY

1 Look at Source A. Why do you think women find it difficult to get the top jobs in the professions listed?

The drawings on page 147 also show that it is not just individuals who can be prejudiced, but that quite often there is INSTITUTIONAL DISCRIMINATION. This is where prejudiced behaviour exists (not necessarily knowingly) throughout an institution such as in employment, housing, education, the police force, etc. So, for example, racist or sexist language or stereotyping might be part of the accepted CULTURE of an institution.

ACTIVITY

2 Look at the information above and Source B. Why is institutional discrimination so difficult to eliminate?

Source B

- The BBC's *Panorama* programme claims a substantial number of minority police officers suffer racism in the workplace (2008).
- Sir Ian Blair, when head of the Metropolitan Police, was taken to an employment tribunal by his Assistant Commissioner, Tarique Ghaffur, who claimed he was the victim of racial and religious discrimination (2008).
- The London branch of the National Black Police Association (NBPA) urged black people not to join the force because of its 'hostile and racist environment' (2008).

Persecution

Persecution is the regular HARASSMENT and mistreatment of an individual or group. It can take different forms, such as:

- Disrespect and verbal abuse – for example, ageist or racist remarks.
- OSTRACISM – for example, not inviting a child to a party when the rest of the class has been invited.
- Violence – for example, in 2007, police recorded 22,151 offences involving knives in England and Wales, including grievous bodily harm, attempted murder, woundings and robbery.
- Murder – for example, Stephen Lawrence, a black teenager, was stabbed to death by a gang of white youths while waiting at a bus stop in London in 1993.
- GHETTOISATION – for example, from October 1941, German Jews were transported to GHETTOS in Poland.
- GENOCIDE – for example, between April and June 1994, an estimated 800,000 Tutsis in Rwanda were massacred by the ruling Hutus in the space of 100 days.

Denial of rights

Prejudice, discrimination and persecution all involve the denial of human rights. Everyone has the right to education, to life, to freedom of expression, etc., and to be treated equally under these rights regardless of race, religion, sex, political views, etc.

Prejudice and discrimination, when taken to extremes, involves 'dehumanisation' – the habit of thinking of people who are different as less than human.

CONCEPTS 1 & 2

There are different causes of prejudice and different forms of prejudice and discrimination against individuals and groups

This section explores the role of individuals, groups and government in forming prejudices in society. It shows you how prejudice can lead to discrimination and persecution.

In this section you will learn about:

- The causes of prejudice.
- The relationship between prejudice, discrimination and persecution.
- A range of different forms of prejudice and discrimination.

The following are ideas and terms that you will need to know from this concept section:

Concept 1: ignorance • group identity • fear of outsiders • stereotypes • scapegoats • role of socialisation • media • peers • family • education • nationalism • propaganda

Concept 2: age • gender • sexuality • disability • race • religion • employment • education • criminal justice system • institutional discrimination

On page 146, you learned that prejudice is an attitude that is usually formed through ignorance and is acquired through socialisation. Prejudice often leads to stereotyping and scapegoating.

What are stereotypes and scapegoats?

Stereotyping

Stereotyping is one way of expressing prejudice. It means labelling a group of people with the same characteristics – as if all the people in the group were exactly the same. Stereotyping can be expressed in different forms such as national STEREOTYPES (for example, labelling all Scotsmen as mean), sexist stereotypes (for example, labelling all blonde women as 'bimbos'), and ageist stereotypes (for example, labelling all old people as grumpy), etc.

ACTIVITIES

1 Sort out the statements below into either fact or stereotype.
   a) Tennis players usually wear white.
   b) All girls are obsessed with clothes.
   c) All Americans are overweight.
   d) Many French people eat garlic.
   e) All England football fans are troublemakers.
   f) Elderly people sometimes enjoy pop music.
   g) Kids today are always noisy.
   h) Some teenage girls drink more than boys.

2 a) How do the cartoons below stereotype the person they portray? For example, the first cartoon suggests all FEMALE librarians are plain and wear glasses. Can you complete the rest?
   b) Can you think of three people who do not conform to these stereotypes?

Many individuals who form stereotyping attitudes would say they are not intended to cause offence and are only meant to be funny. Some groups, such as parts of the media, would say the same.

The media often use stereotypes for comic effect or to create a good headline. This, however, could lead to the stereotype becoming more common, as it makes it seem normal, and therefore influences attitudes. For example, do headlines about teenagers being violent, rude, lazy, drug-takers and heavy drinkers affect the attitudes and actions of adults you do not know towards you?

However unintended, stereotyping can cause offence. More seriously, stereotyping can lead to persecution and scapegoating by groups and governments. This is because it is often easier to create SCAPEGOATS if the person or group that is being blamed can all be labelled the same.

Scapegoating

Scapegoating is where a group is blamed for something because of the stereotypes attached to them. Pressures in society such as unemployment, inflation, depression, defeat in war, etc. usually cause this. Examples are:

- Blaming IMMIGRANTS for a rise in unemployment by saying they are taking 'our' jobs.
- Trying to get rid of a local travellers' encampment by accusing them of a rise in crime figures.
- Blaming a football team's lack of success on the foreign players being only interested in the money and uncommitted.

On a larger scale, scapegoating can be an excuse for ETHNIC CLEANSING. For example, in 1998, Serbians accused Muslims of holding back the development of Bosnia and proceeded to drive out as many of them as possible.

As a group, the press quite often uses scapegoats to help sell newspapers. For example, some newspapers talk about the UK being swamped with 'bogus ASYLUM SEEKERS' taking advantage of its benefit system.

Although scapegoating can be started by individuals or groups, such as the media, it is something governments might encourage:

- so that they are not blamed instead
- to win support by being 'tough on immigration' or 'cracking down on yob culture', etc.

Insiders and outsiders

Scapegoating is usually carried out by the dominant social or cultural group in society. They are in control of the media, the top jobs and the government, and are referred to as the 'insider group'. Examples of insider groups are white settlers in Australia, or the timber companies in the Amazonian rainforest (see pages 46–48). Victims of scapegoating are the less dominant social or cultural group. They are often unwelcome, poorer and disadvantaged in education, housing and jobs. They are the 'outsider group'. Examples of an outsider group are the native Aborigines in Australia and the Yanomani in the rainforest.

Source A

Police stop march

Police in riot gear halted a march by the National Front yesterday …

'We demand the right to put forward our views', shouted one member of the National Front …

A spokesman for a local trade union … said: 'These people are racist, spreading a message of hatred and division. There should be no voice for people who are racist.'

ACTIVITIES

1 a) List six characters from TV soaps, programmes or films and suggest the stereotypes they represent.

   b) Was it easy to compile the list? What does this tell you about the influence of the media in creating stereotypes?

2 The following quotes are from Source A:

'We demand the right to put forward our views.'
'There should be no voice for people who are racist.'

Should every group have the right to express their views in a democracy? Should racists who wish to organise events that encourage hatred and fear have the right to put their views across? Set out the arguments for each of the points of view. Conclude with your own views, with reasons.

The media and prejudice and discrimination in the UK

One of the most controversial issues in this country this century has been the apparent large increase in the number of immigrants. Two kinds of immigrants in particular are the subject of debate:

- Economic migrants from Eastern Europe who started arriving in the UK after the expansion of the European Union (EU)
- Asylum seekers from countries like Iraq and Afghanistan.

The controversial nature of the debate has been seized as an opportunity by the tabloid press to sensationalise, that is, to shock and play on the fears of its readers in order to sell more papers. Broadsheets, on the other hand, tend to take a more responsible role, although not on every occasion. Newspaper headlines and reports often stereotype and create scapegoats, playing on people's prejudices (see Sources A and B). Media coverage of terrorist threats and extremist Islamic groups has suggested to many people that all Muslims are a threat, leading to a general and unfounded suspicion of Muslims in Britain. It is unfortunate that it is not also made clear that an overwhelming majority of Muslims are peace-loving moderates who make a valuable contribution to society.

Source B

Immigration: Advantages and disadvantages

- The UK needs young workers to replace a growing ageing population.
- Immigrants help develop a multicultural society, with diversity of culture, music, etc.
- London has become a melting pot as a third of its population are immigrants.
- Immigrants take approximately 80 per cent of new jobs.
- Through tax and spending economic migrants contribute £2.5 billion to the economy.
- The UK, by providing refuge to asylum seekers, gives the world a moral lead.
- Monocultural ghettos are being created in our towns.
- Economic migrants bring entrepreneurial energy, skills and create business.
- The UK is getting overpopulated, with lack of space and inadequate infrastructure.
- Some bogus asylum seekers have turned out to be terrorists.
- Many economic migrants will take poorly paid jobs which British nationals don't want.
- NHS provision, schooling and welfare for migrants and their children costs £5.6 billion – most immigrants have made no contribution towards this cost.
- Immigrants are often the cause of social disturbances: race riots (e.g. Oldham, 2001), gang warfare between ethnic groups, etc.

Source C

Recent newspaper headlines on immigration

BORN EVERYWHERE, RAISED IN BRITAIN

IMMIGRATION MINISTER CALLS FOR CAP ON NEWCOMERS BECAUSE OF ECONOMIC CRISIS

MIGRANTS SWELLED UK POPULATION BY 500 A DAY

IMMIGRATION BENEFITS MORE THAN IT HARMS UK ECONOMY

ASYLUM SEEKERS' APPEALS COST A VAST AMOUNT OF PUBLIC MONEY

Scrounging the jackpot – a tale of everyday Britain

ARE WE MAD? EVERY ORGAN OF THE STATE NOW SEEMS INTENT ON PROTECTING THOSE WHO WOULD DESTROY US

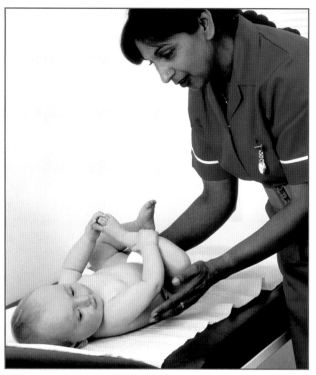

Immigration has many benefits. Here, an imigrant nurse helps care for a baby.

Source D

Two anti-immigration press reports

Afghan refugee Toorpaki Saiedi is given a £1.2 million house by Ealing council at a cost to the taxpayer of £12,458 a month. She and her seven children fled here from the Taliban. If a white person with a job, having lived in the borough all his life, paying thousands of pounds in taxes were to apply for this house, the chances of him getting it would be almost nil.

Sunday Times, 12 October 2008.

Abu Qatada, wanted by Jordan for terrorist attacks, strolls down a London street, carrying groceries paid for by the British taxpayer. He arrived here on a forged passport and claims he would be tortured if sent home.

Daily Mail, 3 September 2008.

The media can help spread prejudice and can encourage persecution. When a government controls the media, there is a danger that it can be used to deliberately attack certain minorities, as was the case in Nazi Germany. In fairness, it must also be remembered that the media can also educate and encourage toleration and further integration in a multi-cultural society.

ACTIVITIES

1 Copy the table below and insert the statements from Source B (page 151) in what you think is the appropriate column.

IMMIGRATION	
The benefits of immigration	**The problems of immigration**

2 Get into groups. Look at Sources C (page 151) and D (above).
   a) List two ways in which immigrants are stereotyped in the headlines in Source C.
   b) Which two headlines match the reports in Source D?
   c) How and why might an economic crisis lead to greater intolerance of immigrants to the UK?
   d) Describe ways in which the media shows a positive view of immigration in the UK. Think about films, dramas and comedy shows, as well as press articles and news programmes.

CONCEPT 3

There are different causes and effects of persecution

This concept section explores the various causes of prejudice and persecution. The case study on the Holocaust illustrates and explains how prejudice can lead to discrimination and persecution in a modern, civilised society undergoing economic and political turmoil.

In this concept section you will learn about:

- The attitudes and actions of governments and states against individuals and groups, leading to persecution.

The following are ideas and terms that you will need to know from this concept section:

the moral, social, political, economic and religious causes and effects of persecution • violence • intolerance • genocide • systematic persecution

What are the causes of prejudice and persecution?

There are many ways individuals, groups and societies can become prejudiced towards each other.

Norms and values

Norms and values are the standard of behaviour and MORAL principles that a group regards as important (see page 5). When a group comes across individuals or groups with different norms and values, it can lead to prejudice, discrimination and persecution. This prejudice is caused by fear and IGNORANCE of the unknown or outsiders, SUPERSTITION, TRIBALISM, or NATIONALISM. So, for example, someone might shun or treat differently someone who is HIV positive and mistakenly believe and fear that any contact can lead to catching the disease themselves.

Political ideologies

Prejudice is often a part of a political ideology – that is, it can form part of the body of ideas that a particular political group have.

Many societies' political ideologies have been built on racial prejudices. They believed they were superior to everyone else, and that other races were inferior. The idea of national superiority is the foundation of most racist regimes. It was behind APARTHEID in South Africa and Nazism in Germany (see pages 154–159).

ACTIVITIES

1 'This town is turning into a foreign land … They are all illegal migrants.' These are the words of a BNP candidate in Sunderland, 2003. Why do you think he held these views? How are views like these examples of prejudice? Discuss this in groups.

2 Choose three of the causes of prejudice discussed in this topic and provide an example of your own for each one.

Religious differences

Religion can also encourage prejudice and persecution. For example, persecution can occur where the religion of the state does not tolerate other BELIEFS, such as the Romans persecuting the early Christians. Another example might be the growth of Islamaphobia (the fear and dislike of Islam) in some Western countries.

In the UK, the concentration of Muslims in certain parts of Bradford, Preston and other cities is seen by some as a threat to British culture. The burqa, mosques and Sharia practices (see page 108) are all looked upon with suspicion.

Economic conditions

Economic pressures, perhaps above all, can foster prejudice. Difficult economic situations where there are high levels of unemployment and inflation can encourage people to turn to extreme political parties for the answers to their problems as these parties tend to blame scapegoats (see page 150). For example, the Nazi Party blamed Jewish people for the harsh economic conditions that Germany faced in the 1930s (see pages 154–159).

The recent recession in the UK brought with it fears for jobs and housing. This in turn increased prejudice and discrimination against immigrants. For example, Polish plumbers were portrayed in the press as putting British plumbers out of work, and more people joined the BNP (British National Party) as a result.

PREJUDICE AND PERSECUTION

Case Study
The Holocaust

The Holocaust is the name given to the slaughter of six million people, mostly Jews, during the Second World War. By learning about it, you might understand how racial prejudice can lead to the most horrendous events and how ordinary people can play their part.

The case study also provides a warning about what can happen and how it is important to act against prejudice. This is shown in the words of Pastor Martin Niemoller, a Christian minister who survived a Nazi concentration camp:

'First they arrested the COMMUNISTS – but I was not a communist, so I did nothing … Then they arrested the trade unionists – and I did nothing because I was not one. And then they came for the Jews and then the Catholics, but I was neither a Jew nor a Catholic and I did nothing. At last they came and arrested me – and there was no one left to do anything about it.'

The persecution of the Jews

Source A

'If I am ever in power, the destruction of the Jews will be my first and most important job.'

Adolf Hitler, 1922

Source B

'We were ordered to dispose of about two hundred Jews. I could see fear in their eyes as we began to unload cans of petrol and forced them into the house … We moved back and threw grenades through the windows.
We listened to the screams as the flames spread from room to room. Dense smoke poured out and some of the Jews jumped out through the windows only to be shot by our troops. Later, many of us were disturbed by what we had done but were told by our commander that Jews were not human.'

A German soldier remembering,
from *The Sunflower* by Simon Wiesental

Source C

'I saw a great collection of bodies, perhaps 150, flung down on each other, all naked, all so thin, their yellow skin glistened like stretched rubber on their bones.'

Richard Dimbleby describing the scene as the British army liberated the concentration camp at Belsen,
19 April 1945

ACTIVITY

1 What do the sources tell you about the Holocaust? List four things.

The Treaty of Versailles

To understand why the Holocaust took place, we must go back to the period immediately after the First World War. Germany had lost the war and had been forced to accept humiliating terms in the Treaty of Versailles, 1919:

- It had to accept the blame for the war.
- It lost 13 per cent of its territories.
- Its armed forces were drastically reduced.
- It had to pay £6.6 million reparations (compensation).

This caused many Germans to feel as Hitler did in Source D.

Source D

'So the war had been in vain. In vain, all the sacrifices. In vain, the death of 2 million soldiers.'

Adolf Hitler, *Mein Kampf*, 1925–26

Hyperinflation

Partly because of the huge reparations bill, Germany was hit by HYPERINFLATION in 1923. Bank notes became worthless and savings were wiped out. People blamed the new democratic government of the Weimar REPUBLIC for having accepted the Treaty. Many turned to new EXTREMIST parties. Source E shows what hyperinflation meant in practice for people trying to buy basic necessities such as food.

Hyperinflation meant the German mark became worthless. This photo shows German children playing with stacks of banknotes in the street in 1923.

Who supported Hitler?

- The working class who were promised jobs.
- Farmers who were promised higher food prices.
- The MIDDLE CLASS who were afraid of a communist revolution.
- The upper classes who resented the Treaty of Versailles.
- Women who were promised a vital role as wives and mothers.
- The military who wanted a bigger army.
- Racists who hated the Jews.
- Young people who found the Nazi methods and military style exciting.

Source E

The cost of a loaf of bread in marks (the old unit of currency in Germany).

Date	Cost of bread
1918	1 mark
1922	163 marks
January 1923	250 marks
July 1923	3,500 marks
September 1923	1,500,000 marks
November 1923	200,000,000,000 marks

Hitler and the rise of the Nazis

Between 1924 and 1929, Germany recovered economically as the USA lent it money. The new extremist parties lost support as the German people became better off. In October 1929, the collapse of the US stock exchange on Wall Street led the USA to demand back the money borrowed and Germany was plunged into depression. Thousands of businesses collapsed, unemployment rose dramatically and living standards plummeted. Many lost their homes and lived on the streets. People were now ready to support alternative parties who promised a solution. The largest of these were the communists and the Nazi Party led by Adolf Hitler.

There were street battles between the parties' supporters as Germany was plunged into political chaos. It was the Nazis who gained most support because Hitler deliberately appealed to many groups.

The Nazis became expert at putting across their ideas. Hitler toured all over the country and spoke to huge crowds in halls and sports stadiums. This was very important when radio was still new and TV did not exist. Dramatic marches, music, searchlights, etc. added to the occasion. Hitler made the most of the economic crisis and appealed to German nationalism. He said things many wanted to hear as he was in tune with people's anger and frustration. The audience were ready to accept the Hitler myth of him as a strong leader or 'superman' who would save their country.

Source F

'I met a poor FAMILY – a couple and their nine children who had to survive on £1.50 a week. They lived on cabbages.'

Reporter for the *Spectator*, 1932

Source G

In such circumstances (the depression), people no longer listened to reason. The German people had fantastic fears, extravagant hatreds and extravagant hopes. In such circumstances, the speeches of Hitler began to attract a mass following.

Alan Bullock, *A Study in Tyranny*, 1962

In January 1933, the political situation had become so desperate that President Hindenburg decided to appoint Hitler as Chancellor. This was because the Nazi Party was the largest in the Reichstag (parliament). The first thing Hitler did was to call for an election in March 1933. Before it took place, the Reichstag fire occurred (possibly started deliberately by the Nazis themselves). A communist was blamed, so Hitler asked Hindenburg to declare a state of emergency and the communists were prevented from taking part in the election.

Source I

A Nazi election poster that reads: 'Our last hope'.

The Nazis won but only managed to get 44 per cent of the votes. Because of the economic and political crisis, Hitler persuaded the Reichstag to pass the Enabling Bill, which allowed him to rule without parliament. Within a few months he banned all other parties and trade unions and closed down all anti-Nazi newspapers. Hitler was now a dictator with total control. When Hindenburg died in 1934, he combined the jobs of Chancellor and President and became known as the Führer (leader). The army swore an oath of personal loyalty to him.

Source J

Growth of the Nazi Party

Date	No. of unemployed (millions)	Nazi votes in Reichstag	Nazi seats
1928	1.8	800,000	12
1930	3.2	6,400,000	107
1932	5	13,700,000	230

ACTIVITIES

Look at pages 150–156 and answer the following questions.

1 a) What is meant by 'scapegoating'?
   b) What factors in Germany in the early 1930s led many people to look for scapegoats? Consider norms and values, IDEOLOGY, economic pressure and the media (see pages 150–152).

2 What factors explain the rise of Hitler to power?

3 Make a large copy of the chart below and complete it.

Group	What Hitler promised
Working class	Employment
Farmers	
Middle class	
Upper class	
Women	
Military	
Racists	
Young people	

The Nazis in power

The Nazis were racists. They believed that the German or 'Aryan' race was the 'master race' (blonde hair and blue eyes). They believed that all Jews belonged to an 'inferior race'.

There were half a million Jews living in Germany, and they made valuable contributions to the economy, science and the arts. Many had fought for their country in the First World War. However, they were undeservedly made 'scapegoats' for the country's woes. The reasons for this are outlined in the box below. It is an example of how racial prejudice can exaggerate a 'threat'.

> ### Why Jews became scapegoats in Germany
>
> - There was a TRADITION in Europe of persecuting the Jews.
> - Jewish people looked, dressed and spoke differently. They had their own CUSTOMS and religion.
> - Many Jews were successful and wealthy, which led to jealousy.
> - Poor Jews were often immigrants and were seen as a threat to jobs.

Persecution

As soon as they were in power, the Nazis began to persecute the Jews. They were not the only ones to suffer – communists, gypsies, homosexuals, homeless people, the disabled and mentally ill were other victims. Not all Germans were Nazis, but their control of the state meant there was little resistance or opposition. Hitler used two methods to gain that control: PROPAGANDA and terror.

1 Propaganda

The Nazis established a Ministry for Propaganda under Dr Joseph Goebbels in an attempt to make every German think the same way by controlling the information they were allowed to see and hear. He was one of the first to realise the importance of radios. They were deliberately made cheap so that every home would have one. Thus millions of people could be brainwashed. The radio, newspapers, books, plays and films were also censored to prevent the spread of alternative ideas.

The Nazi government also attempted to control the minds of the young by introducing Nazi beliefs into the school curriculum. In Biology, for instance, they were given 'scientific' explanations for 'the master race'. In History, the Jews were blamed for almost everything that had gone wrong in Germany since the Middle Ages.

Young people were also forced to join youth movements. Boys enlisted in Hitler Youth and were taught to march and fight. Girls joined the League of German Maidens and taught to become mothers and have babies for Germany. The activities were fun and exciting and meant that they were not aware that they were being brainwashed to believe in Nazi ideas.

2 Terror

Not all Germans would succumb to Nazi methods of social control. Those who would not were either intimidated into submission, sent to concentration camps or killed. The SS (Schutzstaffel or Hitler's bodyguards) and the Gestapo (Secret Police) crushed all opposition.

Today it is difficult to understand how the Holocaust could have happened, in the same way

This Nazi painting of 1939 by Adolf Wissle shows the ideal 'Aryan' family.

Pre-Nazi Period (before 1933)	Jews regarded as a threat and become scapegoats for Germany's economic and social problems.
Nazi Period (before the war)	Nazis come to power and make anti-Semitism official policy. Jews banned from civil service and university positions. Boycott of Jewish doctors, lawyers, teachers and businesses.
1935	Nuremberg Laws take away the citizenship of Jews. They are deprived of basic rights, for example, the right to vote. Marriage and sexual relations between Jews and non-Aryans prohibited.
1938	In the hope of forcing Jews to leave, segregation is introduced. In some parts of the country Jews are banned from theatres, swimming pools, public parks and from attending school. Separate compartments are introduced for them on trains. Jewish-owned properties are confiscated by the state. Jews have to add 'Israel' (males) or 'Sarah' (females) to their names and a large letter 'J' is printed on their passports.
	Kristallnacht (9 November) – 'The night of broken glass'. A carefully organised violence 'erupts' throughout Germany. Rioters burn or damage over 1,000 synagogues and break the windows of more than 7,500 businesses. The police stand by and watch while firemen only make sure that flames don't spread to 'Aryan' property. Ninety-two Jews are killed and approximately 25,000 are sent to concentration camps. This marks the beginning of a systematic attempt to eradicate the Jewish race. It is now obvious that they have no future in Germany. About half of the 500,000 Jewish population emigrate to the USA, Palestine or to other European countries.
Nazi Period (during the war)	The start of the Second World War brings in a new phase in Hitler's attack on the Jews. Germany's conquest of Eastern Europe means gaining control of millions of extra Jews. As a temporary measure many are forced into over-crowded ghettoes where disease, hunger and poverty take their toll. In Warsaw the ghetto population reaches a density of 200,000 per square mile.
1941	The elimination of European Jews becomes official government policy. Special SS killing units shoot tens of thousands of Jews in areas that had once been part of the Soviet Union.
1942	The SS murders are too slow and expensive for the Nazi leaders. They decide on the 'Final Solution'. All Jews are moved to the concentration camps for slave labour and ultimately death in the gas chambers.

that more recent genocide in Rwanda, Bosnia and Sudan is almost impossible to explain. Jews were told they were being re-settled to a new home and were even under the impression they were being taken to the showers as they were led to the gas chambers and their death. Twenty thousand people a day were murdered in Auschwitz alone.

There were Germans who were horrified and brave enough to protest. Some took enormous risks to hide or save Jews. Oscar Schindler (portrayed in the film *Schindler's List*) was a Nazi factory owner who saved thousands from the gas chambers. Many of the SS who carried out the murders later committed suicide, unable to live with what they had done. On the other hand, there were also Germans who knew or guessed the truth, but were too afraid to protest or ignored the situation. Many must have even approved – as far as they were concerned, the Nazi 'New Order' was better than the misery of the Weimar Republic. Germans now felt pride in their NATION – they had jobs, food and security.

During the Allied occupation after the war, all German citizens were forced to watch a film that had been made by the Allies of the concentration camp in Belsen. Many watched in silence, whilst others wept.

ACTIVITIES

1 Why did Hitler personally hate the Jews?

2 Why were the Jews persecuted in Germany in the 1930s?

3 List the different methods used by the Nazis to spread their racist ideas.

4 a) Explain what an 'outsider group' is.
   b) How had the Jews in Germany become outsiders by 1941?

5 Using the sources and information throughout this case study, design a chart that gives examples of different stages in the treatment of the Jews. You could construct your chart by dividing events into the following date ranges:

   • before 1933
   • 1933–38
   • 1938–41
   • 1941–45.

   This will help you see how the situation got progressively worse. Try to show how prejudice leads to discrimination and eventually persecution.

6 In groups, discuss who should be held responsible for the Holocaust:

   • Hitler
   • The Nazis, many of whom claimed to be only obeying orders
   • The whole of Germany.

7 Why do you think German citizens were forced to watch the films shown by the Allies?

8 Can the persecution of ethnic or religious groups be avoided in the future? Use the following questions as guidance:

   • What lessons can be learned?
   • Are things different today?
   • Are the Race Relations Act (see page 163) and the Universal Declaration of Human Rights enough (see page 106)?
   • What else needs to be done?
   • What can *you* do?

CONCEPT 4

Different methods can be used to reduce or resolve prejudice, discrimination and persecution

This concept section considers how individuals, institutions, governments and international organisations can all play a part in ensuring that there will never be another event as horrendous as the Holocaust.

In this concept section you will learn about:

- A range of methods and strategies and their effectiveness in reducing and resolving prejudice and discrimination at an individual, local, national and international level.

The following are ideas and terms that you will need to know from this concept section:

equal opportunities legislation • *sanctions* • *campaigns* • *arbitration* • *force* • *negotiation* • *international action* • *affirmative action* • *reconciliation*

How can we reduce or resolve prejudice, discrimination and persecution?

Prejudice and persecution exists at all levels – personal, local, national and international. People are not born prejudiced. On page 146 we established that prejudice comes from badly formed attitudes. These are acquired as part of a person's culture through agents of socialisation such as family, school, peer groups, the media, etc. These agents have a special responsibility as they provide the role models for the young and impressionable. They must be taught how prejudice has to be challenged before it becomes destructive and leads to discrimination and persecution.

ACTIVITY

1 With a partner discuss:
   a) What point is the poster below making?
   b) How effective do you think it is?

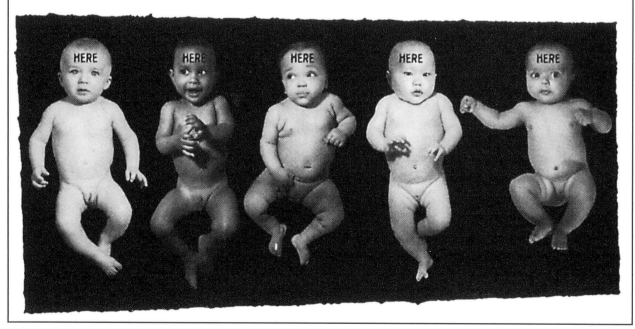

THERE ARE LOTS OF PLACES IN BRITAIN WHERE RACISM DOESN'T EXIST.

HERE   HERE   HERE   HERE   HERE

'Babies' poster from the Commission for Racial Equality, 1997.

At an early age children should learn the importance of RECONCILIATION and accepting that people are different. Where conflict occurs at a local level those with influence or authority should encourage negotiation. For example, two ethnic gangs involved in a turf war could send representatives to a meeting arranged by their ethnic elders. Perhaps a local religious leader might be asked to settle the dispute through ARBITRATION.

At a national level AFFIRMATIVE ACTION needs to be taken by governments. In the UK political correctness (PC) is now almost obligatory – we should aim to avoid expressions or actions that may be understood to exclude or belittle certain people on the grounds of race, gender, disability, sexual orientation, etc. For instance, to avoid accusations of sexism we should avoid words using 'man' or 'men' to refer to both men and women. So, for example, 'chairman' becomes 'chairperson'. Some, however, feel that political correctness has been taken too far and has begun to impinge on our rights to freedom of speech and action.

Another controversial policy, introduced with the best of intentions, is POSITIVE DISCRIMINATION. For example, in the UK a major political party has insisted that in some constituencies a female candidate has to be selected to contest an election in an attempt to increase female representation in the House of Commons. But some feel that positive discrimination makes it unfair for other groups who do not benefit. For example, the cricketer Kevin Pietersen chose to play for England rather than South Africa, where he grew up, because there was a policy there to have a certain number of black cricketers in the team, which meant a lower chance of selection for white players like himself.

International attempts to stop and prevent persecution include SANCTIONS and force. We have seen how both of these were used against the Taliban in Afghanistan with mixed success. Perhaps the most poignant single event in the fight against hatred is Holocaust Memorial Day – an international day of remembrance held annually on 27 January to commemorate victims of the Holocaust and other genocides. On that day we are meant to commit to tackling prejudice, discrimination and racism.

The examples in the table on page 162 are evidence of how attempts have been made to reduce or resolve prejudice and persecution at all levels, both in the present and in the past.

Progress has undoubtedly been made worldwide. Not so long ago it would have been unheard of for someone whose father was a humble goatherder in a remote village in Kenya to become President of the USA. However, in November 2008, Barack Obama achieved that goal. This is testimony to the progress made.

Unfortunately, there are still places in the world where the opposite is true. China has gained international admiration for recent economic progress and in particular for the magnificent 2008 Olympics. However, its human rights record leaves a great deal to be desired.

Barack Obama with his grandmother, Sarah Hussein Obama, outside his father's house in Nyongoma Kogelo in Kenya in 2006.

The Race Relations Act 1976

The Race Relations Act 1976 makes it illegal to discriminate on racial grounds in a range of areas including pay, job applications and housing. The Act also set up the Commission for Racial Equality with powers to examine cases of unfair dismissal and allegations of racial discrimination.

	EXAMPLE	EFFECTIVENESS/SUCCESS
Individual action	• Becoming a school governor to influence decision making on bullying policies in a school. • Socialising your children so they learn that prejudice is unacceptable (see page 160).	• Contribution might help to resolve problem. • Very effective – family plays a central role in moulding our personalities.
Local action	• Local government introducing policies such as providing school meals that take into account everyone's dietary needs. • Employers introducing positive employment policies – for example, B&Q have decided on a positive policy of employing people over 50.	• Shows that minorities are catered for. • Successful as regards B&Q, but example not typical.
National action	• In the early twentieth century, the Suffragette Movement campaigned to gain women the vote. • In the USA, Martin Luther King led the Civil Rights Movement to gain freedom for blacks. • The Commission for Racial Equality started a campaign to tackle racism in soccer, which now runs as a separate organisation – 'Kick it Out' – supported by national football organisations. • The British government has passed legislation to protect minorities, for example, Equal Pay and Sex Discrimination Act 1970 (which led to the setting up of the Equal Opportunities Commission 1976) and the Race Relations Act 1976.	• Women over 30 given the vote in 1918, but mainly due to their contribution in First World War, rather than to the Suffragette campaign. • Civil Rights Act (1964) made segregation illegal but discrimination continued. • Some success but racist chants still heard at certain grounds. • Progress made – new acceptance of minorities in education, work and politics.
International action	• The Human Rights Convention (see page 106) and the International Court of Human Rights promote justice and equality of treatment for all. • The European Union introduced measures and campaigns to fight prejudice. For example, 1997 was made European Year Against Racism as a response to the growth of extreme political parties on the continent, such as the Neo-Nazis.	• Made a tremendous difference in helping to raise awareness of human rights. • Makes it less likely that there will be another holocaust in Europe.

Players from Besiktas and Liverpool Football Clubs in October 2007. How effective do you think tactics such as these are in combating racism in the sport?

Source A

Varied responses to racism in football

- **Humour:** When Everton supporters threw bananas at John Barnes in a Merseyside derby in the 1980s he picked one up, ate it and went on to score two goals.
- **'Turning a deaf ear':** Emile Heskey ignored 'monkey chants' while playing for England in Croatia during the 2008 European Championship qualifiers.
- **Punishment:** UEFA penalised Atletico Madrid for racist abuse by their fans during a Champions League match against Olympic Marseilles in 2008. They were ordered to play two home matches in European competitions at least 200 miles from Madrid.
- **Zero tolerance:** President Sarkozy of France decreed that matches will be cancelled if fans jeer the national anthem. This happened after the *Marseillaise* (France's national anthem) was drowned out by mocking whistles by French-born fans of North African origin during a France–Tunisia friendly in 2008.

The table opposite lists responses to prejudice and discrimination at all levels. It also mentions national action to deal with racism at football, which the Commission for Racial Equality worked for in the form of the 'Kick It Out' campaign. Source A above shows other responses to the problem of racism in the sport made by footballers, UEFA and even a national leader.

ACTIVITIES

1 Study Source A. Which of the above responses to racial abuse was most likely in your opinion to achieve success?

2 Discuss the best ways of challenging prejudice and persecution at either school or work.

3 Most football clubs are taking action against racism. Make a list of six actions individual clubs could take to deal with things such as racist chanting, graffiti, throwing things, etc.

4 Draw a poster or design a website for the 'Kick it Out' campaign.

5 'It is easier to stop discrimination than it is to stop prejudice.' Do you agree with this statement? Discuss it in groups.

GLOBAL INEQUALITY

INTRODUCTION

The global inequality chapter is based on four concepts and we will follow these concepts through in this chapter:

1. There are different features of global inequality.
2. There are different causes of global inequality.
3. Global inequality affects both LESS ECONOMICALLY DEVELOPED COUNTRIES (LEDCs) and MORE ECONOMICALLY DEVELOPED COUNTRIES (MEDCs).
4. The different ways of addressing the problems of global inequality may vary in their effectiveness.

Throughout the world people are living in very different conditions. Some have enough food, have a comfortable income, live in good quality housing and as a result have an excellent standard of living. For others the conditions are the complete opposite. Over recent years there has been much media attention surrounding the issue of GLOBAL INEQUALITY and levels of development throughout the world.

What cultural stereotypes do we have of LEDCs and MEDCs?

From completing Activity 1 below, you have probably established that we form different images of African countries and the USA, and that the media is a powerful influence on the way we 'see' people we have not met in these countries.

The way we can communicate sound and images around the world today means that it is the mass media that provide us with the information that shape the way we come to 'know' and 'understand' people in other countries. But how reliable is this information?

Pictures C and H are scenes of Africa and are probably the ones you chose. These are images most frequently seen on TV and in the newspapers when they cover the latest disaster. We rarely see programmes about daily life that would help redress the balance.

Pictures B and G were taken in the USA and, again, are probably the ones you chose. Images we associate with the USA are heavily influenced by TV programmes and films highlighting the wealth and power of people in that country.

Pictures D and E are also pictures from African countries and pictures A and F were taken in the United States. Does this surprise you?

The pictures highlight STEREOTYPES of rich and poor – which are true in many cases. However, there are also many success stories to be found in Africa, just as there is poverty in the USA.

ACTIVITY

1 a) What images would come to mind if someone started to talk to you about a country in Africa? Make a list of five things.

b) What images come to mind when you think about the United States? Again, make a list of five things.

c) Study the photos A–H opposite. Select those which you think are closest to the images you described in part a) and note them down.

d) Now study the photos again and note down which ones are closest to the images you described in part b).

e) Compare your results in small groups. How similar were your answers?

f) You should have a few pictures left over that do not fit with your images of either Africa, or the USA. Discuss why this is so.

g) As a class, discuss what has made you form these images.

A

B

C

D

E

F

G

H

How do LEDCS and MEDCS see each other?

Many people in LEDCs may have a view of people and governments in MEDCs that we may find completely inaccurate. For example, MEDCs may be seen as selfish, greedy or corrupt. This idea can understandably date back to colonial times, but also develop as a result of unfair trade and exploitation that you will read about in this chapter.

People in LEDCs may also have the impression that those in MEDCs have low MORAL standards, which some would argue can be seen through the increasing amount of sex and violence in the media. In 2008, the President of Zimbabwe at the time, Robert Mugabe, attacked Britain, stating that the British were 'thieves [who] want to steal our country'. Another example can be seen through attitudes of some Muslims towards the West. In 2005, a Danish newspaper published cartoons that offended many Muslims. This sparked worldwide protest and rioting among some members of the Muslim COMMUNITY because they felt a need to defend their religion. Many people at the time linked this need to defend their religion back to the time of the Crusades.

Those in MEDCs are likely to have a certain view of LEDCs, some elements of which you identified in Activity 1. They may also see LEDCs as being primitive. Some people even say that people in LEDCs are lazy; they think that they are incapable of helping themselves, and that this is why they don't have enough food. When MEDCs do offer help, all too often we see the media reports showing the money being spent on weapons and lost through corruption. The events of 9/11 has seen the stereotype of Middle Eastern people as terrorists being developed by media coverage, to the point that two Middle Eastern men were removed from an easyJet flight in November 2006, just because Western passengers thought they looked like terrorists.

The end result of these cultural stereotypes is that a gap in understanding develops. This in turn leads to a rift between LEDCs and MEDCs, fuelled by suspicion and ignorance.

Muslim protests against Danish cartoons of Muhammad, October 2005.

CONCEPT 1

There are different features of global inequality

There are different features of global inequality. In this concept section you will learn about:

- Absolute and relative poverty.
- How we can measure wealth and poverty using DEVELOPMENT INDICATORS.
- What life is like for people living in less economically and more economically developed countries.

The following are ideas and terms that you will need to know from this concept section:

less economically developed countries (LEDCs) • more economically developed countries (MEDCs) • social and economic development indicators • absolute poverty • relative poverty • Gross National Product (GNP) • calorie intake • infant mortality rate • people per doctor • life expectancy • literacy rates • HIV/AIDS

What is poverty?

Poverty is a term used to describe a situation when people don't have the income to buy the basic requirements that they need to live. In order to simply survive you must have food, water and shelter. Without one of these things survival becomes virtually impossible. If people can't afford to buy the basics they need to live, they are said to be living below the 'poverty line'. However, the type of poverty a person is in will depend on where they live in the world.

Relative poverty

Poor people in MEDCs tend to be in RELATIVE POVERTY. Relative poverty means that a person is on less than half the national average income and are therefore in poverty compared to the people around them. For example, the majority of people in the community may have satellite television, but, although they would like to have it, the poorer person can't afford it. So poor people may simply be classed as people unable to enjoy lifestyles that are considered to be the norm in their society.

If you live in an MEDC, the government provides support for people on lower incomes: for example, social security, tax credits and child and disability benefits. This means that – in theory – no one should go without food, water or shelter. In 2008, the UK government were able to negotiate deals with energy companies to provide cheaper tariffs for people on lower incomes and agreed to provide free home insulation as a means of helping those who may struggle to pay their bills.

Absolute poverty

Many people throughout the world live in what is known as ABSOLUTE POVERTY. This is when people are living below the income level needed to buy basic necessities. Absolute poverty is likely to be found where there are many very poor people, where the government cannot provide adequate support for poor people, and where the economy is not strong enough for everyone to earn enough money to buy the basics they need to survive.

Absolute poverty is the type of poverty that you often see in news clips and that charities such as Comic Relief, Make Poverty History and Oxfam campaign to raise money for. There are millions of people around the world who live in absolute poverty, particularly in Africa, Central and South America, and South East Asia.

The map on page 173 shows the North–South divide. This is a term used to describe the difference in wealth and levels of development of countries in the southern half of the world compared to those in the northern half.

ACTIVITIES

1 One definition of relative poverty means being unable to afford what most people in a society can enjoy (NORMS). Make a list of all the things you consider to be norms in the UK today.

2 What do you think are the problems when measuring relative poverty?

How do we measure wealth, poverty and levels of development?

To find out if a country or the people within a country are living in poverty we use social and economic DEVELOPMENT INDICATORS.

Development indicators are statistics that cover a range of different social and economic issues. For example: how many patients there are to every doctor (doctor to patient ratio); what percentage of people can read and write (adult literacy); and how much, on average, people earn if you added all the country's income together and divided it by the number of people (GROSS NATIONAL PRODUCT – GNP).

When looking at development indicators, it is important to remember that they are averages. This means that, although it may look as if the country is poor, there will be some people in that country that are extremely rich, while others will be even poorer than the development indicator suggests. The table below shows development indicators for five different countries.

	UK	USA	CHINA	GHANA	ZIMBABWE
Population (millions)	60.4	295.7	1,306	21.9	12.2
Life expectancy	78	78	72	56	37
Doctor to patient ratio	610	358	610	11,111	16,667
Calorie intake	3,412	3,774	2,951	2,667	1,942
Infant mortality rate (under the age of one)	5	6	21	52	33
Percentage with HIV/AIDS	0.1	0.6	0.1	3.1	33.7
Literacy rate (per cent)	99	97	86	75	91
Average wage ($)	31,460	39,710	5,530	2,280	2,180
Human development index	0.936	0.939	0.745	0.568	0.491
Agriculture (as a percentage of GNP)	1	0.9	13.8	34.3	18.1
Energy consumption per person (oil in tonnes)	3.97	8.33	0.83	0.17	0.41
Internet usage (per thousand)	423	551	63	8	43
Mobile phone (millions)	69	255	547	7	1.2
Percentage below poverty line	14	12	8	29	68

Human development index = a measure of human development decided by the United Nations. It takes into consideration the health, education and standard of living of people within a country. The higher the HDI is the more developed a country is.

The seven measures of child poverty

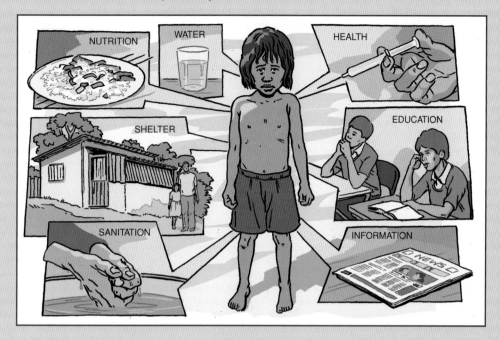

According to a recent UNICEF report, over one billion children suffer serious deprivation in at least one of the following areas:

- 500 million children have no access to sanitation.
- 400 million children do not have access to safe water.
- 640 million children do not have adequate shelter.
- 300 million children lack access to information (newspapers, books, internet, etc.).
- 270 million children have no access to healthcare services.
- 140 million children have never been to school.
- 90 million children are severely deprived of food.

The UN has produced a **Universal Declaration of Human Rights** and more recently the **UN Convention on the Rights of the Child**. Both conventions state that everyone in the world should be able to enjoy the following rights:

UN HUMAN RIGHTS CHARTER – SELECTED ARTICLES
To life.
To privacy.
To protection from being hurt, violence, abuse and neglect.
To the best health possible and access to medical care.
To help from the government if you are poor or in need.
To a good enough standard of living to develop properly.
To education.
To use your own language and practise your own CULTURE and religion.
To play and free time.
To protection from work that is bad for your health or education.

Some development indicators for Kenya, India and MEDCs (average)

SELECTED INDICATORS	KENYA	INDIA	MEDCS
% infant mortality (per 100 live births)	7.5	6.9	0.6
% under-five mortality (per 100 live births)	11.7	10.5	0.6
% HIV/AIDS (15–49)	11.6	0.8	0.4
Female literacy as % male rate	84	65	0
Female primary age group enrolment as % of male	105	86	100
Female secondary age group enrolment as % male	89	68	100
Malnourished (underweight children, under five)	22	53	Not available
% with less than $1 per day per person	26	44	0
% with less than $2 per day per person	62	86	0
Calories per person per day as % of high income countries	58	73	100
% with no access to safe water	56	19	0
% with no access to health services	–	25	0
% with no access to sanitation	15	71	0
Number of people per doctor	6700	2100	400
% GDP public expenditure on education	6.5	3.2	5
% GDP spent on health	2.2	0.6	6.4
% not in secondary education	38.9	40.3	4.4
% people per telephone line	111	45	Under 2
% people per television	47	14	Under 2

Source: UNICEF report: 'Child Rights and Child Poverty in Developing Countries', Summary Report to UNICEF by the Centre for International Poverty Research, University of Bristol

The table above and the 'seven measures of child poverty' (see page 169) suggest that unequal wealth and development can have a big effect on a child's ability to enjoy their human rights. Consider the impact on a child being brought up (socialised) on the brink of, or in absolute poverty.

ACTIVITIES

1 Look at the seven measures of child poverty on page 169. Put the areas of deprivation in order of those that you think would be most important for human development, down to those you think would be least important.

2 Discuss your lists in small groups and try to come up with an order that you can all agree with.

3 In small groups, study the development indicators above and the selected articles from the Human Rights Charter on page 169. Set out your own table of rights, and for each one match one or more indicators to the relevant right. For example:

Human right	Development indicator
Right to Life	Infant mortality

How do lives differ between LEDC and MEDC countries?

The Case Studies that follow will compare the lives of people in the UK (an MEDC) with the lives of people in Ethiopia (an LEDC). Both are examples of people living in the build-up to difficult times: a famine in Ethiopia and a recession in the UK. As you read through them consider the similarities and differences between your own lives.

Case Study
Ethiopia: Ada Hussain

Ada Hussain

My name is Ada Hussain. I am 37 years old. I live in Afar which is a region in the north east of Ethiopia. This region is one of the harshest environments in the world, despite which, myself and my ancestors before me have lived here for generations. I wake about 5.30 in the morning, usually as the children start to chatter. We try and do our chores early, as by midday it is too hot. I have five children, whose ages range from four to sixteen. We did have seven children, but two died before they reached the age of one. We would usually have a breakfast called kinche, which is crushed wheat and butter. Recently, however, food has been in extremely short supply so we can't always eat in the morning.

The temperature here can reach up to 50 degrees Celsius, which is extremely hot. I am a nomad, which means that I move around from place to place in search of water and grazing pastures to feed my camels and cattle.

The region of Afar has been somewhat neglected in terms of development and as a result we have had to be extremely resourceful in how we live. There has been little rain so far this year. The short 'sugum' rains this year were poor and the 'karma' rains are a month late. It is becoming increasingly difficult to find enough grass to feed my cattle and already many have died. Dead animals lie across the landscape and the stench is extremely overpowering in such heat. Even the camels are weak and many are barely able to move.

I have lost 37 of my 40 cattle in the last two months, and the three I have left are on the verge of dying. This means I have nothing to trade with. My children are also getting weaker and weaker as we have no food or milk. The nearest doctor is over 60 km away so there is no chance of any medicine should my children fall ill. All over the region people are saying the same thing. The government has said that the situation is serious but we are still waiting for help. Nearly a million people are without food and unless help arrives soon people will start dying at an alarming rate.

We have been told not to drink water unless we boil it first as there have been outbreaks of cholera due to the dead animals rotting in the Awash River, which is the main source of water for us. This is difficult, however, as wood for fires is scarce. The lack of clean water and food means our immune systems are weak and vulnerable to disease.

We need food, clean water and medical supplies to stop thousands from dying, but the aid agencies have been focused on other crises in the southern half of Africa and we have been forgotten about.

Adapted from a BBC news report.

Paula Johnson.

My name is Paula. I live in Northampton, East Midlands; I am 37 years of age. I was a teacher but gave up work to raise my two children. My husband is also a teacher which means we all get to spend time together in the school holidays.

I live in a semi-detached house in one of the nicer parts of town. We needed to borrow a lot of money for the mortgage; at the time it seemed fine because everyone said house prices would keep going up. Now though prices round here are falling sharply.

My daily routine involves getting up, making breakfast for the children while my husband gets ready for work, taking my eldest daughter Molly to school and then taking my youngest daughter Caitlin to playgroup.

Caitlin had to have her pre-school jabs the other day but had a reaction to them so I had to take her to the hospital. The doctor said it is likely to be a localised reaction but gave us some antibiotics in case it was an infection.

I do a weekly shop at Tesco and we usually have a cooked meal every night, although we can't always have what we want as we are trying to stick to a budget. We usually go abroad but have decided to go camping this year as it is cheaper.

The current recession has made the cost of living more difficult but hopefully my husband will get a pay rise. A few extra bills over the last couple of

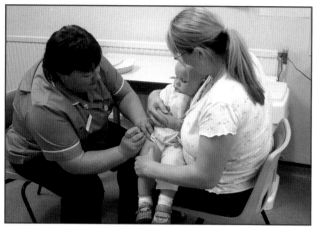

Children in the UK are usually vaccinated against a wide range of diseases.

months have made our finances tight as we had to pay a plumber to fit a new tap, road tax for our car and an MOT. We would like to get our house decorated as it hasn't been painted for three years, but can't afford it at the moment unless we do it ourselves.

We do get some help from the government in the form of child benefits and working tax credits, which help with the cost of living. Once both my daughters are old enough to go to school I will go back to work, which will help our financial situation further.

ACTIVITIES

1 Copy out the table below.

	Relative Poverty	Absolute Poverty
Ada		
Paula		

Read through the case studies above and on page 171, which describe two very different lives. For each person list the examples that suggest they are living in either relative or absolute poverty.

2 Now compare your own life with those of Ada and Paula. Write a paragraph on each explaining the similarities and differences between your life and theirs. Include in the paragraph anything that you may feel you take for granted, such as clean running water.

CONCEPT 2

There are different causes of global inequality

In this concept section you will learn about how each of the following factors contributes to global inequality:

- Human factors – Historical/colonialism.
- Economic factors – CASH CROPS, primary product dependency, world trade, poverty cycle, debt burden.
- Politics and corruption.
- Environmental factors.
- Role of the World Bank and International Monetary Fund (IMF).

The causes of global inequality can be split into two categories: human and environmental.

The following are ideas and terms that you will need to know from this concept:

colonialism • primary product dependency • cash crops • unfair terms of trade • government policy • debt burden • corruption • role of World Bank and IMF • poverty cycle • environmental causes and crises

Human factors

Historical (colonialism)

From the sixteenth century onwards, the leaders of the Western countries of Europe believed it was their right to try to conquer other parts of the world and develop empires. Once a country was conquered, its people lost control of what they grew and made, and were put to work to produce what the colonial power wanted. This process of exploiting the countries in an empire is known as colonialism.

The huge profits made from cheap imports from the colonies and slavery in America helped Europe and the USA become richer and more industrialised, while the countries that became colonies were left behind.

- Between 1500 and 1750, more than $1,500 million in profits and goods was acquired by Western Europe from its overseas colonies.
- Between 1503 and 1660, 185,000 kgs of gold and 16 million kgs of silver were brought to Spain from the Americas. This fuelled European economic expansion.
- Between 1757 and 1815, Britain helped itself to about £1,000 million from India.

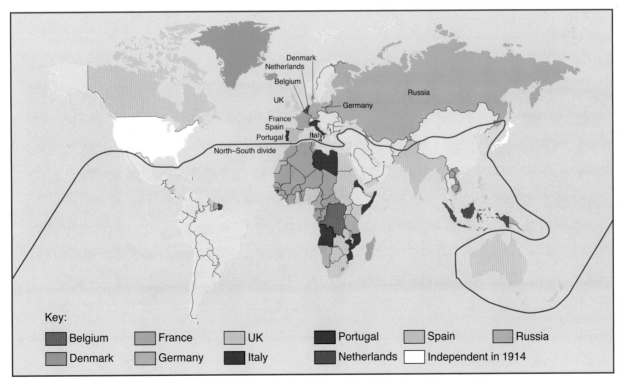

Key:
- Belgium
- Denmark
- France
- Germany
- UK
- Italy
- Portugal
- Netherlands
- Spain
- Russia
- Independent in 1914

Colonial empires in 1914.

From 1945 onwards, many colonies gained their independence. However, little had been invested in developing the economic and political skills of people within the country, and, with the loss of their economic independence, it became difficult for these countries to recover from the effects of a colonial past.

Economic factors

The climate in many LEDCs allows crops to be grown that can't be grown in other parts of the world. These crops include things that we take for granted, such as coffee, cotton, fruit and cocoa, which is used to make chocolate. During the days of the British Empire farmers in these countries were actively encouraged to grow these crops. These crops are known as cash crops as they are grown purely to be sold. With the majority of people in LEDCs involved in the primary industry of farming these products have continued to be grown. As a result, many countries are now dependent on one or two crops as their main source of income. This is known as primary product dependency.

ACTIVITY

1 a) Make a list of ten products you own (this could be clothing, electrical products, food, etc.).

  b) Find out which countries they were made in and add these to your list.

  c) Plot the results on a map of the world to show which products came from MEDCs and which came from LEDCs.

  d) In small groups, discuss where other people's products have come from and add these to your map in different colours.

  e) How much do you depend on world trade, according to your map? Discuss your ideas in pairs, small groups or as a class before writing your answer.

- Raw cocoa beans can be imported into the European Union (EU) and the USA without any tariff being imposed.
- If it is processed in an LEDC country into cocoa butter, the tariff for importing them to the EU or USA goes up to over 10 per cent.
- If the LEDC turns it into cocoa powder, the tariff becomes 15 per cent.
- If it is actually made into chocolate, then the tariff becomes 20 per cent.
- This means that LEDCs are forced to remain as exporters of raw materials: but the real profits are made by those in MEDCs who turn the raw materials into products.

Where are profits highest – in exporting cocoa or in selling chocolate?

Primary products

The price of primary (farmed) products on the world market tends to be low with prices set by buyers in MEDCs. The producing countries have very little control over the value of their crops. The real value is added when the farmed and harvested raw materials such as coffee beans are processed and made into a finished product, such as freeze-dried instant coffee.

Trade gap

The goods that many LEDCs now import cost more than the money they get for their exports; this is known as the 'TRADE GAP'. As a result, they either have to sell more raw materials or borrow the money to make up the difference. This means they are unable to invest their money in new infrastructure such as health, education, transport and energy production. The increasing trade gap is making it very difficult for LEDCs to develop.

Tariffs and quotas

If an LEDC does need to borrow money then the banks or government from the MEDCs will usually attach conditions to their loans. These conditions may state that LEDCs are not allowed to add import tariffs (a tax on particular products that come into the country) or quotas (a limit on the amount of goods that can be brought into their country) on any goods imported to their country. However, MEDCs can impose such tariffs or quotas as the box opposite shows.

Subsidies

Another way in which MEDCS are able to help their farmers is through providing subsidies. A subsidy is when governments give large amounts of taxpayers' money to help keep their farmers in business and ensure they make a profit. In 2003, the USA's cotton farmers received $3.8 billion in subsidies. The farmers produced so much cotton that it could not all be sold in the USA, so they sold it on the world market (called dumping).

The International Cotton Advisory Committee claims that because there was so much cotton for sale around the world it had the effect of lowering prices by about 25 per cent. This in turn meant that in many African countries the millions of people who are involved in growing cotton received less income.

In 2004, Brazil took the issue of cotton subsidies before a World Trade Organisation (WTO) panel who eventually agreed that the subsidies given to US farmers broke world trade rules. The ruling stated that the US government should stop giving money to cotton farmers or potentially face trade sanctions. Sanctions would mean that other countries would not trade with the USA, having a devastating impact on its economy.

But in May 2008, the US government passed a bill that actually increased subsidies received by US farmers to $290 billion. Further WTO trade talks collapsed in July 2008 when China, India and the USA failed to agree to protect farmers in LEDCs from exploitation. The UN estimates that unfair trade rules cost the poorest countries more than $1 billion in lost income each year.

Debt trap

LEDCs want to develop quickly, but, as we have already seen, the income for the products they produce usually leaves them with a trade gap. In order to develop quickly LEDCs need to borrow money from MEDCs or organisations such as the World Bank, or the International Monetary Fund (IMF). The World Bank and International Monetary Fund are organisations that loan money to LEDCs for large-scale development projects.

ACTIVITIES

1 Why do government subsidies to cotton farmers in the USA affect cotton farmers in LEDCs?

2 There are two points of view on the cotton subsidies example. That of a cotton grower in an LEDC and that of an American cotton farmer.
   a) Make a list of arguments to support each of the points of view.
   b) Which argument do you agree with most? Explain your reasons.

3 How would you go about making world trade fairer? Evaluate your ideas by discussing as a class the positive and negative impact of your ideas. Using the points from your discussion, re-think your idea and make changes which reflect your classroom discussion.

Interest payments

But governments or organisations that lend the money expect interest on the loan every year and to be paid back on time. This means that much of the money the LEDC earns from selling the primary products is swallowed up in paying back the loans. If a crop should be destroyed by disease or extreme weather (such as in Nicaragua in 1998 when Hurricane Mitch wiped out 90 per cent of the banana plantations), then the country earns less – leaving less for development after the interest in debts has been paid. A country may even find itself in a situation where it has to borrow more money to pay back the initial loan. This is known as the debt trap.

Loans and their conditions

In 2005, the total debt of the 52 poorest countries was $375 billion. Even though they have actually paid back the money they borrowed, the interest payments keep adding to the total bill. This means they still have to pay $30 million a day between them.

There may also be conditions on what the money can be spent on. Many loans are given on the condition that the money is used on large-scale development projects such as dams or power stations. But large-scale projects do not always help everyone: for example, a dam that produces HYDROELECTRIC POWER is of little or no use to someone that doesn't have electrical appliances.

Some loans are also given for political reasons, for example, Israel receives more money (in the form of loans and aid) from the USA than any other country in the world. In return, the USA has air bases located throughout Israel giving them access to the Middle East.

Another debt problem many countries are now facing is that their debts are being bought from governments by private companies. These private companies are then suing the country as they struggle to pay the debts for even larger sums of money. An example of this is a company called Donegal International who sued Zambia for $55 million following an original debt of $3 million. The company were awarded $15 million. This was money that Zambia needed to invest in its own country. These are known as 'vulture funds'.

ACTIVITIES

1 How does increasing debt affect a country's ability to develop economically and socially?
2 Are the conditions attached to the loans that LEDCs receive fair? Discuss your answer.
3 Do you think the debts of LEDCs should be wiped out? Make a list of the arguments for and against and discuss your ideas in a group.

Poverty cycle

The diagram below shows how millions of people become trapped in a life of poverty from which it is difficult to escape.

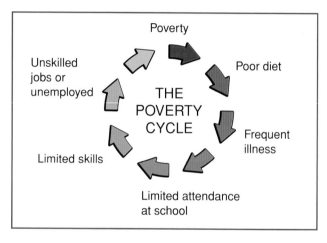

Living at or near to absolute poverty will mean living on a poor diet, which will eventually cause malnutrition. This makes people more vulnerable to diseases, especially when they are very young and very old. Illness causes many children to miss school, but many children also do not attend school because the family needs every child to help in their struggle for survival. So many children spend time working in workshops for very low pay or in the family's field. They help the family to scrape together enough to exist, but when they are older they, too, live on a poor diet and so the next generation continues to struggle. This is the reality of the POVERTY CYCLE.

The poverty cycle can also be used with a table of development indicators to show how they link together in a chain of causes and effects.

1 a) Draw your own copy of the poverty cycle opposite. Choose an LEDC and research the development indicators (see page 168) for that country. You could use websites such as the UN's (www.un.org) or an atlas. Add the information for your chosen country to your poverty cycle. For example, you could choose Zimbabwe and start with the low average income (GNP per capita) there. Next show what this low income might lead to (for example, a lower CALORIE INTAKE).

b) Compare the results for your country to the others in your class.

c) Do levels of development differ between LEDC countries? If so, why do you think this is?

HIV/AIDS

One particular health issue that is having an impact on global inequality is the increasing number of people in Africa with HIV or AIDS. At present, the United Nations estimate that 60 million people in the African continent are infected with the HIV virus. The UN go on to estimate that the epidemic could reach its height by 2025 with 90 million people infected. The lack of readily available contraception and family planning will see the numbers continue to grow. There are medicines available to treat HIV/AIDS (though not cure it), but the majority of people living in Africa simply can't afford them. The unfair trade rules and debts mean the governments are spending money paying back loans rather than using their money to help their own people. Millions of children have been left orphans as their parents have died from this treatable disease. In the UK the treatment would be given free on the NHS.

Political factors

Colonial countries were keen to gain their independence from their rulers. However, since their independence, many countries have been badly run as the leaders have been more concerned with their own wealth rather than the wealth and development of their own people. During colonial control, country borders were clearly defined, but once independence was gained, tribal wars broke out as people wanted their original land back.

This fighting has seen leaders using loans and financial aid to fund weapons and other military hardware to fight the wars rather than developing their country. As a result, food production has been neglected resulting in widespread famine in many parts of the African continent.

The example of Zimbabwe

This can be seen clearly through the example of Zimbabwe. In 1980, following decades of British rule and bitter civil war, the country of Zimbabwe (previously known as Rhodesia) was founded under the leadership of President Robert Mugabe. Throughout his rule life expectancy has fallen from 57 in 1990 to 37 in 2008. This has been due to drought in key growing areas, but also due to a government 'land resettlement' policy in which 4,500 white farmers had their land seized, often through the use of violence, and were forced to leave Zimbabwe.

These farmers accounted for 70 per cent of the country's food and export crops such as cotton and tobacco. The purpose of the land seizures was to give land to the native people of Zimbabwe, but since this process began in the year 2000, much of the land has gone to waste as many of the new owners don't have the financial resources or skills to farm the land.

Zimbabwe has gone from being the 'breadbasket of Africa' to a country that can no longer feed its own people. The World Food Programme predicted that 5.1 million people in Zimbabwe are facing starvation in 2009.

In what many consider desperation, President Mugabe signed an aid deal with Chinese president Hu Jintao in Beijing in 2005. In return for providing aid and funds that Zimbabwe could use to pay back loans, China would be able to exploit minerals from Zimbabwe that it needs in its growing industries. China promised to help Zimbabwe and not interfere with its internal politics (for example, they would not interfere with land resettlement, unlike other countries which have imposed sanctions on Zimbabwe because of it). The Chinese government will now have a great

Chinese President Hu Jintao and Zimbabwe President Robert Mugabe in Beijing in November 2006. What do you think the advantages and disadvantages of an alliance between China and Zimbabwe are for each country?

deal of influence in Zimbabwe, much as the British did when they ruled Zimbabwe.

Following a controversial re-election campaign in June 2008, which many governments throughout the world believe Mugabe lost, Mugabe was able to remain in shared power through the use of corruption and violence. The USA and UK called for sanctions to be imposed on the Zimbabwean leader by all United Nations countries. Russia and China disagreed and vetoed the plan in support of Mugabe. As a direct result of the corruption and violent election campaign in Zimbabwe, food giant Tesco announced in June 2008 that it would stop buying products from Zimbabwe while the political crisis continued. Tesco buy about £1 million worth of produce a year from Zimbabwe.

In July 2009, at the G8 summit in Italy, the US President, Barack Obama, delivered a 'tough love' message to corrupt African leaders. He said that African development had been stunted because Western donors had 'made excuses about corruption and poor governance'.

ACTIVITIES

1 Why do you think Robert Mugabe was keen to strike a deal with China? Use the internet to research your answer. Visit www.bbc.co.uk/news and type in 'Mugabe China deal'.
2 Do you agree with the actions of Tesco? Explain your view.
3 Should financial aid be given to countries which are known to have corrupt political systems? Discuss your ideas in a group.

Environmental factors

Over the past few years the environment has become the biggest global challenge that faces human existence. We frequently hear about global warming and the impact this is having on different parts of the world, particularly in LEDCs, which are least well equipped to deal with weather extremes and the problems associated with them.

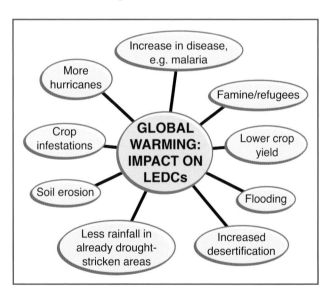

In addition to the problems presented by global warming, localised human activity is making the environmental situation worse. In some parts of Africa overgrazing is leading to increased DESERTIFICATION. As cattle or other animals graze on the vegetation the conditions are so poor that it doesn't grow back. Over many years this process has led to soil erosion, which over time has led to expansion of desert areas.

A second major environmental impact on LEDCs is the effect of earthquakes, volcanoes and tsunamis. As with global warming, LEDCs are the countries least well equipped to deal with these natural hazards as they often don't have the money, equipment, knowledge or INFRASTRUCTURE to help the situation. LEDCs frequently rely on the work of aid agencies and the governments of MEDCs for support in such times of crisis.

The environmental and human factors combined make for a deadly combination in which the governments of LEDCs and people struggle to cope. In the summer of 2008, for example, Haiti (one of the poorest countries in the world) was devastated by four hurricanes in the space of three weeks. Hundreds of people were killed and over 1,000,000 people were left homeless as 80 per cent of homes were destroyed. Widespread flooding contaminated water supplies and impassable roads made it extremely difficult to get aid through. The shortage of food led to rioting as people become increasingly desperate to feed their families. It will take years for Haiti to recover from such devastation.

Case Study
Ghana

Ghana is located on the western coast of Africa between the Ivory Coast and Togo and has a population of 23 million.

Historical causes

The Europeans that arrived in Ghana in 1471 found a land rich in natural resources, which included diamonds and gold. Word of this discovery soon

African slaves working.

Independence Day celebrations in Ghana.

spread throughout Europe and Dutch, Danish, German and British traders arrived to trade cloth, weapons, mirrors, jewellery, rum and guns for gold. As a result Ghana became known as the 'Gold Coast'.

Over time, a new resource was traded that became more important than gold. The resource was slaves. Slaves were needed to work on the plantations in the Americas. By 1660, European traders were buying more than 100,000 slaves per year from Ghana. This caused civil war among the local tribes as they fought with each other to capture native people to sell.

Eventually, after fighting the dominant Ashanti tribes, the 'Gold Coast' became a British colony. The different kingdoms and tribes within the 'Gold Coast' were forced together to make one country.

Not content with the diamonds, gold and slaves, the British further exploited the native people by paying very little for products such as ivory, pepper, corn, timber and metal ores. Railways were built throughout the country to transport these goods to the coast where they could be loaded onto ships and exported to Europe. As the colony developed, greater infrastructure was needed, so some schools, hospitals and roads were built. However, these had to be paid for with taxes paid by the native people, who didn't always get the best use of them.

In 1957 the 'Gold Coast' became one of the first African countries to become independent and it changed its name to Ghana. It was now a free country, but its raw materials had been taken, few people had an education or the skills needed to run a country, and many of the culture and traditions had been changed or wiped out as the colonial powers had forced the natives to follow Christianity, change their language and observe other European behaviour.

Economic causes

After gold, cocoa is Ghana's main export. Cocoa is used to make chocolate and the cocoa produced in Ghana is considered to be among the world's finest. Two million people in Ghana rely on cocoa production, but being a cocoa farmer isn't an easy life. On average a cocoa farmer in Ghana makes about $160 per year. With this they have to pay for food (if they don't grow their own), school fees, doctors' fees, transport, clothes and all the other essentials.

The price a farmer in Ghana gets for their cocoa can change on a daily basis as it is traded on the stock exchange. This means the Ghanaian farmers have little or no financial security. As with other primary products, the price of cocoa has decreased recently and many farmers are finding that they are paid less now than they were in the 1990s. The cocoa farmers are unable to process the cocoa themselves as they don't have the TECHNOLOGY. Even if they did they would be hit by high import tariffs (see box on page 174). Primary product dependency is a major problem for the cocoa farmers. When prices are low, they may not have the resources or skills to diversify and therefore their income falls.

In order to develop quickly, Ghana has borrowed considerable amounts of money, but now finds itself in the debt trap, having to pay back huge amounts of interest each year. Ghana's debt is now over $6 billion.

Environmental causes

Ghana has also seen three-quarters of the rainforest in the south of the country destroyed by logging companies keen to exploit the timber. Farmers have moved on to these cleared areas but have found that the exposed soil soon becomes eroded. In the north of Ghana, the areas that were once savannah grasslands have turned into desert. Poor quality soil means lower crop yields and fewer livestock. This in turn means less food, which could eventually lead to increased dependency on imports.

Tourism is another part of the economy that may help Ghana reduce its dependence on agriculture.

The Ghanaian government is working hard to reduce primary product dependency on crops such as cocoa and its debt burden by encouraging the setting up of manufacturing industries. In 2006, manufactured products accounted for $320 million of Ghana's income. Compared to their debt, however, this is still very little.

ACTIVITIES

1 Copy out the table below.

Historical	Economic	Environmental

   Read through the case study of Ghana and under each of the headings in the table make notes on each of the causes of its lack of development.
2 Why is the Ghanaian government working to encourage exports of manufactured goods?
3 What problems could Ghana face if it wants to export manufactured goods to the USA or countries in the European Union?

CONCEPT 3

Global inequality affects both LEDCs and MEDCs

In this section we will be learning about the impact of the following on LEDCs and MEDCs:

- Global interdependence.
- Multinational companies.
- Global branding.
- Expansion of tourism.

The following are ideas and terms that you will need to know from this concept section:

globalisation • global interdependence • global branding • economic power and technological power of MEDCs • cultural stereotyping in the media • expansion of tourism • multinational companies

Global interdependence

GLOBALISATION is a relatively new term. It simply means the increased movement of people, ideas, goods, services and money between people and countries all over the world. Due to modern-day communication and travel, the world has effectively become borderless, and people and businesses can interact with others from all over the planet. Increased globalisation has led to increased GLOBAL INTERDEPENDENCE. This means that people and countries throughout the world are now dependent on one another. An example of globalisation is the sportswear company Adidas. They design their products in Europe, make them in South East Asia, and then sell them in North America.

The increase of globalisation has led to much debate and even conflict as to whether or not globalisation is having a positive or negative impact throughout the world.

Some of the arguments for and against globalisation are as follows:

ARGUMENTS FOR GLOBALISATION	ARGUMENTS AGAINST GLOBALISATION
• Increased free trade between nations.	• Greater chance of violence to preserve culture which is being destroyed by MEDC and multinational influence.
• Creates employment in LEDCs.	
• Increased communication between countries.	• Greater risk of disease being spread unintentionally between nations: for example, the spread of swine flu in 2009.
• Greater ease and speed of transportation of goods and people.	
• Spread of ideas throughout the world.	• Increase in the spread of materialistic lifestyles (i.e. what goods we have: for example, LCD TVs, mobile phones, money).
• Understanding of other cultures.	
• Easier movement of money between banks, companies and countries which allows for investment.	• Increased damage to natural environment.
	• International organisations such as the World Trade Organisation will tell countries what to do.
• Closer relationships develop between nations reducing the likelihood of conflict.	
• Sharing of ideas, goods, processes and practices.	• Increased chance of civil war within and open war between LEDCs as they fight for natural resources.
• Global mass media ties the world together.	
• Increases in environmental protection in MEDCs.	• Skilled workers leave LEDCs.

Despite the arguments in favour of globalisation, many people believe it contributes further to the causes of global inequality because of the increasing economic and technological power that MEDCs have over LEDCs. Giant global brands such as Nike, Shell, McDonald's and Nestlé are all examples of MULTINATIONAL COMPANIES (sometimes known as transnational companies or TNCs). They have set up offices and factories in LEDCs throughout the world so that they can get the benefits of cheaper labour and lower taxes and land prices.

The negative impact of globalisation can be seen through the following examples.

Shell Oil in Nigeria

Nigeria contributes ten per cent of Shell's global oil production. Shell has been in Nigeria since 1956, providing a much-needed income to the country. However, there has been much conflict over the oil reserves and, in June 2004, following a year-long investigation, Shell acknowledged that it inadvertently caused conflict, poverty and corruption within the country. Other reports allege that Shell was aware of the problems it was causing. For example, some people point to a failure to clear up oil spills quickly enough, which contaminated water supplies. There is also major concern over the way Nigerian governments have treated those Nigerians who protested about Shell's involvement in Nigeria. In June 2008, the Nigerian President Umaru Yar'Adua said that Shell would be replaced by another oil operator by 2009.

The weapons trade

The USA, UK, France, Germany, Russia and China account for 88 per cent of the world's trade in weapons. These countries are involved in a multi-billion-dollar industry that clearly does well out of conflicts throughout the world.

In 2008, China was criticised for supplying weapons to Sudan, which was then in the middle of a humanitarian crisis in which 200,000 people died during five years of war. In February 2008, film director Steven Spielberg resigned his post as an artistic adviser to the Beijing Olympics in protest at China's arms deals with Sudan.

Britain, France and America were heavily criticised in September 2005 following a weapons fair in London in which countries with poor human rights records, such as Indonesia, Colombia and Saudi Arabia, were invited to view and buy weapons battle-tested in the Iraq war.

Sports clothing factory working conditions

Some major sportswear companies have received much negative publicity in recent years for the conditions in which the people that make their products are treated, including:

- Workers may earn as little as a $1 a day.
- Workers are sometimes forced to work overtime.
- Standard working days are up to 14 hours long.
- They work standing up at machines, which creates back problems.
- Workers are not allowed toilet breaks, which can lead to urine infections.
- They must work in dimly lit areas, which can lead to problems with eyesight.
- Workers are often humiliated.
- Workers are not allowed to join a trade union.
- They have to deal with physical and verbal abuse.
- Child labour is common.

The governments of LEDCs are keen to attract large multinational companies as it is a way of generating the much-needed income to help the country develop. With vast sums of money at stake the companies have great influence over the governments – sometimes more influence than the native people have.

ACTIVITIES

1 Work in pairs. One person should argue for globalisation and the other against. Argue your viewpoint with your partner.
2 Write a paragraph explaining your own view on globalisation and global interdependence.
3 Use the internet to research a global branded company. Produce your own case study explaining the impact that company has had on LEDCs throughout the world.

The expansion of tourism

Globalisation has also seen an expansion in the worldwide tourist industry. As a result of better communication and media coverage, people are increasingly aware of the world around them and have a desire to experience new places. With the cost of air travel falling and increased disposable income, people are now able to travel to places throughout the world relatively cheaply.

Due to the warm climates, different cultural experiences on offer, and the cheap cost of holidays and travel within the country, many LEDCs have seen huge rises in the numbers of visitors in recent years. As a result, many of these countries have seen large-scale developments, particularly in coastal areas where tourists want to stay. The expansion of tourism has both positive and negative impacts.

Although there are financial benefits to LEDCs from globalisation and global interdependence, the benefits to MEDCs are far greater. The LEDCs are trapped in a situation where they rely on MEDCs for much of their income, which means that many LEDCs are no longer in complete control of their own country.

POSITIVE IMPACTS OF TOURISM	NEGATIVE IMPACTS OF TOURISM
• Brings in much needed income from overseas visitors, which can help kickstart economies. For example, Spain used tourism to fund huge expansion in the 1950s and 1960s. North Africa and South East Asia have used tourism to help develop more modern economies and expand business opportunities. • Creates employment. • Creates an increased market for souvenirs and crafts. • Improves infrastructure, for example, better roads, airports, sewage systems. • Can help reduce migration as more local job opportunities are available. • Leads to a greater awareness of environmental issues. • Reduces fear/suspicion of other cultures, and can make people more open to new ideas. • Visitors are able to see the wealth gap first-hand. • Promotes trade between LEDCs and MEDCs.	• Leads to destruction of environment for new hotels and infrastructure. • Reduces peace and privacy of locals. • Increases pollution. • Can damage visitor attractions (for example, erosion of coastal areas). • Most financial benefits of tourism go to people from MEDCs who own the hotels, airlines, etc. • Visitor numbers can fluctuate, meaning the boost to the local economy is unstable or seasonal. • Many jobs in tourism are unskilled so there is little training for locals. • The local way of life will change, including job opportunities. • Local traditions may disappear or lose their significance, leading to resentment. • Some tourists may see locals as inferior to them. • Can lead to moral corruption: theft, sex tourism, etc.

The money that tourists bring in can be invaluable to an LEDC.

ACTIVITY

1 Research one of the LEDCs that has become popular with tourists. Find out the following information:
   a) Why it is a popular tourist destination (climate information, attractions, types of holidays available, for example, beach, adventure).
   b) The benefits of tourism for this country.
   c) The drawbacks of tourism for this country.

CONCEPT 4

The different ways of addressing the problems of global inequality may vary in effectiveness

In this concept section we will be learning about:

- Different types of aid.
- The action of pressure groups and the cancellation of debt.
- Fair trade.
- The expansion of tourism.
- Millennium development goals.

The following are ideas and terms that you will need to know from this concept section:

reducing/resolving global inequality • fair trade • cancellation of debt • expansion of tourism • Millennium Development Goals • types of aid • government and non-government organisations (NGOs) • aid: unilateral, bilateral, multilateral, humanitarian

Is aid the best way to reduce global inequality?

One way of reducing global inequality is through the giving of aid. Aid can take many different forms.

1) Development aid

Development aid involves the giving of aid from one country, group of countries or financial institutions to help a country develop. It is sometimes referred to as development co-operation as countries work together to improve the standard of living in the recipient country. Development aid can take two forms: bilateral and multilateral.

a) Bilateral aid

This involves one country giving aid to another. It may involve conditions in which the receiving country is required to spend the aid on products from the donor country. The donor country may use bilateral aid as a marketing tool to increase future trade between the countries. An example of this could involve Britain giving money to Ghana and sending experts to help in the construction of a hydroelectric dam.

b) Multilateral aid

This involves governments from MEDCs giving money to organisations who then decide how the money is spent. Organisations such as the United Nations will receive money and then distribute it to sub-organisations such as the World Health Organisation (WHO) or UNICEF who focus on helping children throughout the world. As with bilateral aid, there are usually conditions attached to this type of aid, but these are decided by the organisation rather than the government. An example of this is the European Union who have given money to the World Health Organisation to help tackle the problem of HIV and AIDS in Africa.

2) NGOs

NGO stands for NON GOVERNMENTAL ORGANISATIONS. These are basically charities that are set up in MEDCs. Money is raised through appeals or events such as Red Nose Day, which is run by Comic Relief. Some people will also give regular donations each month. These organisations also receive tax relief from governments so that more of the money can be put to good use. NGOs often work closely with communities in specific areas rather than the country as a whole. This means the aid can be targeted to meet specific needs making it more effective.

3) Short-term aid/unilateral (humanitarian)

This aid is given by governments or raised by non-government organisations, such as Christian Aid or Oxfam, to help prevent or deal with the suffering resulting from natural and man-made disasters: for example, aid in the form of shelter, food, water and medicine to the Darfur region of Sudan from 2004 to the present day, or to Sri Lanka, India and South East Asia after the Tsunami in December 2004. This aid is a genuine response to human suffering and is in solidarity with those who may have lost their homes, livelihoods and members of their family. It doesn't have conditions attached to it as with other types of loans. Some would argue that there are potential long-term problems with this type of aid. Some of these arguments are outlined opposite (see 'Long-term aid').

4) Long-term aid

Long-term aid is money given to LEDCs to encourage long-term economic growth, aiming to develop their economies through trying to tackle the root causes of poverty, such as weaknesses in agriculture, industry, nutrition, health and education. The idea is that long-term development aid encourages economic growth, which enables the LEDC to develop its industry and participate in world trade and so make profits to develop their own society. However, some would argue that there are potential long-term problems with development aid, such as:

- It leads to the growth of governments and bureaucracies, which use up valuable resources and are slow in giving out the aid.
- It can increase inequality within LEDCs. The powerful ruling elites have greater access to aid and its benefits compared to the rest of society.
- It tends to create economic inefficiency; it damages traditional markets and leads to a waste of resources. An example of this is aid given to Nigeria after 1970, which was used to build up military resources instead of funding schools and hospitals.

ACTIVITIES

1 Copy out the table below. For each of the different types of aid you have just read about, explain in your own words how the aid works and identify the positive and negative effects of it. The first row has been filled out as an example.

TYPE OF AID	HOW DOES IT WORK	POSITIVE EFFECTS	NEGATIVE EFFECTS
Bilateral aid	One country gives aid directly to another	Builds relations between the donor and receiving country	Conditions can be attached to the aid, such as the receiving country must buy products from the donating country

2 Do you think the different types of aid that are given are fair? What would you change about them to enable LEDCs to develop at a quicker rate?

Is more aid really the answer?

Oxfam believes that there is no excuse for poverty in the twenty-first century. As such, Oxfam works closely with others to reduce poverty and bring about lasting change by helping people climb out of poverty.

Oxfam was set up during the Second World War. People all over the UK collected parcels of food, clothes and other essentials that were to be distributed to those whose lives had been destroyed by the war. The group decided to expand their work to include people throughout the world whose lives had been affected by war or other reasons. Oxfam is now one of the main aid agencies in the UK and has branches in 11 countries throughout the world.

Oxfam is largely funded through private donations. People are made aware of the work it does through media campaigns. It also has charity shops within the UK and offers a range of items for sale online, including gifts that can be purchased for people in LEDCs, such as goats, schoolbooks and water pumps. It has also linked up with organisations such as www.bignoisemusic.com and receives a share of the profits from music downloads.

Oxfam has programmes in more than 70 countries. These involve working with local people to improve their standard of living. In local communities it trains health workers, sets up schools and safeguards water supplies. It also responds to emergencies, providing clean water, food and shelter for areas devastated by floods, hurricanes and conflict. Oxfam also represents the views of the poor to governments and powerful organisations, and encourages people to speak up for themselves to change their lives for the better.

Afghanistan
When the war broke out in Afghanistan in 2001, thousands of people were forced to leave their homes. Oxfam set up makeshift camps in Pakistan so that people could escape the US bombing campaign. Clean water and food were brought for the thousands of refugees and Oxfam also helped with the running of schools so that children's education could continue. Once the Taliban had surrendered, Oxfam was able to open its Afghanistan offices again and begin helping the people rebuild their lives. Oxfam has actually been in Afghanistan since 1992. During this time it has regularly distributed food to those who cannot grow or afford to buy their own because of the droughts the country has experienced. It has also provided local water supplies and given training in health and hygiene. Local people have been trained by Oxfam to lead local projects so that the people of Afghanistan don't need to rely on outside agencies.

Ghana
Oxfam has given money to health centres in Ghana to buy fridges to store vaccines. Motorbikes have also been provided to enable the locally trained health workers to visit remote areas of the country to give the vaccines. People have been vaccinated against cerebral spinal meningitis, polio, measles, diphtheria, tuberculosis and typhoid. The vaccines don't cost the people of Ghana a penny. Health centres funded by Oxfam provide a base from which trained staff can give advice on health issues and family planning.

Mali
The Tamachek nomads used to live traditional lives in Mali that involved moving from place to place to find new pastures for the livestock. The government didn't consider them important and, when severe drought killed their cattle, they were forced to settle in villages. Without the skills to farm the land their standard of living was poor. Oxfam provided support to help the new villagers improve their standard of living. They are now able to vote for a government representative, which means their voice will now be heard rather than ignored.

Cambodia
Oxfam, along with the Cambodian government and other NGOs, has partly funded a school in Cambodia, which means that 500 children can receive an education and a way out of poverty. The pupils attend the school in two shifts, morning and afternoon. The children that attend the school get a free school meal, thus ensuring they don't become malnourished. The school has become so successful it is in danger of becoming oversubscribed. Some of the funding from Oxfam provides scholarships and is used to pay for uniforms and equipment if parents can't afford to.

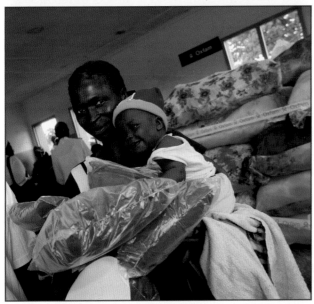

Oxfam are involved in a wide range of humanitarian activities. Here they are shown distributing hygiene supplies in Gaza City (*top*) and passing out mosquito nets to villagers in a malaria-stricken district of Zimbabwe (*bottom*).

Iraq

Oxfam works in areas where people are most vulnerable, providing food, water and temporary shelter. This is often in areas worst hit by violence. It has renovated and equipped primary healthcare facilities and provided emergency healthcare for those in need. It has also been working hard to promote women's rights and has liaised with other NGOs to implement programmes to reduce the conflict between different groups of refugees in the country.

Since its creation in 1942 Oxfam has helped millions of people throughout the world, many of whom would be dead without the help received. Oxfam continues to strive for an end to global inequality and raises money from charitable donations, high street and online shops and events such as Oxjam.

ACTIVITY

1 Oxfam is one example of an aid agency that is working to make a difference. In pairs or threes, produce a presentation about Oxfam or another aid agency which tries to make a difference. You should include the following things in your presentation:
   • When and how did the organisation begin?
   • How is it funded?
   • What does the organisation do?
   • Where does it operate?
   • Give details of a country in which it has worked and the impact it has had there.

Is fair trade the best way of reducing inequality?

The Trade Justice Movement (TJM) argues that trade is not free and fair for the developing world. The Movement is a group of organisations made up of aid agencies, trade unions, fair trade organisations, faith and consumer groups. It is involved with the Make Poverty History Campaign, launched in December 2004, which calls on the UK government to change the rules and practices of unjust trade, cancel poor countries' debts and deliver more and better aid. This is part of a global campaign. Reasons why the TJM argues trade is not free and fair include the following:

• The global system of trade has rules that allow MEDCs and multinational companies to make large profits, but prevent LEDCs from increasing theirs. It is not fair that MEDCs subsidise their farmers to overproduce goods that are then sold cheaply in LEDCs, forcing poor farmers out of business.
• Companies are out to make profits, which may not be to the advantage of local people in LEDCs.

- MEDCs argue that free trade reduces poverty. But when LEDCs open up their markets to free trade, foreign businesses from MEDCs with huge advantages over businesses in the LEDC come to take over local markets by selling cheap goods. Local producers then suffer. When LEDCs do succeed in manufacturing their own goods that do sell well in MEDCs, there is an immediate outcry from threatened businesses in MEDCs. This often leads the governments of MEDCs to put a quota or tariffs on imports. This is what happened in 2005 when China successfully penetrated the European T-shirt market.

- The World Trade Organisation (WTO) is supposed to ensure that all countries keep the global trading rules and it promotes free trade. All 147 members of the WTO are supposed to have an equal say in its work. However, this doesn't happen as the WTO meeting is run as a series of smaller meetings in which delegates from different countries send representatives to negotiate their point of view. Many of the smaller LEDCs can only send a small number of delegates which means their views cannot be represented in all the meetings. Therefore decisions are made without their knowledge. In 2006 the European Union sent over 650 delegates to the meetings.

- The IMF and the World Bank give aid to or cancel the debts of LEDCs but often with strict conditions relating to how LEDCs should trade.

In recent years, public awareness of unjust trade has increased, which has meant a rise in people wanting to buy products that give a fair deal to the people that make them. The 'fair trade' brand has seen its sales grow dramatically. Supermarket products are clearly labelled as fair trade so consumers have the option of supporting this movement. Fairtrade fortnight takes place in March each year and continues to raise public awareness of the plight of many farmers in LEDCs.

However, recent reports suggest that the 2008–09 credit crunch has seen sales of fair trade and organic products fall as customers are looking to get more for their money.

Is the cancellation of debt the best way to reduce global inequality?

A high level of debt among LEDCs has long been seen as a major barrier to development. The Jubilee 2000 campaign was started in the UK in the 1980s. Supported by NGOs, churches and individuals, it campaigned for the unsustainable debts of LEDCs to be dropped by the UK government by the year 2000. By freeing such countries from the crippling effects of debt, they

Campaigns like Make Poverty History help people understand what's going on in the world, and this can lead to action. High-profile stunts such as this help to get the message across.

x

would be able to develop their economies and societies in a sustainable way. As this has not happened, it is now called the Jubilee Debt Campaign, and it is involved with the Make Poverty History Campaign.

The Jubilee Debt Campaign, and other organisations that call for debt cancellation or reduction, argue that the effects include those shown in the diagram below.

However, wiping out debt is not as simple as it sounds. When governments plan their budgets they include money linked to loan repayments. If the debts are cleared the difference has to be found from somewhere else. This could be through a reduction in spending elsewhere, for example, spending less on education or healthcare, or through increasing taxes. This would prove unpopular with the public and could lead to the government being voted out at the next election.

The continued pressure from the Make Poverty History Campaign and others led to an announcement at the G8 summit in Edinburgh in July 2005. It was stated that $1 billion per year would be wiped off the debts of LEDCs. Although this sounds a significant amount, it actually equates to $1 for every person living in the countries with the debt. Make Poverty History states that at least $10 billion per year needs to be wiped off the debt to eradicate extreme poverty.

In 2005, Gordon Brown announced that Britain was to wipe out all of its bilateral debts as a means of reducing global inequality, and in April 2006 he announced $15 billion of aid for education in Africa and Asia over a ten-year period. This was the British contribution to a $50 billion per year increase in aid to Africa, which aims to meet the targets set by the United Nations Millennium Development Goals.

Since the announcement in 2005, world leaders have continued to meet, with global inequality being high on the agenda. In July 2009, G8 leaders met in Italy and agreed to set up a £12.3 billion fund to help the world's poorest countries grow and sell more of their own food, rather than rely on food aid.

Such developments show the impact that pressure groups can have on governments to bring about change. However, despite this, the gap in global inequality is continuing to increase, and as the gap increases so does the money needed to bridge the gap.

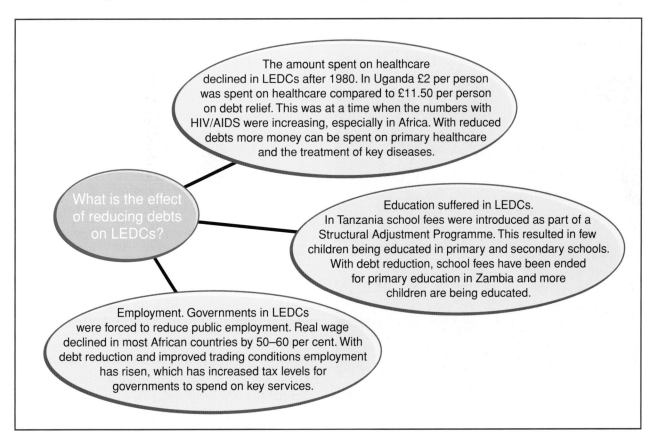

Is tourism the best way to reduce global inequality?

In recent years, a new type of tourism has emerged that benefits the people within a country and has little, if any, negative impacts. This has become known as SUSTAINABLE TOURISM.

Sustainable tourism means that tourists are able to enjoy their holiday while still respecting the local culture and place. It also means that local people are involved in the decisions that could affect them and actually receive a fair share of the earnings. Another benefit is that minimal damage is done to the environment, which is often the reason that attracted tourists there in the first place. This means that the country maintains its character, local people don't feel as if they are being taken advantage of, the tourists are able to experience the real culture as opposed to a manufactured one, and, most importantly, tourism is able to continue indefinitely. This could help thousands of people climb their way out of poverty.

There are two types of sustainable tourism.

Sustainable tourism can help local people by providing an income and the opportunity to teach visitors about their lives and culture.

Community tourism

Community tourism involves small groups of tourists visiting local communities and actually staying with local people. They will eat local food, learn about cultures and customs and live the lives of the people they are staying with. This means that the money that would usually go to the big tour companies will go straight to the local people. Such holidays could involve staying with rainforest tribes and learning their survival skills, or hunting with the Bushmen of the Kalahari desert.

Eco-tourism

Eco-tourists are likely to want to learn about the different species of plant and animal life, and may even work with local people on schemes that help protect endangered animals. There are rules in place, which if followed help preserve the ecosystem (for example, not leaving litter). Eco-tourism helps protect the environment while also bringing in much needed income for local people. In some areas where eco-tourism occurs, there are likely to be limits on the number of tourists. This means that the area can remain sustainable.

Tumani Tenda

An example of both community and eco-tourism can be seen in the Gambia, West Africa. Tumani Tenda is an eco-tourism camp.

The camp is in a Jolla village with around 300 inhabitants. The village owns 140 hectares of land, which is sustainably cultivated. Accommodation is sensitive to the surrounding environment and uses local resources and materials. Activities provided for tourists include historical talks, cultural experiences, cooking lessons, farming tours, tree planting, living with an African family, canoe trips, community forest tours, oyster collecting, fishing, dancing and singing. Tourists staying at the camp are expected to follow sets of rules that respect both the local culture and the environment.

All the money spent by tourists goes to the village development fund. The fund is used for the development, infrastructure and family needs within the village. So far, money from the eco-tourism camp has helped to build a school, pay the taxes for the whole village, take care of emergency problems, buy medicines and support training and education for the village inhabitants.

Despite the clear benefits of sustainable tourism, it is unlikely to significantly contribute to a reduction in global inequality in the short term, as it tends to be on a small scale and helps only a small number of people.

In the longer term, however, this 'bottom up' approach may be beneficial, as people are in control of their own business and depend less on government support.

How can the United Nations Millennium Development Goals help reduce global inequality?

The United Nations Millennium Development Goals are a set of targets that aim to reduce global inequality (see box on p192). They include halving the number of people in extreme poverty, halting the spread of HIV/AIDS, and providing primary education for all children by 2015. The Goals have been agreed by all the world countries and leading development institutions.

A 2008 Millennium Development Goals report suggests that some of the targets set are well within reach:

- The major goal of reducing absolute poverty by half is within reach for the world as a whole.
- In all but two regions, primary school enrolment is at least 90 per cent.
- Deaths from measles fell from over 750,000 in 2000 to less than 250,000 in 2006, and about 80 per cent of children in developing countries now receive a measles vaccine.

ACTIVITIES

1 Copy out the spider diagram below.

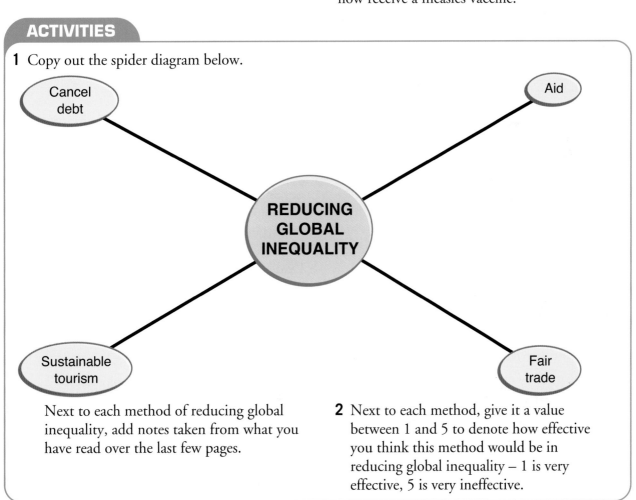

Next to each method of reducing global inequality, add notes taken from what you have read over the last few pages.

2 Next to each method, give it a value between 1 and 5 to denote how effective you think this method would be in reducing global inequality – 1 is very effective, 5 is very ineffective.

- The number of deaths from AIDS fell from 2.2 million in 2005 to 2 million in 2007, and the number of people newly infected declined from 3 million in 2001 to 2.7 million in 2007.
- Malaria prevention is expanding, with widespread increases in insecticide-treated net use among children under five in sub-Saharan Africa: in 16 out of 20 countries, use has at least tripled since around 2000.
- The incidence of tuberculosis is expected to be halted and begin to decline before the target date of 2015.

- Some 1.6 billion people have gained access to safe drinking water since 1990.
- The share of developing countries' export earnings devoted to paying off debt fell from 12.5 per cent in 2000 to 6.6 per cent in 2006, allowing them to put in more resources to reducing poverty.
- The private sector has increased the availability of some essential drugs and has rapidly spread mobile phone technology throughout the developing world.

United Nations Millennium Development Goals

GOAL 1: Eradicate extreme poverty and hunger
- Between 1990 and 2015, halve the proportion of people whose income is less than $1 a day.
- Achieve full and productive employment and decent work for all, including women and young people.
- Between 1990 and 2015, halve the proportion of people who suffer from hunger.

GOAL 2: Achieve universal primary education
- Ensure that, by 2015, children everywhere, boys and girls alike, will be able to complete a full course of primary schooling.

GOAL 3: Promote gender equality and empower women
- Eliminate gender inequality in primary and secondary education, preferably by 2005, and in all levels of education no later than 2015.

GOAL 4: Reduce child mortality
- Between 1990 and 2015, reduce the under-five mortality rate by two-thirds.

GOAL 5: Improve maternal health
- Reduce the number of mothers dying while giving birth ratio by three-quarters.
- Achieve universal access to reproductive healthcare.

GOAL 6: Combat HIV/AIDS, malaria and other diseases
- By 2015, have halted and begun to reverse the spread of HIV/AIDS.

- By 2015, have halted and begun to reverse the incidence of malaria and other major diseases.

GOAL 7: Ensure environmental stability
- Integrate the principles of sustainable development into national policies and programmes, and reverse the loss of environmental resources.
- Reduce bio-diversity loss, achieving, by 2010, a significant reduction in the rate of loss.
- Halve, by 2015, the proportion of the population without sustainable access to safe drinking water and basic sanitation.
- By 2020, achieved a significant improvement in the lives of at least 100 million slum dwellers.

GOAL 8: Develop a global partnership for development
- Address the special needs of the least developed countries, landlocked countries and small island developing states.
- Develop further an open, rule-based, predictable, non-discriminatory trading and financial system.
- Deal comprehensively with developing countries' debt.
- In co-operation with pharmaceutical companies, provide access to affordable essential drugs in developing countries.
- In co-operation with the private sector, make available benefits of new technologies, especially information and communications.

However, some of the targets and perhaps the most significant ones still need greater effort:

- The proportion of people in sub-Saharan Africa living on less than $1 per day is unlikely to be reduced by the target 50 per cent.
- About one quarter of all children in developing countries are considered to be underweight.
- Almost two-thirds of employed women in the developing world are in vulnerable jobs.
- Some 2.5 billion people, almost half the developing world's population, live without improved sanitation.
- Developed countries' foreign aid expenditures declined in 2006 and 2007 and risk falling short of the commitments made in 2005.
- International trade negotiations are years behind schedule and any outcome seems likely to fall far short of the initial high hopes for a development-oriented outcome.

www.un.org/millenniumgoals

Looking ahead to 2015 and beyond, there is no question that we can achieve the overarching goal: we can put an end to poverty. In almost all instances, experience has demonstrated the validity of earlier agreements on the way forward; in other words, we know what to do. But it requires an unswerving, collective, long-term effort.

United Nations Secretary General, Ban Ki-moon, 2008.

ACTIVITIES

1 Do you agree with Ban Ki-moon? Can the Millennium Development Goals really be achieved?
2 What problems can you see that might prevent the goals from being achieved?
3 What else would you like to see done to help reduce global inequality? Discuss your ideas as a class.
4 Using the ideas from this book and your class discussion write a manifesto (a list of things you would do) for reducing global inequality if you were Prime Minister.

Summary

As you can see, global inequality is a complex and fascinating issue. The causes of poverty and unequality in LEDCs are often a result of the actions of MEDCs, are often inter-linked and have been created over a long period of time. Many people would argue that MEDCs should take a greater lead in solving the problem. However, this can be difficult for governments to do because meeting the needs of the people in their own country often comes first.

Recent announcements about increased funding have been welcomed, but many still believe this isn't enough and that we need to fundamentally change people's attitudes and lifestyles. For example, we can no longer expect to buy items at ludicrously cheap prices and throw them away when broken; we need to be prepared to pay higher prices so that those people who make such items can work in better conditions and receive fairer pay.

Also, during the 2009 global economic crisis, the needs of people in developing countries are no longer given as much media coverage. Instead, Western countries have become more focused on their own economic problems.

The UN report on the success so far of the Millennium Development Goals suggests many targets are being met, but these targets won't see people in LEDCs living in the comfort of people in MEDCs, they simply mean that they will survive – but it is a step in the right direction. It is likely to take an extremely long time before the majority of people in the LEDCs throughout the world are living with the comforts that we take for granted, such as clean running water.

FAMILY AND SOCIALISATION

INTRODUCTION

This chapter will help you understand the relationship between families and cultures. The family and socialisation chapter is based on four concepts:

1. There are different types of family and household structures.
2. The family has different functions.
3. There have been changes in the family.
4. There are different influences on the family.

A SOCIETY is made up of individuals, but it is not just a large collection of people living in one area of the world. The chapter on culture and beliefs has shown that a society works as a unit only if it has a shared culture (see page 4). People have to understand how to communicate and co-operate with each other if they want to live together. But how do people learn to live together?

In most people's opinion, it is the FAMILY that should take on the job of teaching babies and children how to live, grow up, and survive in society.

It is not hard to see why most societies are based on the family unit. When they are born, babies are completely dependent on adults and young children take a long time to learn the skills of survival. They need someone to look after them and teach them about society and how to fit in. In most societies, it is the mother and father who automatically take on this job.

Human beings also have social and emotional needs. With very few exceptions, people want support, companionship, affection and social acceptance. Family life can provide all this, which may account for the existence of family groups across all cultures.

Families are part of every society but we know from our own experience, and from what we read and see in the media, that families are not all the same.

CONCEPT 1

There are different types of family and household structure

First, we need to answer some questions:

- What exactly is a family?
- Are all families the same?
- Do people mean the same thing when they talk about families?

The following are ideas and terms that you will need to know from this concept section: *family and households: nuclear, extended, reconstituted, lone (single parent), civil partnerships, student households, single person households, polygamy, monogamy, serial monogamy*

Look at the activity below. It will be more successful if you work with other people.

ACTIVITIES

1 a) Before you read any further, write down your definition of a family.
    b) Discuss your answer in a group. Is your definition the same as everybody else's in the group?
2 Look at the speech bubbles opposite. Which of the examples would you consider to be a family? Organise your answer into two columns – one with the title 'A family', the other with the title 'Not a family'.
3 From your answers and discussion, work out your new definition of a family, for example, 'A family is a group made up of …'

From the activity above, you can see that a family is not easily defined: most people have a clear idea of what a family is but it's not always the same idea. People in the UK and in other parts of the world have different beliefs about what makes up a family.

Man and woman married for 20 years without children.

Two males COHABITING with an adopted son.

Man and woman cohabiting with an adopted son.

Man and woman cohabiting with the children from the woman's previous marriage.

Woman living with her children after her husband has died.

Man and woman married, children living with mother, father living separately but seeing children regularly.

Woman living with her sister and her sister's husband.

Man and woman married and living with their three children.

Man and woman cohabiting with their three children for 15 years.

Man and woman married, both children away working in a different town.

Man and woman married, living together and looking after the 80-year-old mother of the man.

A woman living with her daughter and the daughter's baby.

A family can be parents and children that live together, or a wider group of people linked by marriage and blood relationships, who recognise that they are related but live apart, and may not even have much to do with each other. Think of family gatherings like weddings and Christmas, when relatives who rarely see each other get together.

In most societies the mother and father live with their child or children, and share the work and responsibilities of raising and supporting the children. But is this the only definition of a family? Does a family have to include children? What about married couples with no children, or couples whose children have left home, or a son or daughter looking after their parents? Can these be called families?

There is no single definition of the family that everyone accepts, but most people agree about the basic roles of the family in society and what it should do:

- It should be responsible for reproduction (producing the next generation).
- It should provide affection and personal support for its members.
- The most important role of the family is in the education, SOCIALISATION and care of children.

Don't forget that groups of people living together are not always 'families'. To distinguish these groups from families we call them 'HOUSEHOLDS'.

Two definitions

A family: a family is a group of persons directly linked by kin connections, which means they are related by blood relationships or marriage. The relationships and shared responsibilities are what makes a family different to a household.

A household: a group of people who live together in shared accommodation. The crucial thing about households is that the definition is based on where people live, not their relationships. A household could be a group of students sharing a house, friends living together. A household could be one person living alone.

ACTIVITY

'A household can be a family, but not all households are families, and not all families are households.'

1 Give one example of:
  a) a household that is a family
  b) a household that is not a family
  c) a family that is not a household.

Different types of families and households in the UK

Families found in the UK do not all live in the same kind of household, or have the same relationships with each other. This is because they follow different traditions, or choose different lifestyles because of their wealth, occupations, or personal preferences, or have different values or religious beliefs. Also, family relationships and household arrangements change as people get older.

While there are many different family and household arrangements in the UK, most fall into one of the following categories:

The nuclear family

A mother and father and their unmarried children living together. Most people in the UK will have spent some time in such a family structure, but not everyone. In the UK, this is what most people think of as a 'normal' family. Families like this tend to feel responsible for each other, and the nuclear family is the focus of their activities. They usually are in contact with other relatives but don't necessarily see them on a day-to-day basis.

The extended family

An extended family is one where there are usually three or more generations in the household. Often that would be parents, children and grandparents living together, but the household could include other relatives such as uncles and aunts. Nowadays in the UK, extended families do not always live in the same house, but the wider family share responsibilities for each other and often share finances and ownership of property.

In the pre-industrial past, extended families used to be common in farming areas, where they worked together to keep the farm going. Nowadays, extended families are often families who have recently migrated to Britain and who continue to follow traditions from their original cultures. This often works well as it is helpful for newcomers to a country to have a wide social circle to help them to find their feet and to share resources and property.

The lone parent family

A lone (or single) parent family is a family made up of a child or children living with one parent. In the UK, divorce and family separations have become more common. Some mothers have children and never live with the father, and in some families one parent dies. This means that many children are brought up living with one parent. The lone parent can be either the father or the mother, but most commonly this is the mother. The proportion of children living in lone parent families in the UK more than tripled between 1972 and 2006 to 24 per cent.

The reconstituted family

Many lone parents eventually set up households with other adults, who may also have children. If the new couple decide to stay together and bring up children from their previous relationships, this is called a reconstituted family. In the UK, which has a high divorce rate and many lone parents, this is becoming a more familiar type of household.

Single person households

Not all people live in families. Many people live alone. In fact, in 2005 the number of people in single person households in the UK has more than doubled since 1971, from 3 million to 7 million. Many of these are old people who have lost a partner. But an increasing number are younger working people living in apartments.

Shared households

The large number of young people who are students in higher education has swelled the number of shared households, which are often in university halls or rented houses. Also, the expense of buying a house means that many older single people are sharing houses and flats with friends and work colleagues.

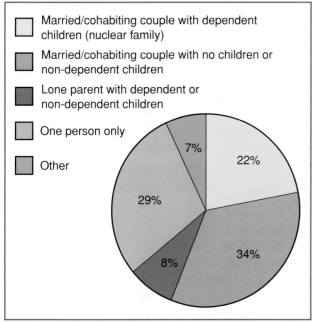

Married/cohabiting couple with dependent children (nuclear family)

Married/cohabiting couple with no children or non-dependent children

Lone parent with dependent or non-dependent children

One person only

Other

7%
22%
29%
8%
34%

A summary of types of households in the UK in 2003.

ACTIVITY

1 From the pie chart above, answer the following questions:
   a) Which is the most common type of household in the UK?
   b) What does 'non-dependent children' mean?
   c) What other type of household is more common than the nuclear family?
   d) What is meant by 'lone parent'?
   e) Give two examples of types of household that could be described as 'other'.

Families and marriage

In many UK families, the father and mother are married. This means they have gone through an official state or religious ceremony where they are bound to each other legally. A husband is allowed to be married to one wife, and a wife to one husband. This type of relationship is called MONOGAMY.

Until the 1950s in the UK, a man and a woman who had children, or even just lived together were expected to be married. If they weren't it was seen by most of the population as being shameful and morally wrong.

However, since the 1950s, many people have lived together and had children, without being married, and without being seen as immoral or shameful. In fact, over the last 60 years the range of accepted family structures in the UK has become very varied:

- Many couples live with several partners before they marry.
- Many couples have children before they marry, and many never get married.
- It has become common for people to marry, divorce, then marry someone else. Many people do this several times. This pattern of lifestyle is called serial monogamy.
- Since December 2005, the Civil Partnership Act has enabled a same-sex couple to register as CIVIL PARTNERS of each other. This means that two men or two women can go through a ceremony that gives them the same legal rights as a married man and woman.

Family life in different cultures

So far we have been describing families and households in the UK. However, in other cultures, families and households may take very different forms. In many cultures a man is allowed to have more than one wife. In a few cultures, women are allowed to have more than one husband, but this is not so widespread.

If a man is married to more than one woman at the same time, or a woman has more than one husband, it is known as POLYGAMY. In the UK, if a man marries another woman while he is still married it, this is a crime and is called BIGAMY. But, if a man or a woman have two or more partners, this is not illegal, even though they are not always easy relationships.

However, elsewhere in the world, polygamy is accepted. For example, some followers of the Mormon church in America still believe in and practise polygamy, as do some Muslims in Islamic states. In many African tribal cultures polygamy is the normal pattern, and a rich or powerful man is expected to have several wives.

Case Study
A family in the UK

Dawn met David at work in Leeds. Before that they had both had a few relationships, but had seen these as not very serious and they never felt they wanted to marry these partners. By the time they met each other, Dawn and David had decided that it was time to settle down.

When they decided to marry, they told their parents and, despite the fact that Dawn's dad thought that David was a bit of an idiot, they agreed to the marriage. Dawn's dad said: 'What can you do? When she makes her mind up, that's it for Dawn.' The couple moved into a flat in town.

After three years Dawn became pregnant and, with their parents' help, they bought a house in a Leeds suburb. Dawn and David stayed there for the next 12 years bringing up their daughter, Elvira, and their young son, Dean.

Dawn was clever and ambitious and was promoted to finance director in the company she worked for, but she had to leave Leeds to work in the head office in Reading. They still saw their parents a few times a year, and got together with the rest of their relatives at Christmas.

David was going nowhere in his career, and decided to start a new life as a landscape gardener. The business didn't go well and tensions grew in the family. Finally, he and Dawn agreed to split up, and later were divorced.

The children stayed with Dawn, and eventually David met a woman who was also a landscape gardener, and moved in with her and her children from an earlier marriage.

Dawn was very successful in the business and eventually became the managing director. Elvira dropped out of university and became a successful DJ and music critic. Dean went to work for his father and became a partner in the landscaping business.

The families still meet at Christmas. Dawn, who also re-married, is still close to her children, and pays for her elderly mother's care in a nursing home.

Case Study
An extended family in the UK

An extended family unit shares responsibilities for the whole family.

In multicultural Britain, immigrants from other cultures often have different patterns of family organisation.

Many people from the Punjab, Gujarat and Bengal who have come to the UK over the last 50 years have continued to organise their families according to their cultural TRADITIONS. Traditionally, these families are extended families, dominated by the older male members who make the important decisions that affect the family.

In the first years as immigrants to the UK, it was common for the families to live close to each other as a large family group made up of several generations of relatives. It wasn't always possible to live in the same house, but the families shared their income and family responsibilities. This was the way they had lived in the past, and in a new country it provided support and a familiar way of life. Many businesses were started using family members as workers to keep costs down. This strategy was often successful and many such families now own flourishing businesses.

Arranged marriages

In the traditional UK family, most children over 18 expect to make their own choices about who they marry, where they live, and the lifestyle they follow. Their parents may try to influence them but, like Dawn's father, they don't feel they can force them into following their wishes.

In many Hindu, Sikh and Muslim families, the older people, particularly the men, try to preserve the traditional extended family and keep control of young people's choices. Many families maintain the tradition of ARRANGED MARRIAGES and a network of obligations to relatives, both in the UK and in their country of origin.

Marriages are arranged by parents because a marriage is important to the whole extended family, not just the two individuals involved. The families of the bride and groom are merged, they have to take on extended family responsibilities, and this is seen as too important to be left to the romantic choices of the young couple.

Arranged marriages may sound strange to people brought up in UK culture, but marriages in many cultures are seen as a practical arrangement, rather than a romantic dream. In many parts of the world, the UK version of family life seems lonely and heartless, where families are distant, and the old are put in care homes.

The modern extended family

The Sikh and Hindu pattern of extended family life is much more centred on close and enduring relationships with a wide range of relatives. The old remain part of the family group and are supported and given respect by the rest of the family. If a member of the wider family group has economic difficulties, or other misfortunes such as bereavement or serious ill-health, the rest of the family would see this as their responsibility and help as much as they can. Childcare is often provided by grandparents and female relatives. In many ways this pattern of family life can be seen as more supportive to the members than the life offered by the isolated nuclear family.

The younger generations of Hindu and Sikh families, who are educated and work in the UK, often challenge these traditional family values. However, this is not easy to do in the face of family pressure. Traditional Hindu weddings are very elaborate ceremonies, a celebration of Hindu

Traditional Hindu weddings are very elaborate ceremonies, which are a highlight of Hindu family life. It would be regarded as a betrayal of the culture if a wedding did not follow the traditions, and young people may feel they cannot ignore these pressures.

family life. It would be regarded as a betrayal of the culture if a wedding did not follow the traditions, and young people may feel they cannot ignore these pressures.

One extreme case of an arranged marriage was widely reported in 2008.

Humayra Abedin, who came to Britain six years ago to study and worked in London as a GP, reportedly went to Bangladesh in the summer after being falsely told her mother was ill. She was then held against her will and, in mid-November, was forced to marry a man chosen by her parents. In the end she was ordered to be returned to England by a Bangladeshi court, and given protection against being abducted again by a British court.

Recent films such as *East is East*, *Bend It Like Beckham*, and *Bhaji on the Beach*, and soaps such as *Coronation Street* and *EastEnders*, have all had storylines which explore these conflicts. What these films show is that a traditional family pattern is hard to break.

It is wrong to suggest that any ethnic group will have the same family structure, and talking about Asian or Sikh families as if they were all the same is very misleading. This applies to families from all cultures and ethnic groups. Families vary according to wealth and class, age group, religion and place of origin.

Family structures and traditions have a big influence on the lives of their members. Research shows that there are fewer divorces or single parent families in the South Asian extended families, and more divorces and children outside marriages among nuclear families in the UK.

However, these patterns are changing over time, and what this research shows is that across the UK (and across much of the Europe and the USA) there is a wide range of family organisations and that these are accepted as aspects of a diverse culture.

The idea of the typical family as being 'a wage-earning father and child-rearing mother' has been replaced by many new family forms. These include: lone mothers; reconstituted families; cohabiting couples with children; lesbian and gay partners; and dual income families where young children are looked after by au pairs, childminders and in a range of childcare institutions (crèches, nurseries, playgroups, etc.).

There have also been some changes that seem to show that the independent young people of British families may be getting less independent. In 2006, 58 per cent of men and 39 per cent of women aged 20–24 in England lived with their parents, an increase of around 8 per cent since 1991. It's a mistake to think that any type of family structure will not change over time.

ACTIVITIES

1 What are the advantages that an extended family offers its members compared with a nuclear family?

2 Give three reasons why there are more than 7 million people living alone in the UK.

3 Why is childcare a booming business in the UK?

Crèches play an important part in modern-day childcare in the UK.

CONCEPT 2

The family has different functions

Families are a part of every society. The fact that families have existed for so long in a changing world shows how important they are in society.

In this concept section we analyse what role the family plays in the lives of its members. You will learn:

- How families are the most reliable way of ensuring that children are born and looked after by caring adults.
- How families provide economic security to members who don't have the resources to support themselves, such as infants and children, mothers looking after children, old or sick people who cannot earn money.
- How families teach children the basic skills, attitudes and values needed to survive in society.
- How families are a source of security and emotional support for their members.

Of course, not all families fulfil these functions equally well; some families are described as 'dysfunctional', which means that they do not perform these roles adequately.

> The following are ideas and terms that you will need to know from this concept section:
>
> *functions of the family: socialisation, economic, reproductive, gender roles, division of labour, childcare, care of the elderly, residential care, social services*

The reproductive role of families

All societies need to maintain themselves by bringing children into the world to replace those who die. This means that there has to be a way of ensuring that these children are kept alive and grow up to fit into society. The most effective way of doing this is through making the family responsible for this process.

Although many single people do have them, raising children is very difficult for a person living alone. The amount of work involved in looking after a baby means that the mother is likely to need help, both financially and to look after the home. If the father of the child is unable to provide this support, the parents of the single mother may have to help.

Nowadays in the UK, the government does give some help to parents and children in need. One of the major jobs of the social services is to help women and families to bring up healthy children, give advice, protect vulnerable people and to help people who have low incomes and poor housing to survive. The NHS provides free medical care, and the government gives financial help to people on low incomes. But in the end it is recognised that for most people the best way to raise children is through the support of a family.

The economic role of the family

All families need economic resources to survive. Such essentials as food, housing and heating are usually provided through the work of family members, either by farming and using the resources in the area, or by working for someone else.

In most families there will be members who cannot do this for themselves, such as the very young, children in school, mothers providing childcare, and the old who are no longer able to work. In a family, sharing resources is the way these individuals can be supported. In most families this is accepted as part of family life. Think of your own family and how they support you as a student, and possibly help and support your grandparents and other relatives.

Most families manage to raise children and keep the home going by sharing out the work. For example, in some families the mother takes on the job of looking after the baby, doing the housework, and looking after older children, while the father provides the income to pay for the family's needs.

However, this isn't the only way it can be done. In many families, both parents go to work to earn money, and leave the childcare to other family members such as grandparents, or pay for childcare by employing someone to look after the children in such places as day care centres or crèches. The way jobs are the responsibility of different members of the family is referred to as the DIVISION OF LABOUR. There is more on this in the section on gender roles in the family on pages 204–206.

Your family and you

Family 1
Diana (14)

My family lives in a big house in Solihull. We have five bedrooms and three bathrooms and a paddock

My dad (he's really my step-dad) works in London three days a week, and spends a lot of time on the phone and working online

My mum teaches at the university and gets tons of free time

School is sometimes boring but I like it because the teachers are nice and I've got loads of friends there. I like languages especially Italian, because I want to live in Italy when I'm older. I try hard at school because my parents say 'without a good education you'll get nowhere'

The family go abroad on holiday at least twice every year. Last year we went to Austria and Barbados

I go riding most weekends, and I sing in the choir at the church

I get on with my parents, but they are always going on about homework, and 'making the most of myself'. They are old-fashioned about clothes, and wouldn't let me get my eyebrow pierced, but my mum says that when I'm 15, I can have a clothes allowance. My dad says I can have a car when I go to university. I want to get married and have children, but not too soon because I want to have a career in the media first

ACTIVITY

1 Although a modern family does not have as much power over the children, the family does have a big influence on your future. Read these two accounts of family life and compare the differences in lifestyle, values and opportunities of Diana and Liam. Then answer the following questions:

Family 2
Liam (15)

I live with my mum and Derek, my step-dad, and my three sisters in a three-bedroom house on an estate in Nottingham. There's not much to do round here, just a corner shop and a pub on the main road

My mum works in a shop, and Derek works for a builder when he's got a big job on. We have a car, but it needs a new clutch so we don't get much use out of it

I work at the chip shop three nights a week, so I've got a bit of money

It's alright at home, but it's noisy and we argue about what to watch on TV. There's nowhere to be on your own to listen to music or just think

I go to a school in the estate and it's not bad. When I was at the junior school I liked it, but at this school I am struggling because I don't do the homework so I sometimes get into trouble. I can't do the homework because there's nowhere to do it in the house, my sisters have their stuff everywhere. I'd like to do A levels, but I don't think I'll do well enough at GCSE. Derek says school is a waste of time because the stuff they teach is useless. He's going to teach me plastering when I leave. My mum wants me to stay on, but they can't afford to keep me until I'm 18, so I'll have to get a job

I don't think I will get married, married people are always rowing about money or something. I'm going to have a good time. When I'm 16, me and my mates are going to have two weeks in Ibiza. It's brilliant out there, dead cheap and you can have a laugh. My mum says that when we all leave home she's off on a cruise. Hope she does, she needs a break

a) How are Diana and Liam's lives at home different?

b) What differences are there in their attitudes to school?

c) How are their plans for their futures different?

d) How would you explain these differences in attitude and ambition?

The role of the family in the socialisation of children

Socialisation is the process of teaching individuals how to fit in with society. Parents are the PRIMARY SOCIALISATION agents. This means that from birth babies are learning how to behave with other people. At this early stage in its life, a baby learns basic skills, how to eat, how to get attention, how to speak, by recognising and imitating its parents' actions. Some of what babies learn is from their parents' deliberate teaching but, as they develop, babies copy their parents' behaviour and pick up their parents' attitudes and beliefs.

What an infant sees a parent do becomes their idea of what is normal. This is how they learn attitudes and values. So if their parents' behaviour is warm and tolerant, this will be how they expect life to be; if parents are violent or angry, this is also what they will learn about life.

By the time a child is five and ready for school, they will have learned some language skills, and have started to learn how to behave with people who are not part of their family. They will also have picked up some of their parents' attitudes and values. This early socialisation is very important in setting the pattern of their reactions to others.

Secondary socialisation

Socialisation doesn't stop with the family. SECONDARY SOCIALISATION takes place when children learn other behaviour, attitudes and values through teachers, their other relatives (especially older brothers and sisters), and through meeting other children. Socialisation continues later in life when they are influenced by peer groups, work relationships, and other groups or organisations that play an important role in an individual's life. The socialisation process is continuous, even carrying on into old age, when you learn how to cope with the problems of ageing, by following medical advice and seeing both how other old people behave and are expected to behave.

But it is what children learn from their parents that is the foundation of their personality, preferences, attitudes and values.

Gender roles in the family

As you have seen from the descriptions of family life in the first part of this chapter, one feature that all families share is that men and women play different roles in the family. One of the reasons is BIOLOGICAL: women give birth to children, and usually feed them in the first months of their lives. Even where women do not breastfeed their children, they tend to be the person that babies rely on and relate to most closely.

This gives women a role that men cannot take on. As a result of this, the male role has tended to be that of protector and provider for the family. In the past this was possibly the result of men's greater strength and size, but in almost every family type the roles of men and women have fallen into this pattern.

One of the reasons this pattern is so enduring is the result of socialisation. Boys and girls are brought up differently in many societies. They are expected to have different skills and boys and girls soon recognise this. They are encouraged by the rest of the family to follow the GENDER ROLES adopted by their parents and other relatives.

Traditional female gender roles in the family

Females often take on the following responsibilities within the family:

- Having babies and nurturing them.
- Raising and educating children, particularly female children.
- Looking after the family's domestic needs: providing food, looking after the home and household goods.
- Giving care, support and affection to members of the family who are in need, such as the old, sick, or depressed.

Traditional male gender roles in the family

Males often take on the following responsibilities within the family:

- Making major family decisions.
- Providing the family with what they need to survive: food and shelter or the income to pay for these essentials.
- Giving protection to the family from outside threats.

- Preparing and training males to take over the roles above.
- Dealing with individuals outside the family and handling any social and economic pressures from the outside world.
- Doing physical work to maintain the family home and sustain the family lifestyle.

The merging of gender roles in the modern nuclear family

If you are a member of a family in a developed society, you will notice that these roles and divisions of labour have become less clear-cut. In the UK, many of these roles are shared between males and females. Later on in the chapter, we will look at why these changes have taken place, but here we can point to some well-known changes in gender roles in recent years:

- Childcare and domestic duties are more likely to be shared by both men and women.
- Many women now are important contributors to the family economy, through regular paid work.
- Major family decisions are often taken jointly, not just by the mother and father and are often influenced by the wishes of the children. For example, decisions about moving house, family holidays, major purchases are often made by the whole family.
- The education and training of children of both genders usually involves the skills and knowledge of both parents.
- Family needs such as meals are often bought in from shops ready-prepared, and household maintenance, such as plumbing and decorating, is often done by paid workers. Both genders take responsibility for this.
- Men are often supportive and caring and women are often fierce defenders against threats to the family.

Despite this, boys and girls are still usually brought up very differently.

Early socialisation into gender roles

There are many families where the traditional gender roles are still followed. This is true of many traditional Hindu, Sikh and Muslim families. It's also true that in most families in the UK, boys and girls are socialised to have different attitudes,

interests and values. This can be seen in children's hairstyles, the clothes they are dressed in, the gifts they receive and the activities they are encouraged to get involved in.

Socialisation starts at a very early age, when baby girls are praised for their prettiness using terms like 'beautiful', 'pretty', 'cute', 'adorable' and 'small', and boys are praised using words such as 'strong', 'big', 'tough', 'lively', 'strapping'. Most researchers agree that parents treat their female and male infants differently. Mothers seem to be more emotionally warm and responsive with girls and more encouraging of independence with boys. Fathers often spend more time with their sons and engage in more physical play with sons than with daughters. Parents commonly see newborn daughters as more delicate than their newborn sons, which may mean that girls are encouraged less than boys to be physically active and to explore their environment. As a result of being treated differently, it's no surprise that children begin to behave differently.

Learning gender roles with Mum and Dad.

Gender socialisation in later years

Parents

In later years of childhood, the strongest influence parents exert on their children is over their education, and their ambitions for the future. The expectations of parents play a large part in forming attitudes to work, marriage, and roles as husband and wives, fathers and mothers. The patterns of behaviour learned through observing your own parents' behaviour, attitudes, and values will be very hard to ignore. But, when most children get older, they find their parents' lifestyle and attitudes outdated, and other socialising agencies also play a part in defining gender roles.

The media

The media is a very important agent of socialisation, particularly for young people. Adolescents, who are often searching for an identity, seize on media images and ideas to shape their own self-image.

When young people see media images of people the same age as themselves, it gives them a guide to how young people behave. Most teenagers want to find a style of life that is unique to their generation, and characters depicted in the media can provide them with role models. A lot of programmes aimed at teenage audiences, such as

Hollyoaks, *Skins* and *Waterloo Road*, seem to give an idea of how young people live. Often the lifestyle, appearance and behaviour of the characters are attractive alternatives to the way the young people's parents want them to behave.

The media present other role models too: the lives and behaviour of celebrities are often the source of people's dreams and aspirations, and their lifestyles can become a guide for how their admirers want to live.

The gender roles played out in TV news, documentaries and dramas may also influence the way many young people behave. Attitudes to relationships, marriage, divorce and having fun have been influenced by what the media depicts as normal and desirable. For example, girls and women have been shown as assertive, determined, tough and rowdy in many recent TV programmes and dramas. This has had two effects. Young women have gained confidence in their own abilities and potential, and have also been more involved in rowdy, drunken behaviour and in criminal activities than they were ten years ago. It could be said that they are beginning to act more like traditional rebellious young males.

The socialising influence of the media is often in conflict with the values and attitudes which parents, teachers and the government want to encourage.

ACTIVITIES

Work in small groups.

1 Copy out the table below and fill it in with your own responses. The first row is filled out as an example of the type of answers you may give.

Programmes/series you like	Characters you like	What do you like about the character?
House	House	Because he doesn't care what other people think of him, he just does what he wants.

2 Compare your answers with those of the rest of the group and see which qualities the group seem to like.

3 Discuss how your attitudes and behaviour are influenced by your favourite characters.

Peer groups

Children and adolescents are influenced by other people of the same age (peer group) they meet in their neighbourhood and at school. Generally, individuals want to be accepted by a group, so they try to fit in.

The group socialises its members into gender roles. Girls learn from other girls how to behave, how they should look and what attitudes and interests are acceptable. The same is true for boys. The media, consumer products and PEER GROUPS work together to identify and reinforce the gender roles young people learn.

However, these gender roles may conflict with the roles that parents try to teach their children. As a result of these conflicts of socialisation, gender roles today can be less rigid and more changeable than they were 50 or even 20 years ago.

The care of the elderly

In the UK and in the developed world, life expectancy has risen dramatically over the last hundred years. In 1901, males born in the UK could expect to live to around 45 years of age and females to around 49. By 2003, male life expectancy at birth had risen to almost 77 years, and for females to just over 81 years.

There are several reasons for this. Our modern lifestyle is much healthier than it was a century ago. In the UK, we have clean water, healthy food, and much better medical care. We are wealthier so we have warmer, drier houses; our working conditions are much safer. We are better educated so are better able to take care of ourselves.

Despite this, elderly people often have health problems or difficulties in looking after themselves. The need to care for the elderly presents many problems for the modern family. Most people over 65 live away from their children. When elderly people can no longer look after themselves, the job of caring usually becomes the work of their sons and daughters. Many families try to bring their parent into their home or move so that they live near enough to provide regular care.

This can cause difficulties for the carer family:

- Many elderly people need full-time care.
- Most houses are too small to provide a private area for an elderly person.
- Looking after an elderly relative can cause stress in the household.
- Many elderly people do not want to cause difficulties for their family.
- Outside care (for example, in a nursing home) is very expensive.
- Many elderly people do not want to leave their own home to live in a nursing home.

Different attitudes to the care of the elderly

Some people argue that a family should look after their relatives because:

- They have a moral duty to care for their parents.
- Care in nursing homes is not always good.
- The elderly deserve to be repaid for caring for their children when they were young.
- The family will provide the best care.

Other people argue that when an elderly person needs care, they should be cared for by the state because:

- The elderly have paid taxes all their life.
- Many people do not have the resources to look after their parents.
- The government have the skills and facilities to do a better job (for example, daily part-time care, 24-hour nursing, medical skills and treatments).

ACTIVITY

1 Read the three accounts of caring for the elderly on page 208 and answer the following questions using the information in this section and your own ideas.

   a) Explain the difficulties that can occur when an elderly relative moves in with the family.

   b) Explain why moving in might be good for both the elderly person and the family.

   c) Explain why a residential home can be a good place for an elderly person to spend their days.

   d) Explain why a care home can be a poor substitute for being cared for by your family.

Janice (43), Wolverhampton

My mother was fine until she fell and broke a hip. When she came out of hospital, she found it impossible to look after herself at home. We decided that we should move her in with us, but we were very worried because our house only has three bedrooms and we have two boys aged nine and seven.

We struggled at first because we were so crowded. The boys felt pushed out and I was so tired I thought I'd have to give up my job. My mother gave us some money for an extension, and once we got used to having her around things got much better. She is the best babysitter and she can look after herself with our help. It's actually better now. My husband and I get out more often, and now she's settled in she's good company.

Fred (83), Leeds

When my eyesight got really bad, I could just about see enough to cook my tea and do the shopping, but that was all. I couldn't read or watch TV so I spent all day listening to the radio and talking books. It was really boring. I had nobody to talk to and I forgot how to talk, nearly. My daughter came over once a week, but she lived 80 miles away and it was too far. Her visit was the big event of the week.

She wanted me to move in with her family, but I didn't want to get in the way. They have their own lives to live. So when my eyes got worse, I decided to go to this residential home.

I must say, it's been a lot better than I expected. The food is good, they look after me well. I like my room, but the real benefit is that I can talk to people again. They're all about my age so we can talk easily, and the days go much more quickly. I'm glad I moved.

Emily (91), Reading

I realised that caring for me was becoming impossible for my son, who was himself 65, and so I decided to sell my house and go into residential care. But it has become a nightmare. I have arthritis in my hands and knee joints so I can't do much for myself and have to rely on the staff here. They are too busy to help me much of the time, so I'm always waiting for someone to do something for me. I feel that I've lost all my life, just sitting around watching TV. A lot of the people here have mental problems and I have found no one I can talk to.

I get fed and looked after, but I feel I'm just marking time until I die. I get very depressed, but I don't tell my son because it will ruin his life if he knows how bad I feel.

CONCEPT 3

There have been changes in the family

In the twenty-first century, families in the UK are very different from families a hundred years ago. Our attitudes to family life, the importance of marriage, the way we bring up children, and our attitudes to divorce have all changed in major ways.

This is the result of many changes in other aspects of our lives. The way we work; our housing; our health and life expectancy; the wealth and technology now available to make our lives easier; changing attitudes to the roles of women, men and children; and government policies and laws – all these things have had major effects on family life in the UK.

In this concept section we will trace the changes that have overtaken families since 1900. You will learn about:

- Changes in health and LIFE EXPECTANCY.
- Changes in family size.
- Changes in the role of children.
- Changing attitudes to marriage and divorce.
- Changes in men and women's roles in the family.
- Changes in households and new types of families.

The following are ideas and terms that you will need to know from this concept section:

industrialisation • life expectancy • teenage mums • dual income households • househusbands • cohabitation • marriage and divorce rates • UN Rights of the Child • child-centred families • pester power

The profile of an average family in 1900

- 3.5 = average number of children per family.
- Average life expectancy for men = 45, for women = 49.
- 90 per cent of houses were rented and 46 per cent of housing was terraced housing.
- 10 per cent of 10–14-year-olds were in work.
- 40 per cent of men over 75 were still working.
- 29 per cent (five million) women were working (mostly as domestic servants).
- Average hours at work per week = 52.
- Average wage for men = £1.40 per week.
- Average rent = 15–20 pence per week
- Pint of beer = 1 pence.

The profile of an average family in the twenty-first century

- 1.8 = average number of children per family.
- 71 per cent of families are headed by a married couple.
- Average life expectancy for men = 77, for women = 81.
- 79 per cent of families live in a mortgaged house.
- 90 per cent of fathers and 68 per cent of mothers go out to work.
- 65 per cent of families have a home computer.
- 52 per cent of families own a pet.
- Average income = £32,779 per year.

ACTIVITIES

1 Compare the average family now with the average family in 1900. What are the biggest changes?

2 How do you think the average family will have changed 50 years from now?

Changes in health and life expectancy

A life expectancy figure is an average figure, which is based on the ages at which individuals die in a particular year. It is used as a measure of general health in a society. In 1900, life expectancy in the UK was 45 for men and 49 for women; by 2006, the life expectancy was 77 for men and 81 for women. This shows that people have become much healthier over the last 100 years.

Why are they healthier?

- Clean water, good SANITATION, better quality food, and warmer, drier housing have kept people healthier. Healthier people can fight off illness and infections, so they live longer.
- Poverty was a major cause of ill-health, and by the end of the nineteenth century people were much better off than they were 50 years before, though compared with our level of wealth now, they were still very poor.
- Better working conditions and cleaner air have kept people fitter in old age.
- Medical knowledge and better medication have controlled infectious diseases, and surgical skills have kept people alive for much longer. A hundred years ago, almost all heart attacks would have been fatal.
- Childbirth is safer and infants get better care, so fewer children die early.

Below, we consider how family life has changed.

Changes in family size

Before 1900, families often contained many children. In the nineteenth century, families had many children because children were the family support system for the future. There was no reliable contraception, and parents knew that some children were likely to die young. In 1900, between six and nine of every 1,000 women died in childbirth, and one in five children died during the first five years of life. Big families were the norm, and tradition and religion supported this belief.

By the twentieth century, people lived longer, lived and worked in better conditions, and were better off, so smaller families made more sense. It was easier to feed a smaller family, and to live in less crowded conditions. Families wanted greater comfort and to live without worrying so much about putting food on the table and keeping the house warm. Fewer children meant that they could all live better lives.

The average family size in the UK dropped from 7.8 children in 1800 to 4.6 children in 1900. In the twentieth century this trend for fewer children has continued as people live longer, and wealth and living conditions continue to get better. Today, two children remains the most common family size, though the average number of children per family in the UK is still dropping – from 2.0 in 1971 to 1.8 in 2006.

Changes in the role of children

As the numbers of children in a family grew smaller, parents' attitudes to children and their role in the family changed. In the nineteenth century, people went through just two stages of life: childhood and adulthood. Childhood was seen as a time when innocent children had to be protected and prepared for adulthood. This was the job of the family and, for some children, schools.

Of course, the lives of children of the upper and middle classes were a lot more comfortable than those of children of poorer families. Richer families had nannies, boys were often sent away to schools, and girls were trained to be wives, mothers and to run houses. But even these children were expected to take on adult responsibilities from an early age.

The children of the working classes had a much harder life, little or no education, strict upbringing and once they were old enough, usually at about 10 or 11 or sometimes younger, they were expected to go to work and be treated as adults.

In the nineteenth century, this work was hard and these 11-year-old 'adults' were expected to provide support for the family, at least until they married and had their own children.

In the past, young children in the UK were sent out to work to earn a living. Nowadays, however, this is more likely to be the kind of work they are involved in.

During the twentieth century, because they tended to have more money, parents were less concerned about their children simply surviving. Instead they became more worried about the welfare of their children.

Parents in the twentieth century recognised the importance of education and of helping children get a good start in life. Governments and parents both realised that better education was vital to improve the economy and lifestyles. Over the last 130 years the length of time young people spend in school has increased gradually.

Year	
1893	Minimum leaving age raised to 11
1899	Minimum leaving age raised to 12
1900	No employment under fourteen without a certificate
1918	Full-time education compulsory from 5–14 years. Abolished half-time schooling.
1936	The school leaving age to be raised to 15 as from September 1939. Not implemented because of Second World War.
1947	School leaving age raised to 15.
1964	The decision to raise the age to 16 was announced and preparations began.
1971	The decision to raise the age to 16 to take effect from 1 September 1972 confirmed.
2008	The government is working to ensure that all young people are in full education or training until the age of 18.

Timeline of changing school leaving ages.

As you can see, changes in education came slowly, but they have had a great impact on the lives of children and their families.

- Children were gradually kept out of the workforce until they were older. Nowadays, the earliest age for full-time work is 16, and it may soon become 18.
- The sudden change from being a child to being treated as an adult has become a much slower process in the twenty-first century.
- Children spend much more of their lives in the family, as a result of spending longer in school.
- Families have become more 'CHILD-CENTRED', which means that the family concentrates more on trying to satisfy the interests and demands of their children. This is recognised by the retail business as 'PESTER POWER' – the influence children have over what their parents buy for them. It's a big market.
- Children's interests have become the priority for many parents when deciding how to live: for example, where to live, what kind of house to buy, what car to buy, where and when to go on holiday.
- Children aged over 11 or 12 have a new status in the family and society and are variously termed 'youths, 'adolescents' and 'teenagers'.
- These young people have developed new youth cultures as part of their transition from childhood to adulthood.
- As the UK population has become richer, these young people have demanded more material goods and greater freedom to behave as they want.
- These social changes meant that much more of the family income is spent on children and young people.
- New groups of young people with their own interests means that new products and technology are created to respond to their demands.
- The 'youth market', centred around clothing, entertainment and consuming food and drink, has become a major part of the economy. Think of trainers, casual clothes, music and movies, mobile phones, fast food, games and software; much of this was created and developed to tap into the interests and spending power of the youth market.

A student apartment.

- The lifestyle period of 'youth' has continued to expand in the twenty-first century as more young people go on to higher education. Many parents are now paying for their children to study and live away at university for three or more years, which may cost them thousands of pounds.

In 1989, the new status of children as individuals who should have human rights was spelled out in the UN Convention on the Rights of the Child. This was an agreement accepted by nearly every country in the world, laying down the rights and freedoms which all children under the age of 18 should have wherever they live.

There are 41 points in the Convention. Some of the most important are given below.

You can find out more about these rights by researching 'UN Convention on the Rights of the Child' on the internet, by contacting UNICEF, or the 'Every Child Matters' government campaign.

The Rights of the Child
Children have:

- The right to life, survival and development.
- The right to non-discrimination
- The right to expect respect for their views and to be treated in their best interests in all matters affecting them.
- Civil rights and freedoms, including the right to a name and nationality, freedom of expression, thought and association, access to information and the right not to be subjected to torture.
- The right to a family environment, including the right to live with and have contact with both parents, to be reunited with parents if separated from them and to the provision of appropriate alternative care where necessary.

- The right to basic health and welfare, including the rights of disabled children, the right to health and healthcare, social security, childcare services and an adequate standard of living.
- Education, leisure and cultural activities, including the right to education and the rights to play, leisure and participation in cultural life and the arts.
- The right to protection covers the rights of refugee children, those affected by armed conflicts, children in the juvenile justice system, children deprived of their liberty and children suffering economic, sexual or other forms of exploitation.

ACTIVITIES

1 Describe how the lives of children have changed since the nineteenth century. Think about health, home life, leisure, education and work.

2 How have parents' attitudes to their children changed over the last 150 years?

3 Do you think the role of parents has become easier or more difficult? Explain your answer using information in this chapter and from your studies.

4 Look at the Rights of the Child (see box on page 212). Explain how stating these rights has changed the lives of children since the nineteenth century.

5 Are all the rights of the child described here being given to all children? Use your knowledge of life in the UK and other countries to give examples of where they have worked and where they have been ignored.

Changing attitudes to marriage and divorce

Marriage

Changes in the size of families and the lives of children were not the only changes in family life that took place in the twentieth century. Before 1950, for most people in the UK, there was a very clear view that the only acceptable way to have children was for the parents to be married. A single woman who gave birth to a child was regarded as a 'fallen woman', someone who was immoral, and who was not respectable. Any other form of family life was seen as scandalous.

We know from the range of households described on pages 196–200, and our own experiences, that this attitude has changed for many people in the UK since 1900. During the two world wars (1914–18 and 1939–45), many women had lived without a man in the house and worked at jobs usually done by men. They gained independence and confidence. Both men and women believed that marriage was not about being respectable; it was about finding happiness and romance.

• Increasing wealth, and new ideas about equal rights for men and women, meant that people started to feel that they could break away from traditional attitudes about how they should live.

• Women realised that they did not have to rely on men to be the 'breadwinner', and that they could support themselves through working for their own wages. Jobs in factories, shops and offices could be done by women at least as well as by men, and the old heavy industries, like mining and ship-building in which men had always found work, were not the only way to earn money.

• There was less pressure to conform to tradition. The Christian Church had always said that people should marry before having sexual relations, but over the last century in the UK, religion and the Christian Church have had less influence on people's values and beliefs. More people have felt that they are free to chose a way of life that they want.

As a result of these social changes in the twentieth century, less people get married, and those who do tend to get married later in life. The changes have been gradual, but have increased more quickly over the last 40 years. The average age of a first marriage has gone from 24 for men and 22 for women in 1970, to 32 for men and 30 for women in 2005.

The shame that used to be attached to having a child 'out of wedlock' used to drive many couples into a marriage that they did not want. As social attitudes and moral judgements became more relaxed, people were no longer prepared to marry for respectability. The number of single parents grew, and fewer people felt that they had to get married before having children. Most people now believe that you should only marry if you expect your marriage to be happy and fulfilling, so nowadays, forced weddings (SHOTGUN WEDDINGS) because of pregnancy are rare.

Cohabitation is no longer seen as a 'sin'. Many people think it is sensible to live together before getting married so that the couple can learn about each other. Older generations were less accepting at first, but because parents had less power to control their children's lives and choices, they were unable to do much about it.

Gradually, cohabitation has gained acceptance in developed societies. The BELIEF that people's private life is their own business has become widespread.

Despite this, marriage remains the most common form of partnership between men and women. In 2006, there were 17.1 million families in the UK; around seven in ten were headed by a married couple.

Divorce

Divorce, which was very rare in 1900, has become easier and cheaper to arrange and divorce rates have increased a thousand-fold over the century.

During and after the Second World War, many marriages fell apart because of long separations and people finding they no longer had much in common with the person they had married. During the 1950s and 1960s, when the divorce laws were changed and the legal process became easier, the number of divorces rose rapidly. Because it has become so common, divorce is now an accepted part of social life and the shame which used to be attached to it has almost disappeared.

The other factor that has encouraged the rise in the number of divorces has been the changing opportunities that the twentieth century has brought, especially for women.

- Women have equal rights to men. They are no longer seen as second-class citizens, or subordinate to men.
- Women have realised that they can support themselves through work, and this freedom means they do not have to depend on marriage to a man.
- There are more opportunities for both men and women to meet other people through work and leisure.
- More access to contraceptives has taken away some of the risk of unwanted pregnancy, so it is less risky to have a sexual relationship outside marriage.
- More people have the money to start a new life if they want to end a marriage.

The number of divorces in the UK has risen from 5000 in 1935 to 166,700 in 2003. There was a massive increase from 1938 until 1970, then the increase in the number rose more slowly. In 2003, for example, the number of divorces rose by 3.7 per cent from 2002. However, that figure has dropped recently: in 2007 there were 132,562 divorces, the lowest figure for 22 years. The reason for this is that more people are now cohabiting, which means that if they want to split up they do not need to get a divorce. The cost of settlement after a divorce has led many people to give up the idea of marriage.

Even with this drop in divorces, it still means that in the UK today more than 40 per cent of all marriages will end in divorce. The rate is higher in the USA and similar in non-Catholic European countries.

For some people, being able to get divorced and start a new life without being criticised as a failure is a major improvement in SOCIAL VALUES and has produced a better society. Divorce is a way of escaping from an intolerable life and has given people the freedom to find a new, happier way of life.

Other people, however, see divorce as a major social problem and as a social evil because it results in broken families, causes unhappiness, and disrupts the raising of children.

The problems caused by divorce

- Children's lives are disrupted by divorce, often causing real grief and misery for children. They may find it hard to cope with new relationships in the family, which may affect their self-confidence. Schoolwork often suffers.
- It causes emotional and psychological distress. The process of splitting up with a partner can be very emotionally disturbing. Leaving someone you once loved is going to cause deep sorrow, will probably cause serious arguments, and both people involved will feel hurt, betrayed, and fearful for the future.
- It is often difficult for a single parent to earn a living and look after the children. Tension between the divorcing couple makes life hard for parents and children. Many say that broken families cause juvenile delinquency, and blame divorces for much social disorder because some children are not brought up in a secure home where there is care and discipline. (Of course, not all families provide this security with two parents.)

- The break-up of households is expensive as well as distressing. A divorce usually means that the family income is lower and somebody has to move out of the family home. Two houses will have to be paid for, probably out of the same money.
- There are still many cultures where divorce is seen as shameful. In such cultures there will be more pressure from relatives and the community.

The positive side of divorce

Some people believe that being able to get divorced is a major advantage in modern society. In the past, when a divorce was almost impossible, there were many sad marriages. Unhappy couples had to stay together. Many people think that being able to leave an unhappy marriage is essential to people's well-being. On the right are three case studies to illustrate how divorce can be seen as a positive step for individuals.

ACTIVITIES

1 From the information in this section and your own knowledge and experiences, list the problems divorce can cause.
2 Why might a religious person object to divorce?
3 Suggest reasons why there are fewer divorces in Asian families in the UK.
4 Explain in your own words why divorce often creates poverty.
5 Read the three case studies. Explain what is meant by:
    a) 'an abusive relationship'
    b) 'to move on'
    c) 'an empty shell marriage'.
6 Explain in your own words why getting divorced can sometimes be a good thing for an individual.

Yvette (34), Sheffield

When we first met, we went out drinking a lot. We both liked being sociable. After we got married and had kids, I knew we had to change. But Dave couldn't get used to staying in and we had rows. Dave got drunk often and sometimes got violent. He wanted life to be the same as it was when we were teenagers and he couldn't grow up. In the end, I left him and took the kids because I was scared for our safety. We couldn't live in an abusive relationship.

Keith (27), London

We were childhood sweethearts. A year after we got married, I was offered a brilliant job in London, but Jane didn't want to move. The job and money were so good, we agreed that I should live in London in the week and come home at weekends. It was fine at first, but soon we were like strangers. In the end, we agreed to part. We were different people than when we were kids. As people grow up they change, and you can't avoid that. You have to move on.

Sarah (54), Dorking

I stayed at home to bring the children up and Simon worked hard in the City making pots of money. We had fantastic holidays and he bought us a beautiful house. He couldn't spend much time with the children because of work, but he said it was for their future. When the children left home, there seemed to be nothing left for me. Simon was at work or the golf club. It was an empty shell marriage. I had an affair and Simon went berserk. The divorce was difficult but at last I feel like a person.

Changes in gender roles in the family

Gender roles are the jobs and responsibilities that people are expected to take on based on their gender (whether they are male or female). The changes in living conditions, working life, and increasing wealth and social attitudes to marriage and divorce have resulted in big changes in gender roles within the family.

In the nineteenth and early twentieth centuries, gender roles were generally fixed and wives were subordinate to their husbands. This was true of all social classes; even in wealthy families, the woman was expected to supervise the housework and the raising of children, though servants often did this work. The women looked after the house and children and the men were the wage earners and the undisputed head of the family, making the decisions and controlling the lives of the rest of the family.

In the twentieth century women's roles and status changed dramatically. The suffragette movement gained the vote for women and women demonstrated their ability to take on traditional male roles during two world wars. Most jobs in the twentieth century did not depend on physical strength, which could have excluded women from them, but on skills in factory production and clerical and administrative work.

Technology also meant that housework, which once had been a full-time task, was made easier by washing machines, vacuum cleaners, gas cookers

A Second World War poster depicting 'Rosie the Riveter' encourages American women to show their abilities and go to work for the war effort. How do you think posters such as these helped to change attitudes to gender roles in the twentieth century?

ACTIVITY

1 **a)** Copy and fill out the chart below to show who mostly does what household job in your family.

b) In class or groups, compare your family division of labour with others. What are the common patterns?

c) If you can, do the same chart with relatives or friends from an earlier generation and identify any changes in family life over time.

Household task	Done mostly by male	Done mostly by female	Done mostly by you	Shared equally
Washing and ironing				
Preparing meals				
Cleaning the house				
Household shopping				
Organising money and bills				
Maintaining and repairing household equipment				
Raising children				
Looking after sick members of family				
Disciplining children				
Deciding on big expenses (such as holidays, car, etc.)				

and central heating. Houses were smaller and easier to run. However, these appliances cost money and it is more expensive to support children, so the 'dual income family', where both husband and wives or partners worked, has become common in the UK.

Attitudes to changing gender roles

For many men and women, the changes in relationships within the family are a good thing. Most women are happy to have lost the lower role of taking care of the man and the family, and are glad that they have more power in the home and in the outside world. Being able to earn a living, having their own money and property, and being treated with respect has made their lives much better. Sharing the work of raising the children and maintaining the home has made the family closer.

Men have also gained by being able to share the responsibility of providing for the family and having a better relationship with their partner. They have become much more involved in raising children, and an equal relationship is closer and more satisfying for many people.

But some people are less happy about these changes in gender roles.

- There is a lot of evidence that although both parents go out to work, many women are still responsible for the housework and most of the childcare.
- Some experts in child development feel that when both parents are at work, they are not able to provide the children with enough attention and care to develop a rounded personality.
- Some people believe that women are better at child-rearing and that men are better as wage-earners, and that taking on both these roles is stressful for both men and women.

ACTIVITIES

1 Read the two extracts below from recent newspaper articles. What criticisms of modern gender roles are expressed in them?

2 Using the material in this topic and your own experiences, what advantages have come about as a result of modern gender roles in the family?

Problem students of working parents

The head of a secondary school in the west of England has caused a row in education circles by claiming that some students were not doing well in school because both parents were working and were too tired to get involved in their children's education. Parents need to make sure they can devote enough time to encouraging and teaching children, or they may find that their children lack a sense of direction.

Mothers working double shifts

A recent survey revealed that many women now do two jobs. There are now as many women as men in the British labour force.

This has brought financial independence to many women, but at a cost.

The survey reveals that 68 per cent of women do 'most of the housework', and 76 per cent of women are 'mainly responsible for childcare'. More than half the women responding to the survey said they were exhausted at the end of the day. 43 per cent of the mothers responding to the survey said they felt their 'quality of life had declined' since they returned to work.

Changes in households and new types of families

On pages 196–200, you read about the different types of families found in the UK.

Now that you know how families have changed you can understand why new types of families and households developed.

Lone parent families

The big increase in the number of lone parent families has been due to the increased number of divorces, and the break up of cohabiting couples who have had a child. There are other reasons for lone parent families, such as the death of one parent, the choice of some mothers to have a child but not stay involved with the father, or women who have a child although the father is not prepared to get in involved, or who is not known to the mother.

Teenage mothers

Britain has the highest teenage pregnancy rate in Europe. The London boroughs of Lambeth, Southwark and Lewisham have the highest number of teenage pregnancies: 10 per cent of women in this area are pregnant by the time they are 20. About 10 per cent of women in Britain are married by the time they are 18. The figure for the USA is 11 per cent but in Brazil the figure is 24 per cent and in Ghana 38 per cent.

Unmarried teenage mothers

Britain tops the world for numbers of *unmarried* teenage mothers. The first worldwide survey of young women's sexual activity showed that 87 per cent of the 41,700 children born to 15 to 19-year-olds in the UK were outside marriage. This compares with 62 per cent in America and 10 per cent in Japan, and is higher than the rate in Third World countries.

The rise in teenage pregnancy has been most striking over the last 20 years. How can these facts be explained? Several theories have been put forward.

- Sex education in the UK is poor and the pregnancies are mistakes.
- Young people are allowed too much freedom by parents and the community.
- The UK system of benefits for single mothers encourages young girls to believe they can bring up a child without too many problems.
- A recent study reveals that girls as young as 13 are making a 'career choice' by deciding to have children, since they see parenting as preferable to working in a dead-end job. Most teenage pregnancies occur in areas where there is high unemployment and low average incomes.

Margaret Jones, chief executive of the Brook Advisory Centres, which offer family planning advice to teenagers, said:

The majority of young women today do not rush into marriage because they become pregnant. Although teenagers are far less likely to have a baby today compared with 20 years ago, they are more likely to have a baby outside marriage. This reflects the trend away from the shotgun marriage, which carried a high risk of divorce, towards cohabitation. In 1995, 67 per cent of babies born to teenagers outside marriage were jointly registered by both parents, suggesting that the majority of teenage mums are nonetheless in stable relationships.

From 'Into a New World: Young Women's Sexual and Reproductive Lives',
International Planned Parenthood Federation, 2007.

Shared households of friends

On the other hand, many people are choosing to not marry until they are into their 30s. Instead, they often choose to live with groups of friends rather than marrying or cohabiting with a partner. Up until the 1960s this would have been rare, but several factors have brought this about:

- Many people want to develop their careers before starting a family. This is especially true for women who now have much better employment opportunities.
- The cost of buying or renting property has risen, so people need longer to save up for deposits.
- Living in shared households has become more common as more young people spend time in higher education, or move away from home to start work.
- Many young people believe they should meet a wide range of people and have more experience of living as a single person before they settle down to a steady relationship.

Today, many young people choose to live in shared households rather than marrying or cohabiting with a partner.

Reconstituted families

The rise in reconstituted families is easy to explain. The increase in the number of divorces has left many people living as lone parents, and the acceptance of re-marriage as a normal part of life means that many lone parents re-marry, often to other lone parents.

Such families are very common in the UK, and marriage trends have certainly changed. Two-fifths of all marriages taking place in the UK in 2003 were re-marriages for both or one partner (109,090 out of a total of 306,200) and the number of such marriages each year are on the increase.

Civil partnerships.

Gay couples have lived together for many years but, until 1967 in England and Wales and 1980 in Scotland, it was illegal. Gay couples often had to be very secretive about their relationship in public. It was also seen as unacceptable by many people in the UK and gay people were often victims of abuse.

Since homosexuality was legalised, more gay people have 'come out' in public, and social attitudes have become much more tolerant, though some prejudice remains. Since 2005, gay people have been able to become partners in a legal civil partnership, which gives them the same rights as married men and women. Between 2005 and early 2008, 26,787 civil partnerships had taken place. The majority were partnerships of women.

Since 1900, there have been so many changes in family and household structure that British society would be completely unrecognisable to someone time-travelling from a hundred years ago.

Civil partnerships are becoming much more common and have been accepted by most of the UK population.

CONCEPT 4

There are different influences on the family

From reading through this chapter, you know that families in a society are not the same and even families in one small area are going to be different from each other. Some differences in families and households are the result of choices that individuals make about how they want to live. For example, children whose parents divorced may feel that they do not want to get married, while children who were brought up in a big happy family may want the same thing in their marriage.

But there are many wider social factors that influence the way families are organised in a society. In this concept section we will examine the forces that shape family life today. You will learn about:

- How social class and differences in wealth affect families.
- How religious beliefs are tightly linked to family life.
- How government policies and laws shape the way families are organised and controlled.
- How the way families are portrayed in the media influences people's expectations of what a family should be, and how its members should behave.

The following are ideas and terms that you will need to know from this concept section:

influences on the family: media, social class, religious beliefs, family size, government policies, the law, Divorce Reform Act, Child Support Act, child benefit, The Children Act, 'the cereal packet family', role models, arranged marriages, contraception, adoption, responsibilities of parents

Wealth and social class

The way families live and the choices they can make depend strongly on their background and their wealth. A family in which the parents are from wealthy families, who are well educated and have good jobs, are likely to be able to buy a house and to ensure their children get good opportunities to follow in their footsteps. On the other hand, a family in which the parents have no jobs or a low income, who struggle to pay the bills, and who live in a rough estate, will find it much harder to give their children the help they need to make a success of their life.

The example of Diana and Liam on pages 202–203 gives an idea of how different levels of wealth can influence the expectations and ambitions of children. This does not mean that rich families are better or happier than poorer ones, but there is no doubt that a family's level of wealth influences how a family is organised, and the kind of support and help the children receive.

Religious beliefs

The role of family is important in most religions, and the stricter versions of these religions are very precise about the way families should live. The Protestant Church of England believes that children should only be born to married couples, and that divorce is a betrayal of the marriage vows. However, many Christians accept that having children out of wedlock is acceptable provided that the parents look after the children with love and care. They also accept that divorce in some circumstances may be accepted, though many churches will not perform the service of re-marriage of a divorced person.

The Catholic Church is much more strict and says that divorce is always wrong, as is cohabitation and unmarried couples having children. They also see having an abortion and the use of contraceptives as sinful.

Many Muslims believe that marriage should be arranged by parents, that children should be brought up with strict segregation of boys and girls, who should not mix in private with the opposite sex until they are married. Strict Muslim beliefs demand that children accept the decisions about their lives that are imposed by the father, and that their lives must follow the teachings of the Qur'an. Divorce is accepted and in some countries a man is allowed to have more than one wife.

Other religions have rules about marriage, childbirth, divorce, and the roles of men, women and children in the family, many of them similar to Christian or Muslim beliefs. However, in all religions there are big variations in how strictly different religious groups follow these rules. Some follow the teaching of the church to the letter, others are influenced by the liberal views of modern societies and are less committed to traditional beliefs.

The way people organise their family life depends on the importance of religion in their lives – if they are very religious, their families will follow the religious beliefs and teachings of their church, mosque or temple. These beliefs will define the roles that men, women and children play in the family and will have much influence on how marriage partners are chosen, and often the way in which people live their lives. If they are less committed to their religion, they will be more influenced by the other values of the society they live in.

The influence of governments on family life

The way we live in the UK is strongly influenced by the government and its policies. Below are some examples of the way the government influences and affects family life.

Government's social policies

1 The welfare state

The WELFARE STATE is the name that is given to a range of government measures that are set up to look after the population of the UK by making sure everybody is provided with housing, food, healthcare and education. The British government has done this since the nineteenth century but until 1948 the help they gave was limited. Education was provided, but healthcare was not free, and only the very poorest were helped with housing and food.

In 1948, the government of the day decided to provide care for everyone who needed it, 'from cradle to grave'. This meant that education, even up to university level, was free, healthcare was free, and everyone over 65 (men) and 60 (women) was given an old age pension. To pay for this everyone who worked paid taxes.

The 'welfare state' also provided other financial help such as unemployment benefits and other social security payments to make sure no one starved. Nowadays, though we have to pay for higher education and some healthcare, the government still spends billions of pounds on housing benefits, income support, disability payments and child benefits to try to make sure that children of low paid, unemployed or single parents are not in need.

How does this affect families?

This means that many of the roles and responsibilities that families used to have, such as education, healthcare, supporting and caring for the elderly, have been largely taken over by government agencies: nurseries, schools, doctors and hospitals, government grants, pensions, residential care homes and so on. While many families still take on some parts of these roles, modern families are now much more focused on providing emotional and psychological support for each other.

It also means that some people have become dependent on being supported by the government. If this dependence lasts for a long time, it is difficult for some people to break out of their benefit lifestyle, and find their way back to supporting themselves. Some politicians and some of the press have suggested that the support that the government gives to single parents and their children is the cause of the large number of unmarried teenage mothers in the UK.

2 The government and children

The government has also taken on the role of protecting and safeguarding children. Examples of the government's attempts to protect children includes the Children Act, 1989, which says that local authorities have a general duty to safeguard and promote the welfare of children (anyone under the age of 18) within their area who are in need. They should try to keep the child living with the parents, but if they believe that the child is not being cared for they have the right to remove them to other care. The welfare of the child is the main consideration. A child is defined as being a child in need if: 'They are unlikely to achieve or maintain, or have the opportunity of achieving, or maintaining, a reasonable standard of health or development without the provision for them of services by a local authority.'

A child will be taken into the care of the local authority where there is ill-treatment or threat to their health or development: 'ill-treatment' includes sexual and emotional abuse as well as physical abuse; 'health' includes physical and mental health; 'development' includes physical, intellectual, emotional, social and behavioural development.

A later act defined the rights of a child very simply. The Children Act, 2004 places a duty on social services to ensure that every child, whatever their background or circumstances, has the support they need to:

- be healthy
- stay safe
- enjoy and achieve through learning
- make a positive contribution to society
- achieve economic well-being.

What does this mean for families?
This means that the way children are raised is not just up to the parents. The government has taken on the role of checking that parents are doing a good job and not neglecting or abusing their children. This is seen by many people as a good policy and enough cases of mistreatment of children have come to light to show that it is necessary.

However, the well-publicised failure to protect some children shows how difficult it is for a government to take on the role and do it effectively. Some people object to government intervention, because they see this as invading the privacy of family life, and they feel that the government has become too involved in trying to control every aspect of people's lives.

3 The government and divorce laws
Over the last 50 years the government has made divorce easier in a sequence of divorce reform laws. From 1857 until 1971, in order to get divorced, a couple had to prove that one or both of them had done something wrong. Usually this was being unfaithful. This had to be proved in a court, which led to a booming business for solicitors, lawyers, private detectives and photographers. Other grounds for divorce were cruelty or desertion.

In 1971, the law was changed – there was no need for there to be a guilty party, and divorce was granted when there was 'the irretrievable breakdown of marriage'. This still had to be proved in court.

The Family Law Act, 1996 said divorce could be granted if a couple were both prepared to state that the marriage had broken down. After a year, if nothing changed, divorce was granted. Therefore, as long as both partners want a divorce, this can be done without using a solicitor and simply by paying about £150 for the cost of the divorce proceedings. If there is no agreement, however, it can be more difficult and expensive.

What effect did this have on families?
Because of legislation changes since the 1950s there has been a big increase in divorce rates. This has resulted in many broken families and this fact, coupled with fewer people marrying, more people cohabiting, and more couples marrying later, might make it seem that the popularity of marriage is falling.

However, there are many signs that this is not so. There are more re-marriages and 80 per cent of children at the age of 16 have been brought up by their parents in the original family. The laws have helped make divorce more acceptable in society, and people now see marriage as a way of finding personal happiness rather than a duty and tradition to be endured even if it turns out to be a disaster.

4 Families and government policy

What does the government think about families?
Politicians often talk enthusiastically about the importance of the family. At election time, political parties will speak about how they will work for the needs of ordinary families.

During the 1990s, the government made many criticisms of the changes in family life which have been described in this chapter. They were particularly concerned about the growing numbers of single parent families. Politicians at the Conservative Party conference in 1993 made speeches that suggested that girls were getting pregnant so that the state could support them and find them homes. The press took this story up and there were headlines such those opposite.

TEENAGERS GET PREGNANT AND WE PAY

Unmarried Mothers Damage Society

Some politicians and psychologists said that children without fathers in the home are more likely to become criminals and truants and end up being a burden on the social services. They argued that when children are not looked after by two parents, they do not get enough discipline, and that boys living with just their mothers do not learn the male role.

In 1993, John Major, Prime Minister at the time, launched a 'Back to Basics' campaign, which said that conventional family life was the best way to put society on the right track again. However, the campaign backfired. It wasn't helped by the fact that several scandals involving MPs at the time meant that the public didn't feel that the government had the right to make moral judgements. Many people sprang to the defence of single parents, saying there was no evidence that girls got pregnant to get a council house and benefits, and that most single parents' biggest problem was poverty, not the absence of men in the household. It was poverty that caused crime and truancy. Research showed that most single parents wanted a conventional family life but were not able to find suitable partners.

Where does the government stand now?
The Labour government in 2009 seems to have mixed feelings about the contemporary family. In 1997, Tony Blair, Prime Minister at the time, made a speech where he said that teenage pregnancies, families not caring for the elderly members, poor parental ROLE MODELS, truancy and poor educational achievement could all be explained by failure in family life. When he said this, most people believed he meant that a strong family was a heterosexual couple bringing up their children in a permanent relationship with an employed male breadwinner.

Do you think that growing numbers of teenage mothers and single parents are a cause for concern?

However, when it comes to policies, the Labour government has done much to support all types of family life. It is gradually giving all families and couples equal rights, whether they are married or not, and whether they are heterosexual or homosexual. Single parents are given both practical and financial help. The government is trying to cut teenage pregnancies by education, not by punishment. In 1998, it wrote a Green Paper (which outlines government policy) that said: 'We also acknowledge just how much families have changed. Family structures have become more complicated, with many more children living with step-parents or in single parent households. They may face extra difficulties and we have designed practical support with these parents in mind.'

Recently, the government has made it possible for homosexual couples to adopt children, and has increased the rights of both men and women to have maternity and paternity leave from work. In other words, the government has made it easier for people to choose how to live rather than pushing them to follow a traditional pattern of family life.

Do media portrayals of weddings help to keep the tradition of marriage alive in modern-day culture?

The influence of the media

Different levels of wealth, social class, background, ethnic cultural traditions, religious beliefs and practices, and government policies all shape attitudes to families and relationships.

However, in modern societies, our attitudes, values and understanding of social life are influenced very powerfully by the media. What we see on TV, in the movies, and hear in songs, and read in the papers all influence our ideas about what is the best way to live.

For many people, role models are people encountered through the media. These are real people such as superstars in sport, music and movies, celebrities, and people working in the media: presenters, interviewers and so on. For some people the lives their role models lead is a guide to what is an ideal lifestyle. The big events in media stories about celebrities are their love lives, marriages and break-ups. This may seem negative, but the basic message is that marriage is important.

The media does more than this. It shows us a version of life, and family life and relationships are a central part of many TV programmes, films, songs and dramas. Here are some examples to illustrate this:

- *Coronation Street, Emmerdale* and *EastEnders* are among the most widely watched programmes on British TV. Their plots and storylines are based around families and their relationships.

Weddings are a regular big event. Although the families in these programmes are often in conflict, the message comes across that a happy, honest marriage is the goal, and that the characters' basic loyalty is to the family.

- There are also a large number of films that centre on relationships, weddings, families: for example, *Four Weddings and a Funeral, My Best Friend's Wedding*, the Bridget Jones films, *My Big Fat Greek Wedding* … you can add to the list. In most of these films the message is that getting married to someone you love is the ideal way of life.

ACTIVITIES

1 Why do some newspapers and politicians think that children who are not brought up in traditional nuclear families (for example, brought up by single teenage mothers) are a problem for society? Use the information on this page and also the information on socialisation and family break-up.

2 Does the UK government seem to think that there is an 'ideal' family? Use information about government policies in this section and any other evidence which you think is relevant.

3 What evidence is there that the majority of the UK population accept different patterns of family life?

An advert for Kingsmill bread, with the comedy duo Mel and Sue, and a family setting.

- Many advertisements, especially those for food, health products and household goods, are based around family scenes. The family is usually the traditional mum, dad and the kids, or wider family members. The images and scenes consistently show families laughing, playing, joking with each other. It might not be realistic, but it presents an ideal that can be made real in everyone's life. The 'perfect' families in these adverts used to be known as 'cereal packet families', after the a long tradition of cereal adverts that showed the whole family having breakfast, glowing with health after eating some cereal, and being nice to each other. Are these advertisements still common or is a different image used?
- Documentaries, which often explore difficulties within families, for example, over raising children, or coming to terms with medical problems, mostly show the value of family bonds.
- Many magazines aimed at women, such as *Hello!, Woman, OK!, Vanity Fair*, either concentrate on the marriages and families of celebrities or run articles that assume all families are traditional in structure.

Media images play a big part in our understanding of what is normal and what is desirable.

ACTIVITIES

Analyse the way families are portrayed in the media.

1 Watch TV for an evening and, for each programme, including news and documentaries, keep a record of each time a family is featured or discussed and what type of family it is. Check your results and see which type of family is most commonly shown or referred to.

2 Watch a soap opera for a week and analyse whether the families shown are shown to be successful and happy, or having problems.

3 Read two or three magazines such as *Hello!, Woman, OK!*, or a celebrity scandal magazine, and cut out stories/articles/ photographs that include or mention families (there will be a lot!). Collect your cuttings and sort into groups according to what types of family they are: for example, nuclear family, extended family, cohabiting couples, single parent family, reconstituted family, gay family.

For each of these projects, try to identify whether the family is depicted as normal or unusual, acceptable or unacceptable.

The media's role in changing ideas of families

The media also show changes in family life. Cohabitation is usually shown without any suggestion that it is not acceptable. Break-ups in relationships are often shown as sad but inevitable as people fall out of love. The real problems in family life are painted clearly, and families that are not working well are the themes of many dramas.

Programmes such as *Shameless*, which depict families that are constantly disintegrating, and films such as *East is East*, which examines the problems of conflicting family values, have played a part in changing people's attitudes towards families, and have encouraged the acceptance of cohabitation, homosexuality, and different attitudes to family lifestyles.

What are British attitudes to marriage?

Most people in Britain have shown that they accept new family and household structures by adopting them, or being tolerant of them. Unmarried mothers and single parents, divorcees and reconstituted families are a familiar part of British life.

People seem to accept that how people choose to live is up to them. There is much less public criticism of lifestyles that used to be seen as shameful, such as having children outside marriage or living together without getting married, or putting an elderly relative into residential care. Most people seem to accept that things have changed. But does the idea that the traditional family is the 'ideal' still exist? There is some evidence from government statistics that it does:

• Many people who get divorced re-marry. They obviously think that marriage is good; they made a mistake but want to try again.
• Most people who cohabit for longer than two years either stay together as if they were married or do eventually marry.

While the following is from a recent survey of adults in Britain aged 20–35:

• Seven in ten wanted to marry.
• Nearly eight in ten (79 per cent) of those cohabiting wanted to marry.
• The main reason why young people wanted to marry was to make a commitment (47 per cent).
• Of those respondents who wanted to marry, only 20 per cent thought that 'married people are generally happier than unmarried people'.

'Young People's Attitudes to Marriage',
Ipsos MORI/Civitas, 2007.

However, other surveys of British attitudes to marriage suggest that our views on family life are changing:

• 70 per cent of people think there is nothing wrong with sex before marriage, up from 48 per cent in 1984.
• Only 28 per cent of people think married couples make better parents than unmarried ones.
• Only 17 per cent of men think that a 'man's job' is to earn money, while a woman should stay at home, down from 32 per cent in 1989.
• Two-thirds of people (66 per cent) think there is little difference socially between being married and living together.

'British Social Attitudes', www.natcen.ac.uk,
24 January 2007.

ACTIVITY

1 Using some of the data here and your own ideas:
   a) Devise a brief questionnaire to discover what your peer group thinks about families. Suggested questions include:
      • Do you want to get married in the future?
      • What is the best age to get married?
      • Is it acceptable for couples to have children if they are not married?
      • Should divorce be made more difficult?
      • Should marriage always be for life?

   Use your own ideas for other questions.

   b) Give the questionnaire to equal numbers of males and females (about 15 of each).
   c) Analyse the answers and write a short report on modern attitudes to marriage using your results.

Examination questions and advice

Exam questions in both papers can be divided into two groups.

1 *Source-based questions* testing your ability to apply your studies to the stimulus material.

2 Questions testing your *recall and understanding* of the examples and cases you have studied.

There are lots of source-based questions of different levels of difficulty running right throughout the book, so in this section we are going to practise the second type of question – all of which are for 12 marks maximum.

You need to practise so that you can write about 160–200 words in fifteen minutes for a top answer.

There are both questions for you to try and candidates' answers to some of the questions for you to discuss in groups.

Culture and beliefs

1 People have different views about the importance of nature and nurture in shaping who we are. Write a short essay about the nature/nurture debate. In your answer you should:

- explain the meaning of the terms
- use examples from your studies
- give your own conclusion on the debate.

Candidate Naomi writes:

Some people say that it is nature that makes you who you are because you get your genes from your parents. The way they act is the way you will act at the same age.

Other people say it is nurture because most young kids have role models and they copy the way they do things and learn from them.

Also, if you are brought up in a tough area, you will be tough yourself.

We looked at how adverts for toys use colours to show which toys were for boys and which were for girls. This is socialisation. There is primary socialisation, which is your parents, and there is secondary socialisation.

I think primary socialisation is the most important because then parents can keep more control over the child. After this, when a child has learned its roles, norms and beliefs, it can socialise itself from media and friends.

ACTIVITIES

1 a) Read candidate Naomi's answer to question 1.

   b) In groups, discuss the strengths of the answer and ways in which it could be improved. Consider the following marking guidelines when discussing the answer:
   - Is there evidence of understanding of the key concepts?
   - Has the candidate used examples from her own studies?
   - Have specialist words/language been used?
   - Has the candidate covered the three bullet points?

2 Now try the question yourself.

   a) First, talk your answer through in small groups/pairs.

   b) Then write down some bullet points or draw a concept map to help you plan your answer.

   c) When you are ready, complete your written answer in about fifteen minutes. You will speed up with practice.

A grade guide and comments on the candidate's answer are given on page 229.

Now try the following questions.

2 Choose a moral issue you have studied. Write about the issue using the following guidelines:

- Explain clearly what the issue is.
- Give examples of the people (individual groups) who hold these views.
- Explain in detail how the views are different.
- Explain why it is difficult for people to agree or compromise about the issue.

3 Explain why people might develop different beliefs and values in different cultures. Use examples from your studies to support your answer.

4 Which of the following have the most influence on teenagers' values and behaviour?

- Parents
- Mass media
- Other

Use examples from your studies to support your answer.

Environmental issues

5 Using your own knowledge, explain why some people have taken action over an environmental issue. In your answer you should:

- identify and explain the environmental issue
- explain the concerns that people have about the issue
- describe the method(s) used.

Candidate Tom writes:

Environmental groups such as Greenpeace affect environmental issues in many ways. Whale hunting is a good example. When this came to the attention of Greenpeace in the 1970s, they found evidence that whales were in danger of becoming extinct and decided to take non-violent direct action. This means they tried to disrupt the whale hunters peacefully and legally.

They got their own ship, Rainbow Warrior, and used inflatables to get in the way of the harpoon gun, all the while videoing what was going on. They influenced people's attitudes towards whale hunting by sending the video to TV channels and using pictures on their own publicity leaflets. They explained how whales have become an endangered species and how this affects the rest of the marine ecosystem. Whales control the numbers of krill, which feed on plankton. Plankton put oxygen in the water, which other fish need to live.

So Greenpeace helped to change people's attitudes. By seeing the video and finding out about how important whales are, the public became concerned. Greenpeace also showed the public that something could be done, so politicians were afraid of losing votes and made an agreement to ban whale hunting.

ACTIVITIES

1 a) Read Tom's answer to question 5.

b) In groups, discuss the strengths of the answer and ways in which it could be improved. Consider the following marking guidelines when discussing the answer:

- Have the three bullet points in the question been covered?
- Has the environmental issue been explained in detail?
- Has the question been answered?
- Is there evidence of own studies and specialist words/language being used?

2 Now try the question yourself.

a) First, talk your answer through in small groups/pairs.

b) Then write down some bullet points or draw a concept map to help you plan your answer.

c) When you are ready, complete your written answer in about 15 minutes.

A grade guide and comments on the candidate's answer are given on page 229.

Now try the following questions.

7 How do people's culture and beliefs affect the way they treat the natural environment? Use information and examples from your studies in your answer to this question.

8 Using an example or examples from your studies, explain how tourism can have both positive and negative effects on the people and environment in tourist destinations.

9 Why are environmental pressure groups campaigning for a reduction in the burning of fossil fuels?

10 Explain how pollution can be reduced on an individual and global level. Use your own studies to answer.

Commentary and grade guide

For question 1

The candidate has a fairly sound grasp of the main concepts. Genes are associated with nature, but not explained very fully. Nurture is linked to the way you are brought up, but this could be explained more clearly. Socialisation is included and reference to own studies is made. It is implied that gender roles are learned, but this is not spelled out. All three bullet points are covered, although reasoning for conclusion is suspect. Answer jumps around a little. Some specialist language used.

Grade and mark guide: C 8/12

For question 5

This is a comprehensive answer that addresses all the requirements of the question. Good use of specialist language and study of Greenpeace. Good detail in the explanation of importance of whales in marine ecosystem. Could have:

- explained how much scientists believe we have yet to learn from whales – we cannot if they are extinct.
- added that some key countries like Norway and Japan are ignoring the ban.

There will always be something to improve, even though grade and mark guide for this is: A 12/12

Humanities Investigation: Controlled assessment

This investigation will count for 25 per cent of the total GCSE grade. The Controlled Assessment is worth 40 marks. These are divided into separate marks for two sets of skills.

1 Investigation, Application and Communication	22 marks (maximum)
2 Analysis and Evaluation	18 marks (maximum)

The Examination Board (AQA) sets seven questions or hypotheses every year. These are different each year. There is one assessment for each of the seven topic areas of the specification. Your teacher will advise which of the areas to investigate.

One example of a possible Humanities Investigation question could be 'Should we recycle more?' from the Core Option of Environmental issues. A hypothesis covering the same area would be 'In the UK we fail to recycle sufficiently to meet the needs of the twenty-first century.'

A good starting point is to place the subject at the centre of a sheet of paper and do a spider diagram of relevant materials that you can investigate. For example:

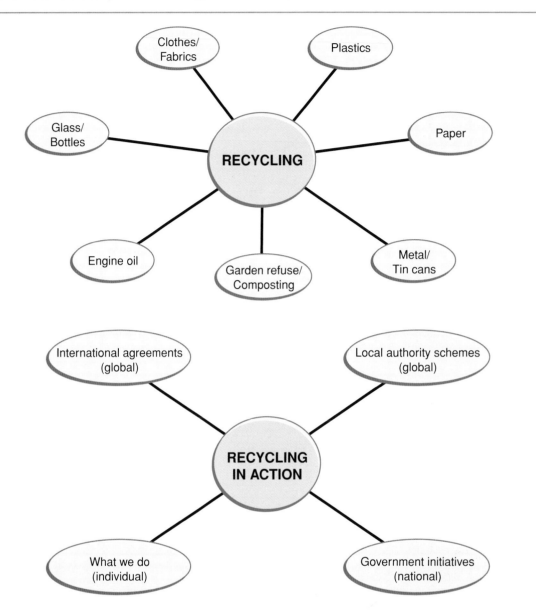

The next step is to formulate key questions on the topic of recycling. For example:

- What is recycling?
- Why is recycling important?
- What materials can be recycled?
- What recycling facilities are there locally?
- How many people recycle?
- How aware of recycling are different age groups?
- Historically – how has recycling developed over time?
- Geographically – how do authorities and facilities compare?
- Political – which pressure groups are involved in recycling?

- How does the UK compare with other countries recycling?
- Is there a difference between more economically developed countries and less economically developed countries?

These are 11 possible questions – but you will have other questions concerning recycling.

To try to answer these key questions you will undertake an investigation. This will involve both primary and secondary sources of information. You should keep your research findings in a file.

Humanities Investigation: Controlled assessment

Primary sources of information

Primary information is material that you find out yourself, such as:

- **Questionnaires and surveys:** You could try to find out how many people recycle. You could see if more older people than younger people recycle. There could also be surveys of how many people are recycling. For example, does your local school have an effective recycling policy? Do your fellow students follow the recycling rules?
- **Visiting recycling sites:** You could visit recycling sites, possibly run by your local council. You could observe and take photographs of the workings of the site.
- **Interviews:** You could interview family members, local officials, or other people involved in recycling. Interviews are quite easy to conduct. You need to work out a series of questions in advance and make sure the answers are retained. An audio tape is useful for this and can be submitted with your research material. You can also look at how effective the interview technique has been in your investigation.

Secondary sources of information

Secondary material on recycling would include:

- **Books, magazines and newspapers:** Books are available from school and local libraries. Magazine and newspaper articles are easily available.
- **Statistics:** These are produced by both central and local government. Your local council is likely to be very useful: all councils have recycling targets.
- **Television and radio:** There are useful programmes on recycling you could watch/listen to.
- **Internet:** There are websites for environmental pressure groups such as Greenpeace. Your local authority, BBC and newspaper websites are also useful.

Answering the question

When you have completed your research, you will answer the question (or hypothesis) originally set. You will use your research information to help you do this. You should have a file of work that you have put together to use.

You will answer the question under 'controlled conditions' at school. The answer to the question should be up to 2,000 words. You can take any of your investigation notes with you. These notes should be presented in a file that your teacher will retain. Your teachers will decide how many sessions will be devoted to producing the controlled assessment.

In marking your assessment, the Investigation, Application and Communication Strand – 22 marks – rewards your research skills. It also gives you credit for thorough and interesting investigation. You will also get marks for good communication and for focusing on the questions or hypothesis. For example, a conclusion on the recycling question might be: 'In our local authority there are many recycling facilities but, although paper recycling is excellent, there is still a long way to go with bottles'.

The markers and moderators are looking for well presented, logical and sustained responses. You will also be rewarded for good spelling, punctuation and grammar.

Eighteen marks are awarded for your analysis and evaluation of the material you have investigated. The aim is to produce material that you can evaluate fully. You could reflect on your key questions and the links between them, and you would be advised to reflect of the adequacy, completeness and usefulness of the sources you have acquired. You are advised to analyse your sources and investigation very widely. The mark scheme at the highest levels refers to a 'holistic awareness' of the issue in the breadth and detail. You would do well to bear this in mind and ensure there are no deficiencies in your sources of information.

GLOSSARY

ABSOLUTE POVERTY When people have less resources (food, water, shelter, etc.) than they need to survive.

ACID RAIN Where gases combine with water droplets in clouds and produce acids (sulphuric and nitric), which rains down, killing plants and damaging buildings.

AESTHETICS The study of beauty in art, music, dance, drama, design, architecture, etc.

AFFIRMATIVE ACTION A policy designed to compensate for discrimination against women and minority groups in the past through measures aimed at improving their economic and educational opportunities.

AGEISM The practice of treating people differently and usually unfairly on the grounds of age, especially because they are old.

AIDS Acquired Immune Deficiency Syndrome. A transmitted disease at epidemic proportions in LEDCs, especially in Africa.

ALTERNATIVE ENERGY A method of producing electrical power that does not use fossil fuels, for example, wind power.

AMNESTY INTERNATIONAL A campaigning organisation, supported by public donations, whose purpose is to protect people wherever justice, fairness, freedom and truth are denied. It works by discovering information about human rights abuses and making this public, and by providing lawyers to defend the victims.

ANTHROPOLOGIST Someone who studies humankind, in particular human cultures.

APARTHEID Racial segmentation in South Africa.

APPEASEMENT Policy of granting concessions to enemies to preserve peace.

AQUACULTURE Breeding and raising fish in a controlled environment. Think of it as farming in water (the seas, lakes, rivers or specially built ponds).

ARBITRATION Settling a dispute by a neutral party.

ARRANGED MARRIAGE A marriage where the selection of marriage partners is done by the parents, or other older relatives, and not left to the individuals who are going to marry.

ASYLUM SEEKERS People who flee their own country because they are being persecuted for reasons of race, religion, nationality or membership of a particular social group or political opinion.

ATTITUDE A state of mind or a feeling; a way of thinking, for example: 'He had a positive attitude about work.' (Can include the way of positioning one's body.)

BALLAST When ships are not fully loaded, they take sea water on board to keep them stable at sea. Often this water contains pollution and oil. When it is pumped out so the boat can be loaded, this pollution ends up back in the water near to a coast.

BEHAVIOUR Manner of acting or conducting yourself.

BELIEF Something accepted as true or valid without actual proof.

BIGAMY When someone marries more than one person at a time in a country where this is illegal.

BIO-DIVERSITY Wide variety of living things: plants, insects and animals.

BIOLOGICAL Anything related to the way human beings work as living organisms.

BIO-MASS An energy resource derived from organic matter. These include wood, agricultural waste and living cell material that can be burned to produce heat energy.

BLACK POWER A movement which believed in the use of force to increase the power of black people in the USA.

BNP British National Party. A far right political party. In their 2005 election manifesto they called for an end to immigration and an introduction of incentives to 'encourage immigrants and their descendants to return home'.

BOYCOTT To refuse to do business or socialise with a person, group or country.

BY-CATCH The name given to any fish that is caught unintentionally.

CALORIE INTAKE Number of calories consumed per person per day. The survival level is 1500–1800.

CANCELLATION OF DEBT An agreement by countries or organisations not to ask for repayment of loans, particularly from poor countries struggling to overcome poverty.

CAPITAL PUNISHMENT Physical punishment (including death) of a crime.

CAPITALISM An economic system based on private, rather than state, ownership of businesses allowing free competition and profit.

CARBON FOOTPRINT A measure of the impact that human activities have on the environment in terms of the amount of greenhouse gas produced by them, which is measured in units of carbon dioxide.

CASH CROPS Crops that are grown only to be sold as exports, not used as food or for other purposes by the local people.

'CEREAL PACKET FAMILY' A way of describing one version of an idealised family. The phrase comes from the common image of a family often seen in adverts for breakfast cereals (mother, father, two children, all eating happily together). Often used to highlight the difference between the media image and reality of family life.

CHILD-CENTRED FAMILIES Families that are primarily organised around satisfying the needs and wishes of the children, with adult interests coming second.

CIA Central Intelligence Agency in the USA. Responsible for external security.

CITIZENSHIP The status of a citizen with attendant duties, rights and privileges.

CIVIL PARTNERS Two men or two women who go through a ceremony that gives them the same legal rights as a married couple.

CIVILISATION A society in an advanced state of social development, having complex legal, political and religious organisations.

COHABITATION Couples who live together without going through any sort of marriage ceremony.

COLD WAR A state of tension and rivalry between nations, stopping short of actual full-scale war. Usually refers to relationship between the USA and the USSR between 1945 and the late 1980s.

COLONIALISM The conquest and ownership (as colonies) by wealthy countries of other countries around the world as part of their empires.

COLONISE To take over land abroad.

COMMUNES Households where several unrelated individuals and couples live together, sharing responsibilities for maintaining the group economically as if they were an extended family.

COMMUNISM A supporter of communism believes in a classless society with all sources of wealth and production owned and controlled by the state.

COMMUNITY 1: A group of people living in the same locality and under the same government. 2: A group of people with a common interest. Includes ideas of sharing, participation and fellowship.

COMPROMISE To settle differences by making concessions.

CONFLICT A state of disharmony between incompatible persons, ideas or interests; a clash.

CONFRONTATION A hostile meeting or exchange of words.

CONGRESS The USA's legislature or parliament.

CONSERVATION Protecting the environment so that it will stay the same in the future. This includes protecting plants, animals, landscapes and mineral resources so they are not damaged or destroyed.

CONSTITUTION A set of rules governing an organisation; the laws and rights upon which a state is founded.

CONVECTION Describes the movement of gases and liquids caused by heating. For example, air rising as the result of heat from the sun is called convection.

CO-OPERATION People working together towards commonly agreed upon goals.

COST/BENEFIT A method of calculating what action to take, based on counting the cost of the action and balancing it against the benefits produced by the action. An example is measuring the millions of pounds that building a wind farm will cost against the billions of pounds that may be saved if it reduces global warming.

COUNSELLING Giving advice and/or support to an individual or group that needs help in resolving a problem.

CULTURAL IDENTITY Knowing who you are through belonging to a group and sharing its values.

CULTURAL RELATIVISM Not putting cultures into a rank order as ethnocentrics do. Judging any culture by its own standards.

CULTURE The shared way of life of a particular society, referring to all aspects of behaviour that are learned and which provide the context in which daily life is lived. Includes values, norms and beliefs as well as the way these are expressed through actions, words and symbols. The aesthetics, customs and traditions that characterise a particular society or nation.

CUSTOM A generally accepted practice or behaviour developed over time.

DDTA Chemical used to kill mosquitoes and other insects and pests. It is not good for people, birds or other animals.

DEBT TRAP Where LEDCs remain poor because much of the money they earn has to be used to pay off debts to MEDCs rather than to develop their countries.

DEFORESTATION Cutting down or burning most trees and plants over a wide area.

DEMOCRACY A form of government in which citizens vote to decide who should form the government and which policies they should put into action.

DEMOCRATIC SOCIETY A society in which all citizens have the right to vote to decide who will run the government, and the right to express criticisms of the government without being punished.

DESERTIFICATION The process where an area becomes very dry (a desert) as a result of low rainfall, rapid evaporation and loss of plants that used to store water.

DÉTENTE A lessening of tension between states.

DEVELOPED WORLD The part of the world where people enjoy a high standard of living as a result of wealth created by industry, services or abundant raw materials.

DEVELOPMENT Process of social and economic improvement that allows people to have an improved standard of living.

DEVELOPMENT INDICATORS Ways of measuring a country's level of economic and social development, for example, life expectancy.

DICTATORSHIP Ruling with complete and unrestricted power.

DISCRIMINATION Discrimination is treating someone differently, usually less well, because they belong to a particular group.

DIVISION OF LABOUR The manner in which necessary work is divided up (for example, housework between a husband and a wife).

DOVES People favouring peace rather than hostility to settle conflict.

DRAFT Conscription or call-up to the US army.

DRAFT-DODGING Avoiding conscription or draft.

ECOLOGY The study of the interdependency between different parts of the natural environment.

ECONOMIC DEVELOPMENT To do with increasing the wealth of a country and improving living standards of the people. It usually means expanding trade and developing technology. Tourism may also be a way of starting development.

ECOSYSTEM A range of biological and chemical elements that works together to create an enduring natural environment.

EMIGRATION Leaving a country to settle in another. The term is sometimes used when someone moves to a distant part of the same country.

EMPIRE A group of countries conquered and ruled by a wealthy power – the imperialist country.

ENDANGERED SPECIES Any plant or animal species that is in danger of being wiped out.

ENERGY Power, usually electrical power.

ENERGY GENERATION The method in which electricity is produced, for example, by burning fossil fuel or using wind power.

ENVIRONMENT The sum of all external conditions and influences affecting survival and development.

ENVIRONMENTALISTS People who are concerned about changes and damage to natural environments and who try to make people aware of what is happening.

EQUAL OPPORTUNITIES LEGISLATION Laws that try to ensure everyone is treated fairly, regardless of gender, ethnicity, class, sexuality, etc.

ETHICS A system of moral principles, rules or standards that governs the conduct of members of a group.

ETHNIC CLEANSING Genocide or forced removal of an ethnic group or groups by another.

ETHNIC GROUP A group with a distinct cultural identity, for example, their own language, traditions, religion.

ETHNICITY Racial status or distinctiveness.

ETHNOCENTRISM An attitude of cultural superiority, which implies that one's own culture is better than some other culture. It is the basis of racism, nationalism and tribalism.

EXPLOIT To make use of for the benefit of individuals or groups. The word can also mean 'use to make a profit'.

EXPORT Sale of goods produced in one country to others.

EXTREMIST Someone who has extreme opinions, especially in politics or religion.

FAMILY The family is a group of persons directly linked by kin connections, the adult members of which assume responsibility for caring for children.

FEDERAL GOVERNMENT The central government of a group of states such as the USA.

FEMALE INFANTICIDE The killing of girls at or soon after birth.

FEMININE Behavioural characteristics associated with being a woman in a specific culture.

FERTILISERS Chemicals sprayed or spread onto farmland to help crops grow.

FOOD CHAIN Describes how different species both eat other species and provide food for other species. For example, small fish eat plankton, herrings eat small fish, cod eat herring, seals eat cod, dolphins and whales eat seals.

FOSSIL FUELS Materials found occurring naturally underground. They were produced millions of years ago by organic matter such as trees, plants and animals, which have decayed and been compressed. These are coal, oil and natural gases.

FREE TRADE Trade without artificial protection of prices of goods.

FULLY EXPLOITED This is when a resource, such as a species of fish or a raw material, has been caught, extracted, or used to such an extent that any further exploitation will wipe it out.

GENDER Gender identifies behaviour associated with a specific sex in a specific culture. The term is often used incorrectly as an alternative to the word 'sex'. 'Gender' refers to social or cultural categories whereas 'sex' refers to biological categories.

GENDER ROLES These are the expectations by a culture of the way in which people will behave according to their sex (whether they are male or female). This will include how people participate in social activities, the work they do in the home or in employment, and will usually involve expectations of personal style and manners.

GENES A sequence of DNA that occupies a specific place on a chromosome and determines a particular characteristic in an organism. Genes are hereditary (i.e. passed on from parents biologically).

GENOCIDE The deliberate killing of a whole nation or people.

GEOTHERMAL ENERGY Power produced using the heat produced deep in the Earth, especially in volcanic area where the hot materials are close to the surface.

GHETTO A slum section of a city occupied mainly by a deprived minority group, usually racial.

GHETTOISATION Forcing a certain group of people to live in certain areas.

GLOBAL INEQUALITY The difference in wealth and development between different countries. For example, the wealth gap between the USA and Zimbabwe.

GLOBAL INTERDEPENDENCE The fact that most people in the world today depend on the rest of the world for survival, for example, because of the trading of vital goods, or because of reliance on other nations to protect the environment.

GLOBAL RESPONSIBILITY Where a situation can only be dealt with by people across the world accepting that they are the cause of the problem and taking action to solve it.

GLOBAL WARMING The theory that average temperatures around the world are rising steadily.

GLOBALISATION The increase of international trade and the worldwide sharing of information, social norms and cultural values. Globalisation as a term includes the spread of multi-national companies, such as Shell and Nike, and the spread of brands and fashions.

GROSS NATIONAL PRODUCT The value of all the goods and services produced in an economy, plus the value of the goods and services imported, minus the value of the goods and services exported.

GUERILLA CAMPAIGN A method of warfare making use of surprise attacks.

HAPPY SLAPPING A custom of videoing on mobile phones acts of bullying for amusement and further humiliation.

HARASSMENT Pestering or tormenting.

HAWKS People favouring force to settle conflict.

HIGHWAYS AGENCY (HA) The government body that manages, improves and builds all major roads in the UK.

HOUSEHOLD A group of people that lives together in shared accommodation.

HOUSEHUSBAND A man who takes on the family roles usually done by a housewife, such as cleaning and cooking.

HUMAN RIGHTS ACT 1989 Incorporated the European Convention on Human Rights into UK law.

HYDROPOWER Makes use of the movement of fresh water in rivers, using the flow of water to generate electricity.

HYPERINFLATION Extraordinarily high inflation or increase in prices.

IDENTITY The individual qualities and relationships that a person has which makes them unique, and which also indicate the groups and communities that the person is a part of.

IDEOLOGY Ideas and beliefs which form the basis for a social, economic or political system.

IGNORANCE Lack of knowledge or awareness.

IMMIGRANT Someone who comes to a foreign country to settle.

IMPORT Buying goods into a country.

INDUSTRIAL TRIBUNAL A body set up to hear complaints and make judgments in disputes between employers and employees.

INDUSTRIALISATION The change from producing materials using manual labour and human skills, to producing materials in large factories and industrial plants using powered machinery, automated equipment, and computerised processes.

INFRASTRUCTURE The organisation of the services needed to run a community. It would include such things as clean water supply, provision of electricity, rubbish and sewage disposal, roads and transport systems, medical care facilities and some sort of social control to prevent crime and violence.

INJUSTICE Unfairness or lack of justice.

INNATE CHARACTERISTICS A feature of being a human being that is possessed at birth. For example, your sex.

INSTITUTIONAL DISCRIMINATION Discrimination within an organisation, for example, the police force.

INTELLIGENCE The capacity to acquire and apply knowledge. The ability to think and reason.

INTEREST Percentage of money to be repaid in addition to the amount lent. Gives the lender a profit from lending.

INTERMEDIARY Someone who is brought in to settle a dispute or bring both sides into agreement.

INTERNATIONAL CONFLICT Conflict between two or more different countries, often a war, but sometimes a war of words, such as the Cold War between the USA and the USSR.

INTERNATIONAL MONETARY FUND (IMF) A world financial organisation that guides and/or supports LEDCs.

INTERPERSONAL SKILLS The ability to relate to other people.

INTOLERANCE An inability to accept differences of opinion or lifestyle.

ISLAM The religion of Muslims, or all Muslims collectively.

ISSUES Situations in societies that are the source of disagreements, often based on strongly held values and beliefs.

KIN AND KINSHIP GROUPS Another word for relatives. This often refers to more distant relatives who play a role in influencing and helping other members of the wider family e.g. uncles, cousins, in-laws and so on. They are connected genetically or through marriage.

LEARNED RESPONSE A reaction to something which has been taught.

LEDCs Less economically developed countries: countries that are significantly less wealthy than MEDCs. They have lower levels of technology and industry, and the population has a lower standard of life. Usually lower life expectancy and lower levels of health care and education. Not all LEDCs are at the same level. Some suffer from famine and widespread diseases, others are better off but still below the wealth level of MEDCs.

LIBERAL DEMOCRACY This is based on two values.
1: that the government operates with the freely given consent of the people. 2: that the government is somehow responsible to the people who elected it. In a liberal democracy, we would therefore see government chosen through regular and fair elections; that all men and women over a certain age would be entitled to participate in the election process; that elections would be open to a number of political parties to compete in; that the government would be held accountable through a parliament or congress; that the rights of individuals would be respected in society and possibly protected through a constitution; and that the rule of law would be respected.

LIBERALS Those in favour of political and serial reform.

LIFE EXPECTANCY The average age at which members of a country's population die.

LOAN The lending of money: often with interest repayments expected.

LYNCHING To kill (a person suspected of crime), especially by hanging, without a proper trial.

MAJORITY The amount by which the greater number of votes cast in an election is more than the total number of remaining votes.

MALNUTRITION Inappropriate food intake. The average calorie intake falls below that required to stay healthy.

MASCULINE Behavioural characteristics associated with being a man in a specific culture.

MEDCs More economically developed countries: countries that have high levels of wealth and well-developed technology and industry. People in these countries have a high standard of living and good services such as health care and education.

MEDIATION An attempt to bring together two sides in a dispute.

MEDIATION TECHNIQUES The skills of mediation.

METEOROLOGIST Someone who studies weather patterns and their causes.

MIDDLE CLASS A description of a section of a population who share similar wealth and influence (power) in society. They are called 'middle class' because they are more wealthy and powerful than the 'working class', but not as wealthy and powerful as the 'upper class'. Examples of middle-class people could be doctors, or senior managers in industry.

MIGRATION Departure from a person's native land to settle in another.

MILITANT Willing to take strong or violent action.

MONOGAMY The custom of being married to/in a relationship with only one person at a time.

MORAL (ADJECTIVE/ADVERB) Virtuous, doing the right thing (opposite: immoral). Personal standards or rules that guide an individual towards making judgements about permissible behaviour with regard to basic human values (for example, individual freedoms, respect for others).

MORALITY Concerned with the distinction between good and evil or right and wrong.

MULTI-CULTURALISM The belief that all cultures (including values, traditions and beliefs) should be respected and accepted by other cultures. A multi-cultural society is one in which this belief is put into action

MULTINATIONAL COMPANIES Large-scale business organisations that have factories, sales outlets, etc., in several different countries. Examples include Sony and Toyota.

MUTUALLY EXCLUSIVE Incompatible.

NAACP (NATIONAL ASSOCIATION FOR THE ADVANCEMENT OF COLOURED PEOPLE) American organisation whose goal is the end of racial discrimination and segregation.

NATION A group of people living together in a certain area under the same government; a country. Once a synonym for 'ethnic group', designating a single culture sharing a language, religion, history, territory, ancestry and kinship. Now usually a synonym for state or nation state.

NATIONAL CONFLICT Conflict between countries, sometimes involving war, such as the conflict between the Hutu and Tutsi tribes in Rwanda.

NATIONAL GUARD An organised force of military reserves in individual American states. They can be called up by the state or by the federal government.

NATIONALISM Loyalty to one's nation.

NATIONALIST Someone who believes in independence for his/her own country.

NATIONALITY A person's nationality is the country of which a person is a citizen. This is the country that issues their passport and which is their official homeland.

NATURAL ENVIRONMENT Any part of the planet that has not been altered or much changed by human intervention. It could refer to land, sea or water, or the atmosphere.

NATURAL RESOURCES The raw materials that we take from the natural environment and use to help us live. Sometimes we use natural resources as they are found in nature (for example, we eat berries and fruit, and drink water). Sometimes we use them to make things or energy.

NATURE The characteristics and behaviour someone inherits, rather than learns.

NATURE AND NURTURE DEBATE The argument about which is the most important influence on an individual's personal development: the genes they are born with, or the way in which they are raised and socialised.

NEGOTIATE To discuss in order to reach an agreement.

NOBEL PEACE PRIZE A prize given annually for the promotion of world peace; started by Alfred Nobel (1833–96), Swedish discoverer of dynamite.

NGOs (NON-GOVERNMENT ORGANISATIONS) These are charities such as Oxfam, which provide aid to LEDCs.

NON-RENEWABLE RESOURCES Simply explained by saying that once we have used up this type of resource, there will be no more created, for example, coal and oil.

NORMS Rules that define behaviour that is expected, required, or acceptable in particular circumstances. May be written or unwritten.

NUCLEAR FAMILY A description of the basic family group: mother, father, and their children.

NURTURE What a person learns from their experiences, environment or training.

NUTRIENTS Substances that promote growth on plants or animals.

OMBUDSMAN An official appointed to investigate complaints against public authorities or government departments or the people who work for them.

OSTRACISE To refuse to have anything to do with someone.

PACIFISM The belief that violence is unjustified and war is wrong on moral or religious grounds.

PARLIAMENTARY HEALTH SELECT COMMITTEE Appointed by the House of Commons to examine the expenditure, administration and policy of the Department of Health. It has a maximum of 11 members.

PCBS A manufactured chemical used in many products such as lubricants, paints, sealants and many electrical products. Exposure to it causes medical problems in people such as a severe form of acne called chloracne, numbness in the arms and/or legs, muscle spasms, chronic bronchitis and problems with the nervous system.

PEER GROUPS A friendship group with common interests and position, made up of individuals of similar age.

PEER PRESSURE Compulsion to do or obtain the same things as others in one's peer group.

PERSECUTE To ill-treat, oppress, torment or put an individual or a group to death because of religion or politics.

PERSPECTIVES Different ways of looking at or evaluating a problem, issue or course of action.

PESTER POWER The influence children have over parents' choices of what to buy.

PESTICIDES Chemicals sprayed or spread onto land and crops to kill insects and wildlife that could damage crops or people.

PHOTOCHEMICAL SMOG Petrol and diesel fuels produce many chemical by-products. These chemicals combine with water vapour and sunlight to produce a dangerously polluted atmosphere.

PLANKTON Microscopic plants used by many sea creatures as a basic food source.

POLLUTION Describes a situation where the natural environment is contaminated by harmful substances, often as a result of human activity.

POLYGAMY The custom of being married to more than one person at a time.

POVERTY CYCLE OR TRAP The results of being poor (like poor health and lack of education) that trap poor people into continuing poverty – a vicious cycle.

POVERTY LINE The level of income below which a person cannot afford to buy all the resources they need to live.

PRIMARY SOCIALISATION Socialisation is the process of teaching people how to fit in to a society. Primary socialisation is the first stage of this process and it is usually done by the parents who teach children how to speak, behave with others, and many of the attitudes and values they will live by in later life.

PROPAGANDA The organised circulation by a political group, etc., of ideas, information, misinformation, rumour or opinion by means of the media.

PUSH AND PULL FACTORS Push factors are those things that encourage people to leave a place to settle elsewhere (e.g. poverty, political threats). Pull factors are those things that attract people to move to a new place (e.g. more jobs, less crime).

QUOTA The specific quantity of goods that a country's government allows to be imported.

RECONCILIATION To bring people together after a conflict.

RECONSTITUTED FAMILY A family that is made up of people who have divorced or separated from an earlier partnership and formed another family, bringing up children from one or both previous marriages.

REFUGEES People fleeing from a country or area because of a threat, such as famine, war or natural disaster.

REGENERATED When plants that have been cut down grow again. It can also refer to any natural environment that recovers after it has been damaged.

RELATIVE POVERTY Being poor compared to the average or norms of a country. Poverty moves up or down depending on what the 'average' is. A common measure: relative poverty is less than half the average income (GNP pc).

RELIGION Belief in and reverence for a supernatural power or powers regarded as creator and governor of the universe. May be based on the teachings of a spiritual leader. Usually includes an organisation and special buildings.

RELIGIOUS PRACTICES Activities that are part of following a religion, such as praying daily or attending a church/synagogue/mosque/etc. Other examples include attending ceremonies such as religious wedding and funerals.

RENEWABLE ENERGY SOURCES Sources of energy that occur naturally and are always available. They do not run out with use.

REPUBLIC A form of government without a monarchy in which supreme power is held by the people or their elected representatives.

RESISTANCE GROUPS Underground organisations fighting for the freedom of a country occupied by an enemy force.

RITES OF PASSAGE Ceremonies and activities that mark a change in a person's status and lifestyle. For example, an 18th birthday party or a young Masai going hunting alone for three days to mark becoming an adult.

ROLE The behaviour expected of a person with a certain social position or status (for example, child, group leader).

ROLE MODELS People who are viewed as examples of the right way to behave or live, and who are imitated by others.

SANCTIONS An economic or military measure taken against a nation as a means of coercion or force, usually to stop aggression.

SANITATION Cleaning, washing, getting rid of rubbish, dirt and sewage.

SCAPEGOAT A person or group wrongly accused of causing a problem. Scapegoats are often used to deflect the blame away from the true cause of the problem. For example, Hitler incorrectly blamed the Jews for Germany's poverty in the 1930s.

SEGREGATE To set apart or isolate a race, class or minority from the rest of society.

SELF-ESTEEM Pride in oneself; self-respect.

SEPARATIST A person who wants independence from an established church, organisation or state.

SEX Identifies the biological differences between women and men: male or female.

SEXUALITY A sexual state or condition.

SHOTGUN WEDDINGS Weddings that took place because the woman was pregnant. They were called 'shotgun weddings' because of the stereotype of the father of the pregnant bride going to the wedding with a shotgun to make sure the groom went through with the marriage.

SINGLE-PARENT FAMILY A family where only the mother or father is involved in bringing up the children. The other parent is not generally present.

SMALL-SCALE CONFICT Conflict at an individual or local level.

SOCIAL CLASS This is a way of dividing up the population of a society into groups which have similar levels of wealth, power and lifestyles. See MIDDLE CLASS.

SOCIAL EVIL 'Social evil' is a term which can be used to define any behaviour, lifestyle, or group which is seen as being a threat to social stability or well-being of society or any accepted group within society.

SOCIAL ORGANISATION It is not a precise term and is often used by the media or politicians or the forces of law and order to identify a particular situation which is seen as dangerous and threatening to other members of society. An example could be widespread binge drinking.

SOCIAL OUTCAST This is someone who, as a result of their behaviour or personality or social status, is not accepted by the rest of society. This may result in their exclusion from many events, activities and rights which most people in society enjoy.

SOCIAL ROLES Activities and responsibilities that individuals and groups take on as part of their membership of a social group.

SOCIAL VALUES Social values are what most people in a society consider desirable and acceptable attitudes, beliefs and behaviour.

SOCIALISATION Some social groups may have different social values and this could cause tension in a society.

SOCIALIST Someone who believes in socialism – the political and economic theory that advocates the state ownership of industry and capital and the distribution of that wealth in the community.

SOCIETY A community of people interacting with each other. May include more than one culture.

SOCIOLOGIST A sociologist is someone who studies the way a society works. They attempt to observe how social organisations operate and how people are influenced by these organisations. They try to look at social life in an unbiased way and say what is happening, rather than what should happen.

SOLAR ENERGY Makes use of the heat and light of the sun to produce heat and electricity.

STATE GOVERNMENTS The governments of the individual states of the USA.

STATE LAWS The laws of the individual states of the USA.

STEREOTYPES A simplified and fixed image of all members of a culture or group (based on race, religion, ethnicity, age, gender, etc.). It is usually a negative image, based on prejudice and lack of information.

STEWARDSHIP Where the people using the natural environment understand what it needs to survive and treat it with respect and concern for the future.

SUBSIDIES Payment of money to producers in your own country so that they can produce their goods more cheaply than foreign competition, for example, Italian tomato growers are subsidised and can sell tomatoes more cheaply than unsubsidised Tanzanian tomato growers.

SUPERSTITION A belief, practice or rite unreasoningly upheld by faith in magic or chance.

SUPREME COURT The highest court in a country or state.

SUSTAINABLE DEVELOPMENT Using resources and working in the environment in such a way that the resources can be replaced, and the environment is not permanently damaged. Preserving the environment for future generations.

SUSTAINABLE TOURISM Also called eco-tourism, nature tourism, green travel, environmentally responsible tourism. All these terms describe attempts to organise travel and tourism in ways that minimise the environmental damage that the travel and tourism business causes.

SUSTAINABLY Methods of working in a natural environment that do not damage the health of the ecosystem and make it possible for the environment to survive and thrive.

SYSTEMATIC DISCRIMINATION Discrimination that is the result of deliberate intentions.

TARIFF A tax on the goods of another country by the country importing those goods. This forces up the price of the imported produce and protects the home producers.

TECHNOLOGY Any product or process that extends the power of a human being, for example, in terms of survival, comfort level and quality of life.

TRADITION Customs, legends or beliefs that are handed down from generation to generation, often by word of mouth or by example.

TRADE GAP When the goods that a country imports cost more than the income they get for their exports.

TRIBALISM A sense of belonging or loyalty to a tribe.

UN CONVENTION ON THE RIGHTS OF THE CHILD Designed to ensure the survival, development and protection of children worldwide.

UNCONSTITUTIONAL Against the principles set forth in the constitution of a nation or state.

UNITED NATIONS (UN) An association of most of the countries in the world, formed in 1945 to promote peace, security and economic development.

UNIVERSAL DECLARATION OF HUMAN RIGHTS A declaration adopted by the United Nations in 1948 which sets out the basic human rights to which everyone is entitled.

URBANISATION The movement of people from the country into cities. Also the growth of cities as centres of commerce, industry, entertainment and political control.

USSR Union of Soviet Socialist Republics, i.e. Communist Russia.

VALUES Standards by which members of a culture define what is desirable and undesirable, good or bad, beautiful or ugly, important or unimportant, etc.

WEALTH The accumulation of past income, natural resources and financial resources. According to the rich, it does not bring happiness; according to the poor, it brings something quite closely resembling it!

WELFARE STATE A range of government measures set up to look after all members of society and to ensure everyone has adequate housing, food, healthcare and education.

WMD Weapons of Mass Destruction.

WOMEN'S LIBERATION MOVEMENT A movement to free women from the disadvantages they suffer in a male-dominated society. Aimed at achieving equality, for example, with regard to job opportunities and pay.

WORLD BANK A world financial organisation that guides and/or supports LEDCs.

WORLD HEALTH ORGANISATION (WHO) The United Nations' specialised agency for health, established in 1948. It aims to promote the highest level of health for all peoples.

WORLD HERITAGE CONVENTION An international agreement created to protect unique sites such as Stonehenge or the Pyramids.

WORLD TRADE ORGANISATION (WTO) International organisation that tries to regulate trade between different countries. Sometimes accused of being dominated by MEDCs and looking after them at the expense of LEDCs.

INDEX